George Eliot in Society

George Eliot in Society

Travels Abroad and Sundays at the Priory

Kathleen McCormack

The Ohio State University Press
Columbus

Copyright © 2013 by The Ohio State University.
All rights reserved.

Library of Congress Cataloging-in-Publication Data

McCormack, Kathleen, 1944–
George Eliot in society : travels abroad and Sundays at the Priory / Kathleen McCormack.
p. cm.
Includes bibliographical references and index.
ISBN 978-0-8142-1211-0 (cloth : alk. paper)—ISBN 978-0-8142-9313-3 (cd)
1. Eliot, George, 1819–1880. 2. Novelists, English—19th century—Biography. I. Title.
PR4681.M34 2013
823'.8—dc23
[B]
2012036644

Paper (ISBN: 978-0-8142-5666-4)
Cover design by Laurence J. Nozik
Text design by Juliet Williams
Type set in Adobe Granjon

*For
Michael and Andrea
Rose and Lily
with love*

CONTENTS

List of Illustrations   ix
Acknowledgments   xi
Abbreviations   xiii

CHAPTER 1	Introduction: The Big "S"	1
CHAPTER 2	Travels Abroad: Taking the Waters	37
CHAPTER 3	Months of Sundays	57
CHAPTER 4	Between *Middlemarch* and *Daniel Deronda*: Singers, Lovers, and Others	79
CHAPTER 5	The Salons, the Spas, and *Daniel Deronda*	111
CHAPTER 6	John Cross and the Last Spa	137

Appendix   The Leweses' Travels Abroad: A Chronology   155
Bibliography   157
Index   168

ILLUSTRATIONS

Chapter 1

1. George Eliot. Portrait by Frederic Burton — 5
2. George Henry Lewes. Courtesy of the National Portrait Gallery London — 11
3. Frederic Burton. Courtesy of the National Portrait Gallery London — 13
4. Herbert Spencer. Courtesy of the National Portrait Gallery London — 24
5. Charles Lee Lewes. Courtesy of the National Portrait Gallery London — 25
6. Barbara Bodichon. Courtesy of the National Portrait Gallery London — 26
7. The Priory, exterior. From photo by Cassell & Co., Lim. — 27
8. The Priory drawing room. From J. W. Cross's *George Eliot's Life in Letters* — 29

Chapter 2

9. Baden Baden. Author's collection — 39

Chapter 4

10. George Du Maurier. Courtesy of the National Portrait Gallery London — 84
11. "The Two Thrones." *Punch,* 7 June 1879 — 86

Chapter 5

12. Lady Castletown. Portrait by G. F. Watts 112

13. The Elisabethenbrunnen, Kurpark, Bad Homburg 114

Chapter 6

14. Bad Wildbad, the Bad Hotel on the Kurplatz 147

ACKNOWLEDGMENTS

The society (less extensive than George Eliot's, though only a touch less illustrious), both personal and professional, which I have kept during the years I've been writing this book, has contributed much to its completion. On the professional side, I would like to thank my institution's President Mark Rosenberg, always reliable for his dedication to the university and for a good-humored response to an e-mail. Provost Douglas Wartzok, Dean Kenneth Furton, and Associate Dean Nicol Rae have gratified me through taking generous and much appreciated notice of uninterrupted effort. James M. Sutton, Chair of the Department of English, provided singularly welcome fairness, as well as financial support for travels to collections and conferences.

Among George Eliot specialists, Nancy Henry deserves hearty thanks for her constant accessibility and reliability as she drew on her formidable expertise concerning the life and works of George Eliot. Bill Baker's interest and readiness to help and advise remains indispensable to myself as to every George Eliot scholar. To Dinah Birch and Kathryn Hughes, I offer thanks for timely help when urgently needed and also to George Griffith for sharing materials on several occasions. Finally, no Victorianist can do without thanking Patrick Leary, founder and list owner of the VICTORIA listserv, ever vigilant, always good-natured, and impeccably scholarly. I am also grateful to him for his permission to include excerpts from his personally transcribed diaries of Shirley Brooks in chapter 4.

At Florida International University, I am perennially thankful for the integrity and interest in my work shown by Faculty Senate President Tom Breslin, as well as to FIU founding faculty member Darden Asbury Pyron, who has for more than three decades offered encouragement, inspiration, and amusement in the face of daunting circumstances. With Meri-Jane Rochelson and Tometro Hopkins, at once good friends and invaluable colleagues, I have worked happily and productively side by side for more than twenty-five years. I could not do without them. I have also welcomed the congenial professionalism and intellectual companionship of Lynne Barrett, Ken Rogerson, Dan Guernsey, Marilyn Hoder-Salmon, Lauren Christos, and others too many to name. With office staff Marta Lee and Térèse Campbell, day-to-day matters in the Biscayne Bay English Department invariably receive instant attention and quick resolution, while they create a workplace atmosphere that remains ever tranquil, industrious, pleasant, and tolerant of eccentricities.

Institutions and organizations which have helped my research either materially or in spirit include the collections (the Beinecke Rare Book and Manuscript Library at Yale University and the British Library in London) where I conducted the majority of my work. Thanks as well to J. E. Flower, editor of the *Journal of European Studies* for permission to reprint parts of the article, "George Eliot: Poetry, Fiction, and European Spas," which appeared in March 2010. I thank guest editor Kyriaki Hadjiafxendi for soliciting my work for placement among the illustrious contributors to the special 2011 number of *George Eliot–George Henry Lewes Studies: The Cultural Place of George Eliot's Poetry,* as well as for the plenitude and originality of the essays it contains. In 2009 the FIU Faculty Senate Honors and Awards Committee created a high point in my life to spur me on: the University Faculty Research Award.

More personally, I cannot omit Mary Free, who, in 2003, performed a miracle so potent that I can never thank her enough. FIU graduates Brenda Silva and Alicia Carazo, whose success in their fields of authorship and law have rewarded pedagogical efforts of years ago, are grown into friends in whose good will I have eternal confidence. The memories which I cherish of George Valcarce and Richard Fantina, though full of regret at their loss, sustain my belief in the continued existence on this earth, however too briefly, of genuinely good people.

Among family members, thanks to my mother Regina McCormack who continues to inspire us all with her courage and independence of thought and action. I cannot overrate the happiness I gain from my beloved son and daughter-in-law, Michael and Andrea Gilbert. For Rose and Lily Gilbert, I declare my ineradicable love and the hope that, as they grow into women, we can share our lives in ever more meaningful ways.

ABBREVIATIONS

GEL   George Eliot Letters
GHLL   The Letters of George Henry Lewes
GHLJ   Diaries and Journals of George Henry Lewes
H&J   The Journals of George Eliot
JWC   George Eliot's Life as Related in Her Letters and Journals
ODNB   Oxford Dictionary of National Biography

CHAPTER 1

Introduction
The Big "S"

Social acceptance could hardly go further.
—Gordon Haight

I light up every Sunday to see my friends but go out smokily, like a lamp out of order, on Monday.
—*George Eliot Letters*, 1 January 1874

In June of 1877, freshly arrived in Surrey for their first summer at a country home of their own, George Eliot and George Henry Lewes delighted in their new "property" (*GEL* 6:386). Lewes, writing to John Walter Cross, describes it as "more ravishing than we fancied it—especially in this splendid weather—and the walks and drives are so much better than Society! (With a big S)" (*GEL* 6:386). In addition to his satisfaction with the Heights, Lewes's letter affirms that he and George Eliot had by this time acquired a group of friends and acquaintances of such stature that they regarded themselves as moving in Society—with the capital letter. Having outlived and overlived the period of social ostracism that followed their non-marital union in 1854, they now mixed comfortably, not albeit at the most elite (royal) levels, but nevertheless in an exclusive urban and international circle.

This progression from ostracism through celebrity occurred partly at the Leweses' own well-attended gatherings, famously known as Sundays at the Priory. From the time that George Eliot and Lewes began cohabiting, through his death in 1878, their social life reflected the most extreme contradictions: from social exclusion directed at their legally non-marital status in their earlier years together, through the 1870s, when they enjoyed a program of frequent social events—concerts, opera, dinners, weekends, recitals, excursions, and salons—crowded with many of the most important and respected of Victorian contemporaries. George Eliot's fiction reflects this gradual but extreme change, as the social level of her central characters rises from the simple rural folk of *Adam Bede* through the lords and ladies of *Daniel Deronda*.

Ever since the mid-to-late 1860s, when George Eliot's novels had firmly established her as one of England's most successful novelists—and with only *Middlemarch, Daniel Deronda,* and *Impressions of Theophrastus Such* left to write—the Leweses had been dividing their years into three (not necessarily contiguous) seasons, which consisted of their winter residence in London at the Priory, their travels abroad, and their summer leases, usually in Surrey. Of the three locations, only the last offered respite from their active social lives. Abroad, they often encountered well-to-do friends and acquaintances from their London circle. Many of these friends regularly visited at the Sunday salons that began occurring according to a rigorous schedule in the late sixties no matter what physical or mental ills one or the other might be suffering at the time. Indeed Lewes's journals often note that headaches troubled him on the very Sunday afternoons they entertained, although he concealed them so bravely that all commentators on the parties describe him as lively and voluble. Some years, as in 1871, the couple conducted the salon for five solid months (January through April, plus November and December), receiving hundreds of visitors.

Heretofore, versions of Sundays at the Priory, both the memories of guests who attended and the conclusions of twentieth-century biographers, have left impressions of the afternoons as supremely dull occasions, with few women in attendance, and guests approaching the Sibyl one by one to express their almost pious devotion. But this version conflicts with the neglected evidence of the lists of Sunday guests which appear in Lewes's as yet unpublished diaries and journals held in the Beinecke Rare Book and Manuscript Library at Yale University which provide the source for my conclusions concerning the numbers and identities of the visitors to the salon.[1] The host's sense of the importance of the occasions appears in these conscientious records, kept Sunday by Sunday, recording names in their order of arrival. Together with his descriptions of their travels, they occupy the majority of the space in his later diaries and show his eagerness about additional newcomers because each list ends with a comma that suggests he anticipates still another visitor's arrival. The extensive remi-

---

[1] Although currently unpublished, Lewes's diaries and journals are being transcribed and will appear under the editorship of William Baker.

niscences of the guests, both the volumes written by themselves and their biographers, as well as some of the excerpts contained in K. K. Collins's groundbreaking *George Eliot: Interviews and Recollections,* provide details of the happenings at one or the other of the Sundays. The "Letters to and about George Eliot," also in the Beinecke collection, provide additional information from the Leweses' friends. These supplement Lewes's lists, which seldom describe events or conversations, and add new material from the reminiscences and comments that have survived in most previous George Eliot biography.

These sources reveal that the traditional version of the salons as at once dull and scandalous ignores much of what went on at Sundays at the Priory, specifically: for the uninterrupted effort required to overcome physical and mental disturbances so as to welcome their guests gracefully; for the significant numbers of women in attendance; for the substantial gay and lesbian contingent; for the literary self-promotion George Eliot— and even more actively, Lewes—engaged in Sunday after Sunday; for the usefulness of the gatherings in furthering Lewes's scientific/psychological interests; for the liveliness provided by the circulation of Lewes himself; for the occasional musical recital; or for the amount of publishing business conducted among the guests, the majority of whom—as editors, authors, reviewers, and fiction writers—had some connection with one or more Victorian periodicals. Sundays at the Priory served many purposes and occurred during many months of the Leweses' lives, specifically the last decade of their time together. In time and effort alone, they occupied a substantial portion of George Eliot's energy during the years of her maturity, fulfilling multiple needs ranging from affectionate intimacy to pure business.

Partly because of the importance of the pivotal event of George Eliot's life, her decision to live with Lewes despite his still-legal marriage to another woman, her biographies, both long and short, have paid most attention to her early years, especially the period leading up to her momentous decision and the time immediately following when she began her career as a fiction writer (Haight, Ashton, Karl, Taylor, Hughes, Redinger, Henry, Bodenheimer).[2] In addition, the Victorians themselves, notably in

[2] Among the biographies devoting less than a quarter of their space to the years after which George Eliot had gained literary eminence, the last ten years of her life, Haight includes 131 out of 551 pages for *Middlemarch* and beyond; Hughes, 59 of 348; Ashton, 86 of 382; Karl, 190 of 641, and Henry, 89 of 270. Mary Deakin (*The Early Life of George Eliot*), Elfrida Vipont (*Towards a High Attic*), and Ruby Redinger (*George Eliot: The Emergent Self*) focus exclusively on the early life. Among the shorter versions, Henry's "Life" section in her *Cambridge Introduction to George Eliot* devotes nearly ten of thirteen pages to the period leading up to the serious commencement of the writing of *Middlemarch*, while the "life of George Eliot"

their 1881 obituaries, often expressed their preference for her more pastoral earlier fiction with its physical and temporal settings in the Midlands, a preference that directed attention to her girlhood as Mary Ann Evans of Warwickshire rather than to Mrs. Lewes of the Priory.[3]

Skimping on George Eliot's later years has encouraged the misconception that she remained outside of respectable society all her life. Even Virginia Woolf, an admirer, believed that in her adulthood she escaped an existence of little event, "but only to a secluded villa in St. John's Wood" (76). More recently, William Hughes and Andrew Smith assert that George Eliot remained "unvisited by most women of her status up until her marriage to Walter Cross [sic] in 1880" (57). Lewes's carefully kept guest lists prove otherwise. Although certain of the men never did bring their wives to George Eliot's salons, the majority of the married guests did, and the (social) status of these women easily matched, if not exceeded, that of George Eliot herself. Indeed the comings and goings at the Priory, along with the acquaintances George Eliot made as she traveled both in England and abroad, identify her not as a sheltered or ostracized recluse but as a member of a large and elite, if slightly Bohemian, international social circle, in which she moved as a literary celebrity and through which she stimulated her creative imagination as she composed her later poetry and fiction.

In *Interviews and Recollections,* Collins calculates that "as a rule, modern biographies of George Eliot quoted, or quote from, about forty recollections of her" (xvii). His work, like mine, seeks to add to these forty stalwarts a wide variety of "unfamiliar sources" which, for him, "complicate her character and circumstances . . . often in richly modulated ways" (xviii). Some of his "unfamiliar sources" overlap with mine, and the recollections he presents often come from afternoons at the Priory.[4] Collins's format (quotations from the individuals followed by notes explaining their identities), differs radically from my roughly chronological narrative of the ways the guests and their activities grew and changed over the years and

---

entry in John Rignall's *Oxford Readers Companion,* arranged in double-columned pages, accumulates twenty-three columns before George Eliot begins writing *Middlemarch* and devotes but four to the remainder of her life. Barbara Hardy's *A Critic's Biography* largely eludes the pattern through her topical rather than chronological organization ("Three or Four Love Stories," "Acquaintances and Friends," and so on). Rosemarie Bodenheimer (*The Real Life of Mary Ann Evans*) also takes a non-chronological approach. She devotes six pages to the Cross marriage in chapter 4 (111–18), then detours into a discussion of *Daniel Deronda.* Afterwards, she returns to the 1860s in the chapter, "George Eliot's Stepsons." In chapter 8 she goes so far as to call 1870–80 George Eliot's "posthumous decade" (233).

[3] Because George Eliot died late in December 1880, most obituaries appeared in 1881.

[4] See, for example, the passages by Lucy Clifford, Soph'ia Kovalevskaia, Matilda Betham-Edwards, James Sully, and Charles Waldstein.

Figure 1
George Eliot. Portrait by Frederic Burton

how some of the guests make plausible models for George Eliot's composite characters. At the same time, between us, we double or triple the forty sources and in the process deliver a much more socially active version of George Eliot.

Haight's Sources: Letters to America

Gordon Haight, in his standard biography, in addition to the occasional remark, presents two long descriptions of the Sundays, one from 1869, the second from 1873. They both come from letters written by Americans who did not revisit once their London holidays ended. The later, by John Fiske, "Spencer's American disciple" (467), concentrates on the couple themselves, rather than the gathering. Fiske likes both of the Leweses enormously.[5] Though not like a "bluestocking," she speaks wonderfully of Homer. She describes herself reading Fiske's book, which arrived while she was sitting on the floor, and remaining so absorbed as not to move for hours. He concludes, "I call them a wonderful couple" (468). Charles Eliot Norton, four years previously, delivered a more checkered account.

Haight devotes two pages to Norton's description of the early 1869 afternoons. Members of the Norton family presented themselves at the Priory throughout January 1869, for lunch or tea, and Norton wrote the letter excerpted by Haight on 19 January (409–10). Norton's generally negative description of the Leweses and their home depends partly on his efforts to establish a morally disapproving yet insouciant tone in his letter to his friend G. W. Curtis and partly on the timing of his visit just at the point the Leweses were devoting their efforts to establishing a more regular schedule and a more comprehensive guest list. He finds Lewes "very ugly, very vivacious, very entertaining" with "an air that reminds you of vulgarity" (quoted in Haight 409–11). The word recurs in his description of the Frederic Burton portrait of George Eliot hanging over the fireplace in the study: "an odious vulgarizing portrait." He regards the Leweses' taste in the visual arts, as demonstrated by the engravings, prints, and portraits on the Priory walls, unimpressive.[6] His hostess herself he describes as talking without brilliance but with simplicity and intensity.

---

[5] In the absence of mention of another Haight title, references come from the *Biography*. Similarly, for Edith Simcox, references cited by page number alone come from the *Autobiography of a Shirtmaker*.

[6] Kathryn Hughes describes Norton's letter, especially the part about the painting and prints, as "spiteful" (282).

Early in this description Norton addresses the scandal still lingering around George Eliot's living circumstances with Lewes. Though people respect her and her decision, he opines, the couple's male guests tend to arrive unaccompanied by their wives, so as to show respect for the virtue of their own women and mitigate George Eliot's effect as an example of a transgressor who suffers no consequences. He concludes that "the women who visit her are either so emancipée as not to mind what the world says about them, or have no social position to maintain" (quoted in Haight 409). His estimate of an emancipée woman guest again shows his reluctance to be pleased. The first women the Nortons met at the Priory included Eleanor Sellar, Emilia Pattison, and Eliza Lynn Linton, none of whom at the time held or practiced radical ideas about female emancipation. Nor had they abandoned their social status as Norton suggests. Sellar, married to Professor William Sellar of the University of Edinburgh, had family connections to the Crosses. Pattison, married, though unhappily, to the Rector of Lincoln College Oxford, maintained the position of the distinguished don's wife. Linton's status depended on her position as an independent literary figure, but she hardly advanced radical ideas.

Indeed, the women at the Priory during 1869 made up a mixed bag, the majority of them authors and other intellectuals and/or social activists, but also women primarily occupied with husbands and children, often many children.[7] Norton's determination to represent them as mannish, heedless,

---

[7] Although I will discuss the motivations and varying experiences of many of the women who came to the Priory in later chapters, Norton's remarks, as reinforced by both contemporaries and later biographers, have achieved such wide circulation that I provide here an uninclusive list of women who attended George Eliot's salons with some regularity over a substantial period of at least a year or two. Repeat women visitors at the Priory included Barbara Bodichon, Bessie Raynor Parkes Belloc, Bodichon's sister and her partner Isa Craig; old friends Rufa Call and Eliza Lynn Linton; most of the wives of the dedicated Positivists including Emily (Edward) Beesly, Ethel (Frederic) Harrison, Frances (Alexander) Bain, Lucy (Henry) Crompton and the wives of the Lushington twins, Godfrey and Vernon; women with Pre-Raphaelite associations: Georgiana Burne-Jones, Rosalind Howard, Alexandra Orr (Frederic Leighton's sister), artist Helen Allingham; and education reformers Anne Jemima Clough and Kate Amberley. Wives of the most frequent male singers, George Du Maurier and Richard Liebreich, often joined the audience when their husbands sang. Sets of sisters added to the number of women: Lady Louisa Colvile and her sister Jane Strachey, the four Cross sisters and their cousin Eleanor Sellar, and the women members of the Chambers/Lehmann/Benzon family complex. Additional couples included the Frederic Harrisons, the Justice Charles Bowens, the Alfred Morrisons, and the Charles Roundells. As for the big S, no one could deny a place in Society for Lady Augusta Castletown and her daughters Lady Sebright, Mrs. Skeffington Smyth, and the Honourable Cecilia Wingfield, nor to the dependents of Henry Huth the bibliophile, a mother and daughter who also arrived as a pair. Women who would find material for their own writing, in addition to Browning specialist Alexandra Orr, included Olga Novikoff, Edith Simcox, Emilia Pattison, Kate Field, and Matilda Betham-Edwards. Later additions included new brides of regularly attending men,

or vulgar reveals a standoffishness, what Haight calls "Brahminical indifference" (411) inconsistent with his repeated January visits, made together with women of his own family. For their part, the Leweses did their best to beguile the Nortons. Lewes trotted out some of his liveliest prose in the notes of invitation that followed his first meeting with Norton in Oxford the previous August and presented the family with a letter of introduction to the Leweses' acquaintance the Countess Ida von Baudissin of Freiburg when the Norton family moved on to the Continent.

John Fiske, Haight's other main source, experienced a more typical afternoon in 1873 as the Sundays were reaching their peak of popularity after the publication of *Middlemarch*. He comments favorably on George Eliot's brilliance, which he could appreciate personally as the group on his first Sunday remained small, only eight people. He visited twice more that season, seeing slightly larger groups that included many of the regulars. In January 1874 he unfortunately chose the second Sunday of the month, missing Anthony Trollope who came on the first and Robert Browning on the last. These three visits made up his entire experience of the Priory. Both Norton's and Fiske's descriptions come from a total of no more than six visits between them, while Haight ignores a slew of regulars whose comments would proceed from a long series of afternoons, some of them stretching over more than a decade, guests whose repeated attendance guarantees that they did not regard the afternoons as either a scandal or a bore. For the rest, Haight's biography scatters a few lists here and there, usually to illustrate the illustriousness of the guests.

Nineteenth-Century Biographers

Expanding the number and variety of sources who comment on Sundays at the Priory also creates a livelier version of the afternoons. To be sure, salon participants such as Oscar Browning, Leslie Stephen, Sidney Colvin, and others among Collins's forty sources acknowledge a heaviness pervading the drawing room. Stephen thought the tone of the day depended on the number of guests. Of George Eliot he writes, "If rainy weather had limited the audience, and the tentative sparks of conversation had been fanned into life, she could be as charming as any admirer could desire" (143–44). Mathilde Blind emphasizes solemnity: "The deep seriousness of her nature made her Sunday afternoon receptions, which became more

---

Lucy Clifford, Kate Gurney, as well as several of the younger women friends and protégées always associated with George Eliot's maturity: Alice Helps, Elma Stuart, Phoebe Marks (Hertha Ayrton), and Bice Trollope.

and more fashionable as time wore on, something of a tax to one who preferred the intimate converse of a few to that more superficially brilliant talk which a promiscuous gathering brings with it" (205). Colvin concedes that the afternoons were "not always quite free from stiffness, the presiding genius allowing herself—so at least some of us thought—to be treated a little too markedly and formally as such" (Collins 90). On the other hand, some of the most negative descriptions come from people whose names seldom if ever appear on Lewes's lists. Memoirist Walter Sichel quotes John Everett Millais concerning the heaviness both of general atmosphere and of George Eliot's "Elephantine" (47) piano technique, but, unlike Edward Burne-Jones, Frederic Leighton, George Howard, and other Pre-Raphaelites, Millais appears but once on the guest lists in Lewes's diaries.

Repeatedly, sources emphasize the dearth of women guests or categorize the few they acknowledge as outsiders of some kind.

Robert Buchanan endured a falling out with Lewes over his negative comments about the Pre-Raphaelites, so his visits occurred mainly in the late sixties before the salon hit its stride. Lewes's diaries show no evidence of enough visits to justify the harshest of Buchanan's conclusions about the Priory, which he saves for his review of Cross's *George Eliot's Life as Related in Her Letters and Journals*. Then he lets loose. One of the admirers of the early fiction at the expense of the later, he finds that George Eliot's inspiration deteriorates into mechanical construction. As a result of an isolation in which George Eliot's "female acquaintances might have been counted upon the fingers of one hand" (320), she lacks, of all things, sympathy (315). In her later novels she was becoming too much the scientist, her novels a matter of "dissection and vivisection." In this, she shares the inclinations not only of Lewes himself, but also of many of the psychologist/guests (Alexander Bain, James Sully, George Croom Robertson, George Romanes) that his interests help draw to the Sunday afternoons during the writing of *Problems of Life and Mind*.[8] Buchanan's belief that

---

[8] Several scholars have recently drawn parallels between Lewes's science and George Eliot's art that include the contributions of several of Lewes's colleagues among the English proto-psychologists of the late nineteenth century. They include Glenda Sacks's "George Eliot's Boudoir Experiment: Dorothea as Embodied Learner" (2009), Peter Garratt's *Victorian Empiricism: Self, Knowledge, and Reality in Ruskin, Bain, Lewes, Spencer, and George Eliot* (2010), and Kay Young's *Imagining Minds: The Neuro-Aesthetics of Austen, Eliot, and Hardy* (2010). Stella Pratt-Smith also notices these interactions in the poetry: "'I Grant You Ample Leave' bears considerable resemblance to contemporary developments in brain science and the imaging of its internal structures" (69).

Describing, or even providing parenthetical identifications of the men involved with Lewes's project, creates a challenge of nomenclature because they fit so many categories. "Physiologist psychologist," awkward but accurate, competes with "philosopher," or, more

the makeup of the Priory social circle led George Eliot's fiction in unfortunate directions implicitly acknowledges the importance of the gatherings to her writing.

The memoirs of one frequent guest, the artist Rudolph Lehmann, include no suggestion of a motivation similar to Buchanan's for disparaging the Priory and its residents. As part of the Benzon/Lehmann/Chambers complex of married brothers and sisters, he both issued and accepted invitations to and from the Leweses, including his own dinners and musical entertainments, even inducing George Eliot to accompany Lewes on a few evenings out. Yet in the prosopographic section of *An Artist's Remembrance,* "People I Have Known," when he describes Sundays at the Priory he chooses a clownish tone that deviates from his other biographical snippets. Whereas he narrates incidents concerning artist Edward Burne-Jones and actor Helen Faucit straightforwardly, he switches to the present tense for George Eliot and George Henry Lewes and applies the common metaphor of the salons as religious ritual. He concludes, "Only one or two exceptionally high-minded or high-born women are in the room. As a rule, so-called 'Society' does not visit this sanctuary" (235). While Lehmann's comments do apply accurately to the absence of significant numbers from the very upper echelons of the aristocracy, from 1869 on, Lehmann himself visited the Priory at least twenty times.[9] During those visits, he shared afternoons such as 24 March 1872 with a total of thirteen women guests. Five years later, still in steady attendance, both Rudolph and Amelia Lehmann visited the same afternoon as Frederick Locker(-Lampson) and his daughter Eleanor, soon to be a principal in the society wedding of the year, to Lionel Tennyson (Haight 508). Lehmann's wife, Amelia, sang more often than any other woman guest, and Lehmann's unexpectedly harsh and heavy-handed humor exemplifies the caution necessary when evaluating the varying degrees of reliability among Priory guests' descriptions. At the same time, even the authors who speak of stiffness often acknowledge a perpetual periphery of liveliness encircling the seriousness at the fireside end of the core semicircle. All of the guests agree with versions of well-attended afternoons that place George Eliot next to the fire speaking to callers one by one while Lewes gyrated about the edges keeping things going with the group in general. According to Leslie Stephen: "George Lewes, in the first place, was unquenchable. He was

---

specifically "positivist," which also would apply in most cases. The attraction these men have drawn recently proceeds from their similarities to current neuroscience which, like theirs, addresses the mind/brain problem.

[9] Only rarely do Lewes's lists of guests fail to specify which of the Lehmanns visited on any given Sunday, but the Rudolph Lehmanns appear most frequently.

Figure 2
George Henry Lewes. Courtesy of the National Portrait Gallery, London

always full of anecdotes and vivacious repartee; and while more serious interviews were taking place at the centre of the circle, there would be a little knot on the periphery which was a focus of laughter and good-natured fun" (143). Kate Field, the American journalist, remembers how "Lewes pervaded the atmosphere, speaking first with one and then with another, always interesting and frequently brilliant" (Whiting 397). Blind calls Lewes the "social cement" of the gatherings: vivacious, tactful, and a relentless raconteur (206). Neither Colvin, nor Buchanan, nor Lehmann disputes the stimulating liveliness Lewes contributed.

Nor could George Eliot have remained as stiff as usually described, nailed to the chair beside the fireplace, rather than moving around the room at least at times. Sophia Kovalevsky remembers her leading the young mathematician to a seat near Herbert Spencer. Other younger women describe her as tactile. Kate Field reports that George Eliot took her hand upon their first meeting and talked sympathetically about the ambitions of young women (Whiting 397). Edith Simcox, Georgiana Burne-Jones, and Lucy Clifford exchanged kisses with her. Whereas the standard narrative presents her as utterly humorless, the prank of bringing together Kovalevsky and Spencer (described below) shows a sly mischief in arranging her guests. Lewes would tend to call her "Polly," and the use of the diminutive also subtracts a bit of the stolidness from the usual representation of an unsmiling, immovable idol granting audiences.

Indeed the youthfulness of the party in general also contributed some of the life to the afternoons. Most of the guests were younger than their hosts, some of them associates of Lewes's eldest son, Charles Lee. The most senior and among the most regular, on the other hand, Frederic Burton could share childhood memories with Herbert Spencer, Anthony Trollope, and the rarer visitors, Robert Browning and later Tennyson. But the majority were born in the 1830s and 40s, putting them (in reverse order) in their own thirties and forties during the Priory period, many of them still young enough to be pursuing romantic attachments, whether to men or women.

George Eliot relished engagements among her younger friends and had a standard practice for welcoming new brides to the Priory. When Lucy Lane married the popular mathematician W. K. Clifford of University College London in 1875, the couple waited fruitlessly for a Priory invitation for the bride until Positivist Henry Crompton, drawing on his own experience, explained the procedures to the groom: "She'll never invite her . . . you must ask to be allowed to take her, and show that you would consider it a great honour" (110). George Eliot also had reason to perceive that crushes, flirtations, and love matches were often proceeding

Figure 3
Frederic Burton. Courtesy of the National Portrait Gallery London

during Sunday afternoons at the Priory. In 1875 when Emily Cross became engaged to Francis Otter, she wrote happily to the Leweses: "My Dearest Aunt & Uncle, I must write at once to you, and tell you that I have given my whole heart to someone I met first at your house" (ms. letter, Beinecke, 12 Jan 1875). Along with science, art, literature, and politics, love had its place at the Priory on a Sunday afternoon.

As time went on, the afternoons began to offer music, with several regular or repeat performers, sometimes of international fame, and on several occasions George Eliot read from her works in progress: *Middlemarch, Daniel Deronda,* and her poetry as well. Now and then Lewes solicited subscriptions for worthy charitable projects, such as funds for the care of George Du Maurier's eyes, a lifelong burden especially troubling to a visual artist. People took light refreshments, advanced their ideas, fell in love, quarreled, confided their troubles, and talked and talked and talked through the Sunday afternoons at the Leweses' Priory.

Of course John Walter Cross's version of Sundays at the Priory in his *George Eliot's Life* carries the authority of a regular guest and an intimate of the family. At the same time, its rhetoric, here as elsewhere in his biography, suggests that the motives for his project, universally regarded as sanitizing, included creating an image of George Eliot as far from the social butterfly as possible.[10] Cross relies on italics to assert of his wife that "she was eminently *not* a typical mistress of a *salon*" because "she took things too seriously, and seldom found the effort of entertaining compensated by the gain" (3:272). He, too, gives Lewes, always effortless in his conversation whether the group was small or large, credit for the liveliness of the afternoons. But Cross's conclusion, that "her *salon* was important as a meeting-place for many friends whom she cared greatly to see, but it was not otherwise important in her own life," fails to account for many of the activities that occurred at Sundays at the Priory.

Travels Abroad

Meanwhile, like the entertainments at the Priory, the travel seasons of the Leweses' year also helped raise their social center of gravity, as well-off and sophisticated *Inglesi* abroad encountered each other in Bellosguardo,

---

[10] Haight, as well, prefers to present the Leweses as reclusive. His *Biography* asserts that they "avoided as many engagements as possible" (462), then follows up on the next page with a description of the 1873 season during which "guests over-flowed the drawing-room of the Priory" (463). In volume 9 of his collection of George Eliot's letters, he captions one period (February 1878) "A Month of Parties for GE and GHL" (*GEL* 9:209).

or on the Spanish Steps, or taking the cure in the Black Forest. Compatriots who had become expatriates often included people less likely to make the same moral judgments abroad that they would deliver in London or who perhaps were themselves living abroad to avoid similar judgments. As early as 1861, T. A. Trollope, the more famous novelist's elder brother, along with his friend, the social magnet of Bellosguardo, Isa Blagden, welcomed the Leweses to the Florentine group. Later, Trollope's daughter Bice became one of the Priory singers who performed for their guests. In 1864, the traveling couple conducted their artistic explorations of Italy—over a northern route that included a three-week-long stay in Venice and stops in Turin, Padua, Verona, Milan, and the northern Italian Lakes region—accompanied by National Gallery art expert Burton, who became one of three or four Priory guests who seldom missed a Sunday (Haight 377). In 1869, the year the salons began in earnest, George Eliot and Lewes met members of the Cross family in Rome, an encounter that initiated the most important family friendship they sustained during their mature years and which swelled the Sunday groups because John Cross often arrived at the Priory with one or more of his siblings.

One kind of foreign venue in particular, the health-oriented mountain spas that the Leweses patronized with fidelity if not always with positive physical effects, facilitated acquaintance with other English invalids and their friends and companions. The opening scene to George Eliot's *Daniel Deronda,* set in a gas-stifled, over-ornamented European spa casino, permeated by greed, vanity, and obsession, has led scholars to conclude, as E. A. McCobb has put it, that George Eliot regarded such places as "infernal" (537). Certainly, during their frequent interludes at the European spas, George Eliot and George Henry Lewes did express repulsion toward the gambling at Bad Homburg and Baden Baden. Nevertheless, the other activities available at the mountain spas attracted the couple, and, from the mid-sixties when they had both the time and the means to choose their travels as they would, they returned again and again to spas in France, Belgium, Switzerland, and especially Germany.

While traveling to enjoy the spa culture of (supposedly) healing waters, concerts, dining, society, and long walks in the gardens and hills, as well as the artistic/historical culture available elsewhere in the capitals of Europe, George Eliot also found creative inspiration that reached her literature. Not only do the spas turn up occasionally in her poetry and fiction before becoming an important setting in *Daniel Deronda,* but her frequent visits raise questions about the generally accepted belief that Bad Homburg forms the only model for the novel's Leubronn. Finally, her last stay at a European spa helps explain her response to one of the most sensational and provocative events of her life: the mental illness of her much younger husband that marred the Venetian phase of the honeymoon of the sixty-year-old novelist in 1880. Indeed, far from shunning the European spa culture in favor of the Continental capitals, by the late sixties George Eliot and Lewes were among the most devoted habitués.

"Madame de Sablé"

No discussion of George Eliot's salons can omit the importance of "Woman in France: Madame de Sablé," in which the then–Marian Evans expressed her distinct approval of salonizing in an essay written in 1854, when she had only limited experience with contemporary salons of the kind she and Lewes eventually came to host.[11] She wrote the piece for the *Westminster Review* while living with Lewes in their first lodgings together: a set of oddly shaped rooms on the Kaufstrasse in Weimar. Indeed the commission to write "Woman in France" came in good time to Evans. Just arrived in Weimar, she received a letter from John Chapman requesting the review for the *Westminster*.

As Thomas Pinney asserts, this important essay signals her change in role from the periodical's de facto editor to one of its money-earning contributors (52). Adding to the finances that enabled the newly declared couple to live comfortably in Germany, the commission pleased them so much that they instantly sought out the inadequate Weimar bookstore to gratify Chapman's request. They rushed down to the Markt Platz to order the book at the quaint little Hof Buchhandlung, and Evans sat down to write in their lodgings near the Herderplatz as soon as the book arrived from London.

As in many of her essays, in this one Evans chooses a male persona. Of his own society, he admits, "We read the 'Athenaeum' askance at the tea-table, and take notes from the 'Philosophical Journal' at a soirée; we invite our friends that we may thrust a book into their hands, and presuppose an exclusive desire in the 'ladies' to discuss their own matters, that we may crackle the *Times* at our ease" (Pinney 60). But, unlike these gender-

---

[11] When referring to my subject before she assumed her pseudonym, I call her by her birth name, either Mary Ann or Marian Evans, depending on which she was going by at the time. Afterward, I call her George Eliot, but, following Barbara Hardy's practice, without ever shortening it to the surname alone, as she was not really a person called George Eliot. Accepting the obligation of calling people what they want to be called would require applying the name Marian Lewes, which she preferred for most of her adult life, and shortening it to "Lewes," which could not help causing confusion between herself and her life's companion. Meanwhile my own preference lies with "Marian Evans." See bibliography.

divided English parties, the salons of France, he goes on, successfully blend men and women in literary and political conversations.

The essay begins with the assertion that the women of France, rather than those of England, Spain, Germany, or Italy, have produced the work most worth saving from a hypothetical general burning of literature written by women. After a typically nineteenth-century analysis of physiology that attributes the intellectualism of French women partly to their small, quick brains (and partly to the unsentimental French marital customs), he mentions the French salons of the seventeenth century as an important source of this superiority.

The essay persona goes on to define salons: "As all the world knows, [they] were *reunions* of both sexes, where conversation ran the whole gamut of subjects, from the frothiest *vers de societé* to the philosophy of Descartes" (Pinney 57). The Marquise de Rambouillet "was the very model of the woman who can act as an amalgam to the most incongruous elements; beautiful, but not preoccupied by coquetry or passion; an enthusiastic admirer of talent, but with no pretensions to talent on her own part; exquisitely refined in language and manners, but warm and generous withal, not given to entertain her guests with her own compositions, or to paralyse them by her universal knowledge" (57–58). Naming some of the guests at the salon, "Richelieu, Corneille, the Great Condé, Balzac, and Bossuet," the persona admires how the Rambouillet parties did not separate into groups according to gender, but mixed, to the advantage of both. Together with conversation that extended to non-literary topics such as politics and religion, he names one advantage of this custom: that "women would not become *bas bleus* or dreamy moralizers, ignorant of the world and of human nature, but intelligent observers of character and events" (58). Imitators who failed to match the Hotel de Rambouillet failed because of a tendency to succumb to an "affectation" (59) that differed from the simplicity maintained by the Marquise.

The essay continues its exemplification by moving on to the gatherings at the Palais de Luxembourg, hosted by Mademoiselle d'Orleans. On these occasions the women agreed to write their own literary self-portraits. Indeed, Evans anticipates gender/genre discussions initiated by feminist analysis in the second half of the twentieth century by observing that the standard genres may not suit women's experience as well as more personal kinds of writing such as these portraits and, later in the essay, letter writing.[12] Evans connects the ladies' portraits with Jean de la Bruyère's

---

[12] Alison Booth, in *How to Make It as a Woman: Collective Biographical History from Victoria to the Present,* begins by connecting salons and women's collective biography through a description of the self-portrait project pursued by Christine de Pisan and her friends. Later,

"Characters," an influence she herself demonstrates in her very last book, *Impressions of Theophrastus Such* (Stange) which describes one character after another.

At this point the persona moves to the publication that has created the occasion for the review, the research of Victor Cousin, specifically concerning Madame de Sablé: "Few better specimens of the woman who is extreme in nothing, but sympathetic in all things; who affects us by no special quality, but by her entire being" (62). Good at letters, confidante of both men and women, she nevertheless has what Evans regards as a virtue: "no ambition as an authoress" (73). Subjects of conversation at Port Royal included theology, physics, metaphysics, and morals, "varied by discussions on love and friendship, on the drama, and on most of the things in heaven and earth which the philosophy of that day dreamt of" (73–74). De Sablé converses in "epigrammatic" observations and in a "sententious style, to which we owe, probably some of the best *Pensées* of Pascal" (75). Indeed, "it is clear that but for her influence the 'Maxims' of La Rochefoucauld would never have existed" (75). Madame de Sablé served more to inspire than to write her own thoughts and maxims.

The essay persona acknowledges a falling off in the value of salons during the eighteenth century. Having become "a recreation, not an influence" (61), they lost their distinct moral grounding during the age of Voltaire and Rousseau. Nevertheless, the persona concludes with a Wollstonecraftian assertion: "Women become superior in France by being admitted to a common fund of ideas, to common objects of interest with men" (80). This idea, which echoes *A Vindication of the Rights of Woman,* recurs in Evans's comments on the condition of women, including in the problematic 1856 *Westminster Review* essay "Silly Novels by Lady Novelists."[13]

The de Sablé essay anticipates Sundays at the Priory, and, more importantly, helps explain one of the traditional trouble spots of *Middlemarch,* the conclusion that relegates Dorothea Ladislaw to a supporting, "diffusive" ("Finale") role vis-à-vis her MP husband, Will. George Eliot's essay on Madame de Sablé, together with the experience of her own salon, suggests a less trivializing future for Dorothea beyond the purely domestic

---

she accounts for the heavy presence of French monarchs in English and American royal prosopographies: "I suggest that this French infiltration—the ubiquitous Joan of Arc aside—results from the continued impact of the salons and the written recognition of French women since the seventeenth century, as well as the conspicuous roles women played in the events of the French Revolution and Napoleonic era . . . the English-speaking prosopographies served, it seems, as a middle-class Victorian substitute for the riskier and more rarefied salons" (43).

[13] See "George Eliot's Wollstonecraftian Feminism" and "George Eliot: Wollstonecraft's 'Judicious Person with Some Turn for Humour.'"

one the "Finale," on the face of it, anticipates. At Sundays at the Priory and elsewhere, George Eliot fulfilled her own prescription as a salonière by receiving the confidences of both her male and female guests, though the crises about which they confided differed. While the men often shared their struggles regarding loss of faith and hence, as a consequence, their university positions, the women guests, many of them a decade or more younger than George Eliot, more often described desires to contribute something to society on a monumental scale thwarted by their gender. More specifically, as the wife of a politician, Dorothea Ladislaw's duties would include welcoming political guests to her London home.

Dorothea's construction as nun-like also echoes the de Sablé essay because its persona believes the French woman intellectual's path often ended at the convent. Dorothea reverses the pattern. Though in the opening to *Middlemarch,* she dresses with habit-like simplicity, prays often, and has a St. Bernard called Monk, she ends up in London participating in a social circle that would include much political chatter. George Eliot discarded a draft of a "Finale" representing Dorothea's life in London in favor of her reflections on women and ambition. Nevertheless, the wife of Will Ladislaw, MP, in London, like a substantial number of Priory guests who already were or eventually became Members of Parliament, comes to move in a world of social gatherings that would not exclude politics.

Previous Parties

George Eliot, even as a young Londoner named Marian Evans, and later as a well-traveled intellectual in her mid-thirties, sampled some social occasions that helped prepare her to conduct her own salon.[14] When Evans went to live at the establishment of John Chapman at 142 Strand in 1851, she entered a working place, a family home, a boarding house, and a site that plunged her into London literary/social activities. In *142 Strand,* Rosemary Ashton describes Chapman's frequent parties as "soirées . . . regular Friday evening gathering[s]," concluding that "nowhere was the speech freer and the speculation more serious and intelligent than among the authors who gathered round Chapman at his headquarters at 142 Strand" (13). Here Evans met Horace Greeley, Frederika Bremer,

---

[14] As generally associated with eighteenth-century France the term *salon* carries a narrower meaning than had become the case in Victorian England, in particular its emphasis on leadership by a woman. Many nineteenth-century hostesses perceived their gatherings as salons, although both *reunion* and *conversazione* would serve as plausible equivalents.

Ralph Waldo Emerson, and, at the meeting Chapman called of the committee to reduce the power of the Booksellers' Association in 1852, Charles Dickens. She also encountered people who later became guests at Sundays at the Priory, notably Eliza Lynn Linton, Herbert Spencer, and William Ballantyne Hodgson. Meeting Evans elsewhere in 1844, Hodgson praised her knowledge of languages and concluded of the evening they shared at the home of Richard Rathbone: "a delightful party" (JWC 1: 364). Later professor of economics at the University of Edinburgh, Hodgson went on to join the group in St John's Wood once or twice a year for many seasons.

Marian Evans had known Rufa Brabant all during the 1840s when they both joined the Bray-Hennell holiday excursions to such spots as Malvern and Tenby. She, too, appeared at Chapman's, and, as Mrs. Mark Call (after the death of her first husband Charles Christian Hennell), came once or twice a year to the Priory well into the seventies. Another visitor to 142 Strand, artist/art critic Philip Gilbert Hamerton, describes how Chapman relied on Evans to play the piano for his guests, and, although he doubted that her published work at that point offered "anything beyond good ordinary literary abilities," she played "remarkably well" (Hamerton 160). He, too, met up with George Eliot years later, visiting at the Priory in 1866 and again, with his wife, in 1877. As de facto editor of the *Westminster Review,* Evans went beyond contributing to the musical entertainment at the soirées: she participated conversationally in groups as heavily literary and as closely involved with Victorian publishing as her own salons would later become.

On Lewes's side, his travel as a young scholar introduced him to salons during the period of study in Berlin when he attended the most prominent of that time and place, the salon of Henriette Solmar. Later, as young marrieds, Lewes and his wife Agnes attended Sunday open houses at the home of Thornton Hunt (Ashton 57). In London during the next few years, Alexander Bain notes meeting Lewes at the "weekly bachelor dinners" of physician Neil Arnott, where Lewes's "arrangements" made him, along with author George Craik, "habitués of the party" (125). During the 1840s, according to Ashton, Lewes participated in journalist Douglas Jerrold's "literary clubs, where good food and drink were conducive to good literary talk" (65). Another set of gatherings that attracted people who also turned up at the Priory occurred at the home of Richard Monckton Milnes, later Lord Houghton. Haight's description of an 1863 group includes Lewes, Spencer, Swinburne, Froude, Browning, Arnold, and Ruskin (388). Other parties hosted by Milnes included the Lushington twins, Robert Lytton, Thomas Henry Huxley, and Montstuart Grant Duff, longtime friends or acquaintances. In June 1864, Milnes, the man whose gatherings were often considered outré or louche (and who introduced Swinburne to the pornography of the Marquis de Sade), came to the Priory and met George Eliot for the first time (Haight 389). He attended Sundays about once a year thereafter, sometimes accompanied by Lady Houghton.

After Evans moved away from the Strand and cast her lot with Lewes, their elopement to Germany introduced her to salonizing on a sophisticated international level in Berlin. Gerlinde Röder-Bolton describes Henriette Solmar's salons during the bitter 1854–55 winter when the Leweses attended. Refreshments were light, business talk verboten, and social inclusion prevalent: "Together with the empowerment of women as both salon mistresses and as guests in their own right, the disregard of class distinctions and the informality of salon hospitality contrasted starkly with social conditions elsewhere and has led to the salon being described as a *Freiraum*: a space beyond social classifications, where tolerance reigned, and religious and political bigotry were unacceptable" (121). She attributes Solmar's shaping of her evenings to an imitation of Rahel Levin's, which took place at her home in Berlin at Mauerstrasse 36 roughly between 1790 and the 1820s and gained fame for their (and her) intellectualism (Bilski and Braun 28–32). Indeed Varnhagen von Ense, Levin's husband, creates a link between the two because, after his wife's death in 1833, Varnhagen continued to enjoy salons and attended Solmar's alongside the Leweses. Röder-Bolton's comments that Solmar's replication of the salons of Levin made her salon "the last of its kind ... socially inclusive, unpretentious hospitality with a focus on wide-ranging, stimulating conversation and the free exchange of ideas" (126). In "Recollections of Berlin 1854–1855," George Eliot describes Solmar as "the true type of the mistress of the *salon*" (H&J 245, emphasis in original), a conclusion she bases on Solmar's "cheerfulness and intelligence" rather than on her "warmth," which is lacking, or on the unprepossessing looks of the middle-aged woman.[15]

The Solmar salons, by means of this connection with Rahel Levin's, demonstrate that George Eliot not only qualified as a successful salonière according to Victorian definitions of the term, but that Sundays at the Priory had their place in the more widespread and ongoing European salon culture. In addition to the German link, they had a direct line of descent from Madame Juliette Récamier herself. Just a few seasons before the 1869 debut of the Leweses' regular Sundays, they made a journey to Spain that began, as did many European itineraries, in Paris. There the couple

---

[15] The similarities among Levin's, Solmar's, and George Eliot's salons include their lack of beauty in the hostesses, the "modest" refreshments served (Bilski & Braun 28), and the intellectual loftiness. Bilski and Braun also mention that some guests at Levin's regarded Varnhagen (like Lewes in London in the 1870s) as the "chief architect of the 'Rahel cult'" (32).

attended the salon of the English expatriate Mary Mohl, familiarly known as Clarkey, who conducted her afternoons on the Rue du Bac for several decades.

George Eliot arrived at her first afternoon there with a specific literary goal in mind, for she brought with her a set of letters she had received from her best friend, Barbara Bodichon, about which she was seeking opinions regarding the likelihood of their publication. Bodichon had traveled Spain from north to south the previous year, and the content of her letters offered encouragement for a potential traveler by emphasizing the ease of the route. When she later converted some of the series of letters into an article that appeared in *Temple Bar,* she entitled the piece "An *Easy* Railway Journey in Spain" (my italics). Having circulated the letters at Clarkey Mohl's salon, George Eliot concluded that they should appear in a "good organ" (*GEL* 4:329) and wrote to tell her friend so. This errand on behalf of Bodichon anticipated some of the similar publication-related exchanges that occurred on Sundays in St John's Wood.

Although the Leweses preferred the smaller groups in which Mohl included them after their dissatisfaction with her regular salon, the regular salon brought George Eliot to an event that has its place in a line of descent that reached a generation back to one of the most famous of French salons, that of Madame Récamier. In her thirties, having leased rooms from Récamier at the Abbaye-aux-Bois, Mohl made acquaintances worth carrying forth when she moved to the Rue du Bac and began her own "internationally famous" afternoons (Waddington). Both Mohl and her guests saw her as carrying on the Récamier tradition, just as Solmar was doing the same with the Rahel Levin tradition. It is thus no overstatement to claim that Sundays at the Priory had links not only to its contemporary competitors in London such as those at Pre-Raphaelite artist G. F. Watts's Little Holland House (whose guest list often overlapped with the Priory's), but also to the best known of the eighteenth-century European salons, those of Levin in Berlin and Récamier in Paris.[16]

Any Given Sunday

The Sundays that flourished in St John's Wood continued to follow the pattern of a core of serious discussions of philosophy, science, and art encir-

---

[16] Frederick Locker-Lampson connects her with the salonière for whom she had expressed admiration in her 1854 essay. Of George Eliot's Sunday afternoon manners, he asserts (whether or not he was remembering her own essay of many years ago), "Madame de Sablé might have said of her, 'ella s'écoutra en parlant.' She was a good listener" (308).

cled by Lewes's stirring the perimeters into vivacity. But they also grew and changed over the years.[17] In addition to the lifelong regulars, people might attend the Sundays with intensity and regularity for a season or two and then drop out to be replaced by other similarly semi-faithful coteries. A handful of celebrities (Dickens, Bagehot, Ruskin) might make a single appearance, while others (Trollope, Browning, and Tennyson) reappeared for at least a season, often more. Barbara Bodichon, Herbert Spencer, Frederic Burton, and Charles Lee Lewes participated from the first gatherings in the mid-1860s through to the more sporadic kinds of visits George Eliot's friends continued to pay at her country home at Witley after Lewes's death.

But throughout their existence, George Eliot's Sundays remained emphatically literary salons. Editors, authors, and reviewers conducted discussions and made contacts that might result in a forthcoming article, review, or editorial position for any of the dozens of periodicals represented. Nor did authors for these periodicals hesitate to engage in critical in-print exchanges with their fellow guests.

Substantial numbers in attendance helped people with reasons for literary or other antagonisms to mingle without conflicts. Edith Simcox's antipathy to Johnnie Cross and indifference to George Eliot's other young friend, Elma Stuart, did not deter her from taking the ever-present chance of meeting them at the Priory. Du Maurier conversed alongside some of the members of the group of aesthetes whose work he satirized in the pages of *Punch*. Leslie Stephen's brother, James Fitzjames (whom Millicent Garrett Fawcett attacked for arguing that the physical strength of men requires the submission of wives) joined parties that included feminists as radical as Bodichon (20 April 1873) and Simcox (25 May 1873). Simcox herself wrote "The Capacity of Women" in 1887 to counter the assertions of psychologist George Romanes (who dropped in at the Priory several times in the spring of 1877), in his piece on "Mental Differences Between Men and Women" (Broomfield and Mitchell 583). On 18 February 1877, his visit coincided with Simcox's in a group of twelve guests.

Nor did the Priory guests shrink from writing reviews of publications by each other or by their hosts. Alexander Bain's close relationship with James Sully went back many years before Sully first visited the Priory and shared afternoons with Bain in St John's Wood. Bain reviewed Sully's

---

[17] Acknowledging the difficulty of ascertaining the accuracy of the reports of his "unfamiliar sources," Collins concludes that sometimes they conflict on the subject of the Priory Sundays: "Here it may be reasonable to conclude that since no one report is likely to be definitive, they are all true in the sense that if her receptions followed some basic script, it simply changed in details from time to time" (xx).

Figure 4
Herbert Spencer. Courtesy of the National Portrait Gallery London

Figure 5
Charles Lee Lewes. Courtesy of the National Portrait Gallery London

Figure 6
Barbara Bodichon. Courtesy of the National Portrait Gallery London

Figure 7. The Priory, exterior. From photo by Cassell & Co., Lim.

Pessimism: A History and a Criticism in *Mind* in 1877. Several of the psychologists reviewed Lewes's first volume of *Problems of Life and Mind* when it appeared in 1874. Sidney Colvin, who began visiting in 1869, reviewed *Middlemarch* glowingly in January 1873 for the *Fortnightly Review,* as did Lord Houghton for the *Edinburgh.*

Indeed, Lewes shamelessly made the Priory an arena for publicizing George Eliot's own writing, first with *The Spanish Gypsy,* then, more aggressively, with *Middlemarch,* sustaining interest by circulating word of mouth, seducing likely positive reviewers, and initiating read-aloud sessions by George Eliot herself. Lewes and his efforts offer one explanation for the grueling schedule of salons because, for all their talk about the joys of seeing guests in the most efficient and pleasant way they could contrive, Sundays at the Priory were hard work for both of the busy, sickly hosts. The exhaustion their letters express as they turn to the seasons spent at their cottages in Surrey resulted naturally from long, crowded, but immensely productive Sundays rather than, as sometimes suggested, from a general dislike of entertaining, a suggestion in any case belied by the many months of Sundays.

At the same time, the conversation at the Priory did not always go as smoothly as George Eliot might desire. When she regretted something she said or did during an afternoon, some piece of what she regarded as tactlessness or neglect, she hastened to pen an apology or an explanation as soon as possible, either Sunday night or Monday morning. In January 1874, she wrote a follow-up letter to John Cross and posted it on Monday. After inviting Cross and his sister Emily to lunch for the following Sunday, George Eliot confesses her anxieties about Mary Cross and the previous afternoon's gathering: "I was rather miserable yesterday fearing that dear Mary had a very dull visit. My small capacity for looking after my guests is always absorbed by the least interesting persons who happen to be present, and after Mr. and Mrs. Cornish came in, I lost sight of everybody else's fortunes and could only wonder whether they were as little amused as I was" (*GEL* 6:7). The Cornishes, he an Eton master (*GEL* 6:7, n. 6), she a novelist and collector of William Thackeray's letters, did not charm George Eliot and did not return to the Priory. In June of 1876, George Eliot admitted to Elma Stuart that the day's entertainment had made her "rather melancholy ever since you left, that your visit was spoiled. For me, at least; because I could not say one word to you of my gratitude for all your goodness to me" (*GEL* 6:259). At least twice she addressed Bodichon with notes that regret a flippant remark that conveyed more ill will than she intended. One guest, Sydney A. Gimson, recollected hearing from Henry Crompton of an antagonistic "discussion concerning the origin of

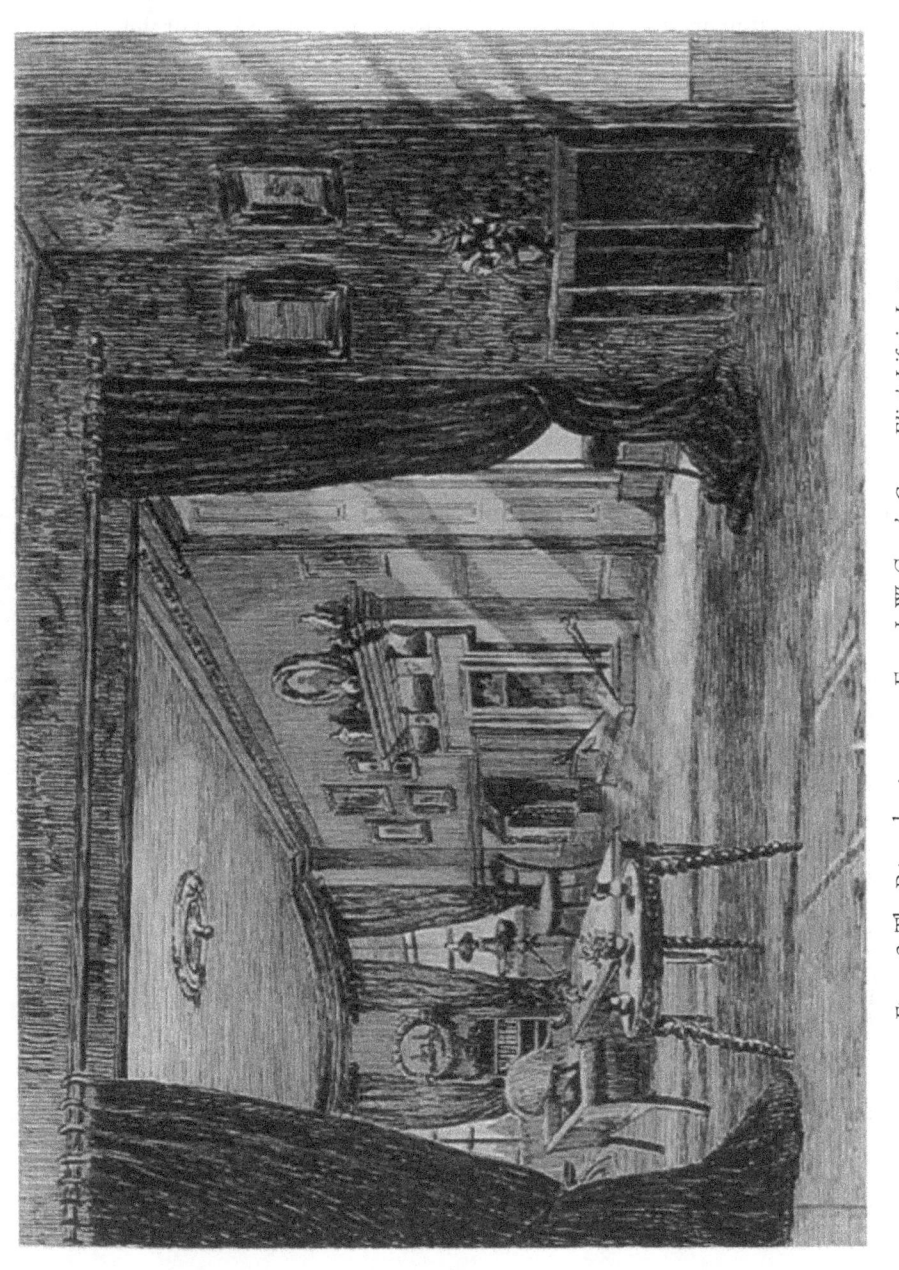

Figure 8. The Priory drawing room. From J. W. Cross's *George Eliot's Life in Letters*

music" between George Eliot and Spencer that likely occurred during a Sunday afternoon: "Crompton thought that Spencer was getting the worst of the argument and eventually he jumped up and rushed out of the room, banging the door after him!" ("Henry Crompton" Web page). As with her anxious morning-after notes to various guests, George Eliot made a lifetime project of smoothing things over with Spencer as well as other Priory guests.[18]

Indeed, the four most regular regulars (Spencer, Bodichon, Burton, and C. L. Lewes) each made specific contributions to the afternoons, Spencer's being his prickly demeanor. When the conversation verged on conflict, Spencer was often involved. The segment of guests composed of young Lewes's friends and acquaintances, on the other hand, contributes a family element, as George Henry Lewes put himself out to entertain the guests brought along by his son. Bodichon helped swell the guest list in different directions because she often invited artists, educators, and feminists of her own acquaintance, many of whom became regulars themselves. Among the artists and their critics, the fourth regular, Frederic Burton, could find an excellent audience for the progress of his current project, adding to the collection at the National Gallery. By the 1870s, having given up painting entirely, Burton nevertheless often gets mentioned in descriptions of the Priory, not for his most famous canvas, "The Meeting on the Turret Stairs," but for the portrait of George Eliot that overlooked, from a remote point in the study, the activities of Sunday afternoons.

The Place

Many guests' descriptions of the Sundays begin with the Priory itself, mentioning its situation and decor as encouraging visitors. Among the wealthiest and most social guests, Lewis and Cecilia Wingfield, for example, who met the Leweses in 1871, introduced themselves as neighbors, their having recently moved nearby to Maida Vale. Soon after, family members, most frequently Cecilia Wingfield and her mother, established themselves as regular visitors. In 1869, recommending the NW London postal code to scholar Emmanuel Deutsch (nearly always identified as the model for Mordecai in *Daniel Deronda*), George Eliot cited its convenient proximity to several Underground stops, then wryly concludes her letter: "In a word it is detestable; but less detestable than most parts of London and its

---

[18] See Nancy Paxton's *George Eliot and Herbert Spencer*.

suburbs" (*GEL* 5:73).[19] Matilda Betham-Edwards, Bodichon's friend and an ever-struggling author, comments on the Priory's seclusion as "one of the many St. John's Wood villas almost to be called country retreats. The comfortably proportioned two-storeyed residence, approached by a drive, stood sufficiently apart from the road as to ensure its inmates comparative quiet" (38–39). Robert Buchanan specifically mentions the effectiveness of "a high front wall facing the street, to which it communicates through a massive doorway" (218) in reducing obtrusive city noise. Haight and others describe a walled garden full of roses surrounding the house, isolating it and sheltering it from both street and canal traffic.[20]

The Leweses bought the Priory in 1863 and did it up with great care. Photographs show an exterior adorned with the fashionable neo-Gothic touches that justify its name. Convenient for the zoo in Regent's Park and walks up Primrose Hill, it occupied a site on the bank of the Regent's Canal, a working waterway accommodating various kinds of vessels, but mostly the barges for which the canals were originally built. Most sources describe a gate with a jingling bell for announcements, and Lucy Clifford adds "a watch-dog of a servant who knew uncommonly well how to dispose" of interlopers (112).[21] Earlier, the young Russian mathematician Soph'ia Kovalevsky had described the servant as "a young chambermaid, crisp and stiff, as are all English chambermaids" (537). Between 1869 and 1877 there had been a change in gate-keeping personnel at the Priory.

The engraving that Cross includes in the *George Eliot's Life in Letters* reveals that inside, prints and portraits crowded the walls in the Victorian style, walls covered in custom-made, Owen Jones–designed wallpaper and otherwise covered with shelves of books upon books. Lucy Clifford detects an air of Morris in the colors of the decor, while others remember an abundance of flowers decorating the room (Collins 106, 117). The often published engraving shows a theatrically broad archway hung with heavy curtains pulled aside and falling to the floor, their extra length accumulating in folds on the carpet. Light flows in strong rays through the long windows, especially those positioned in the curving wall that protruded into

---

[19] Haight places the year of Deutsch's notes in brackets to indicate that the date proceeds from his own gathering of evidence rather than from a date inscribed by George Eliot.

[20] George Eliot's 1869 poem, "In a London Drawingroom," invites comparisons between the location of the room and the Priory drawing room. But the poem positions its persona within view of the "houses opposite" (1.2) and of the pedestrians and vehicles hurrying along the street, presumably beyond the wall and therefore normally invisible to the Priory residents.

[21] According to Collins, several guests, including James Sully and Charles Warren Stoddard, attributed magical powers to the jangling bell at the gate, which "once the bell was rung mysteriously unlocked on its own" (xxi).

the garden beyond the fireplace. An advantage on a sunny Sunday, when the room could look "bright and pretty" (Simcox 71), the windows provided less cheer when the rain came heavily or the frequent fogs shrouded the garden.

Sources agree unanimously that on crowded afternoons George Eliot took the low easy chair next to the fireplace, while an even lower rush-bottomed chair to her left would accommodate the individual conversations accorded in particular to first-time guests. Regarding the other furniture, Charles Lee Lewes's daughter Blanche remembers especially well "the enormous number of armchairs in the drawing-room at the Priory, which mother told me were there because George Eliot and Grandpapa didn't like to sit in armchairs themselves unless everyone else in the room could do so too" (Paterson 250). Arthur Paterson continues, "This is a characteristic touch, for not only did George Eliot dislike feeling that she was more comfortable than others, but she hated still more to be in any way enthroned, even at her receptions" (250). The effort at anti-regal egalitarianism could not always have succeeded. Betham-Edwards creates a dramatically opposite first view of the drawing room scene: "There in the center of the room, as if enthroned, sat the Diva; at her feet in a semicircle gathered philosophers, scientists, men of letters, poets, artists—in fine, the leading spirits of the great Victorian age" (42).[22] The sofa, placed at right angles to the low chair in the Priory engraving, became an occasion of irritation for Oscar Browning because it often accommodated "fashionably dressed" ladies who "seemed to fill the room" (90). He again complains about the sofa's occupant when he notes that, Récamier-like, Barbara Bodichon "generally reclined upon the sofa" (*Memoirs* 192). In fact, the dress of the women guests varied from the deliberately plain Pre-Raphaelite styles worn, for example, by Georgiana Burne-Jones and Rosalind Howard, through George Eliot's own simple but carefully designed

---

[22] This description follows with a physical description of George Eliot that comes oddly from an observer who saw her as frequently as did Betham-Edwards. On her first meeting the novelist in 1867, she found herself confronted by a "tall, prematurely old lady wearing black, with a majestic but appealing and wholly unforgettable face. A subdued yet penetrating light—I am tempted to say luminosity—shone from large dark eyes that looked all the darker on account of the white, marble-like complexion. She might have sat for St Teresa" (40). The dresses worn by George Eliot show a stature far from "tall," while her pale gray-blue eyes, memorably described by Georgiana Burne-Jones as appearing "washed by many waters" (*Memorials* vol. 2, 4) should not have appeared "dark" to her visitor. As another example of faulty reliability, Betham-Edwards wonders at the lack of pets at the Priory (59), although the Leweses adored their dogs as Beryl Gray has noted. Haight emphasizes some of Edwards's inconsistencies in *GEL* volume 5 and elsewhere. By the time she wrote her reminiscences, she was over eighty years old, and so her memory may have faltered on several matters.

dresses accessorized with good lace, to the crinolines and bustles of which George Eliot makes fun in her second Saccharissa essay, "Modern Housekeeping," by mentioning the enlargement of drawing rooms as an effect of the fashion for hooped skirts. Oscar Browning claims that the redecoration of the Priory by Basil Champneys in 1871 (by which the Priory gained the decorator as an addition to the guest list) included expanding the drawing room, which he claims was increased in size to accommodate the crinolines worn by some of the women guests (90). Simcox noted that a larger crowd necessitated pushing the sofa back against the wall, away from its usual position closer to the fireplace, to create more floor space for expanding parties of guests (71).

Catering

Because the salon afternoons followed luncheons attended by a selected four or five guests, they did not offer heavy refreshments. Two reports suggest that the other arrivals had to wait at least an hour before receiving so much as a cup of tea. Lucy Clifford put tea-time at 5:00 P.M. and agrees with Betham-Edwards that Lewes did the pouring and that "Mrs L. was reverently served" (115). Then, according to Betham-Edwards, the company would drift "towards the lower end of the room, Mr L presiding at the teapot" where he signaled his readiness to serve: "'To make tea, my friends,' he said laughingly, 'I hold is the whole duty of man.'" (44). The tea also signaled a relaxation in the atmosphere: "All now was comparative frivolity, gaiety, and persiflage; mirth and music replaced Socratic discussion and talk worthy of being Boswellised" (Betham-Edwards 44). Writing of the salons that occurred some five years after Betham-Edwards's period of attendance, Clifford found less relaxation ensuing after tea. Guests accepted their cups and "sat solemnly down again" (115) to resume serious talk. As for food, Clifford reports that each saucer accommodated a "bit of doubled thin bread and butter" (115). Although the Leweses themselves drank alcohol on occasion and had plentiful assortments of glassware in which to serve it to their guests, no one mentions convivial consumption occurring on the Sundays.[23]

---

[23] Both George Eliot and Lewes drank alcohol (See *George Eliot and Intoxication,* 29–32). They included wine and beer on their shopping lists and sampled different varieties as they traveled in Belgium, Germany, Italy, France, and Spain. Brandy, too, appears at least once in their notebooks: on the menu of a simple supper in May 1861 in Florence (*GHLJ* 22 May).

Sources and Themes

In addition to Lewes's diaries, which provide both the Priory guest lists and journals of their travels, the indispensable letters and journals, as collected primarily by Haight, William Baker, and Margaret Harris and Judith Johnston, provide material concerning both the salons and the spas. Reminiscences of many Victorians whose associations with the Lewseses have gone unnoticed add more of Collins's "unfamiliar sources" (xviii). For the sections about the Leweses' foreign travels, the voluminous nineteenth-century guide books help differentiate one spa from another and provide background for the information contained in the couple's letters and journals. Far exceeding the presentation of information about railways, hotels, and dining, *Murray's* and their ilk often add anecdotes, histories of the sites, excerpts from literature set at the locales, and such moralizing interjections as those about the horrors of gambling in the spa guides as detailed in chapter 5, which concerns *Daniel Deronda*. As they traveled, the Leweses could not get on without their guide books. When they left one behind at a shop in 1875 (GHLJ 24 September), they were dismayed enough for Lewes to note the loss in his diary even though their destination on that occasion, Wales, would not require as much useful information as they needed, for example, in Spain or even Italy.

The shift in George Eliot's social status that occurred during the mid-sixties coincides with the Leweses' beginning regular visits to Black Forest spas and forms the point at which I take up my narratives of their travels abroad, accompanied by descriptions of some of the people they met and the creative results in George Eliot's poetry and prose.[24] Roughly chronological, the descriptions of the Priory Sundays begin with their launch in

---

[24] George Eliot responded early in her career to efforts to find models for her characters with the assertion, which she repeated often, that she assembled them as composites from "widely sundered elements" (*GEL* 3:55). Hence conclusions such as Haight's concerning the Pattisons as models for the Casaubons, can fall into the hazards that accompany any attempt either to substantiate or demolish proposed models because they attempt to draw one-on-one correspondences that George Eliot's composite method precludes. Lewes himself several times acknowledges this strand to George Eliot's creativity. In 1876, he refers to Anton Rubenstein as "Klesmer" (*GEL* 9:177), and, also in 1876, teases Robert Lytton about his similarities to Daniel Deronda. Currently, Kathryn Hughes is repeating the trend of the earliest audiences in looking for Warwickshire models for characters, specifically the Dodsons. Haight goes so far as to reify some of the usual identifications on the caption pages inserted in the *Letters*, such as "GE sees 'Gwendolen' at Homburg" (9:27) and "GE and GHL meet Rubenstein ('Klesmer') at Lehmann's" (9:169). Henry's commitment to observing connections between characters and models in her 2012 biography leads her to offer, among others, the original and irresistible suggestion that George Eliot based Rosamond Vincy on Agnes Jervis Lewes (82).

1869 in the regular form they would take for the next decade. Because this launch coincided with George Eliot's continuation of her poetry writing, the group, which often included Robert Browning, conversed much about poetry, its theory and practice.

During the period later that year when Thornton Lewes's terminal illness precluded the couple's usual retreat to a summer lease in Surrey, the salons continued through the summer, and new additions to the guest list included some important potential regulars. Meanwhile, George Eliot was writing *Middlemarch* volume by volume, and Lewes was depending partly on the Priory afternoons to encourage its success. The swell in numbers of visitors after *Middlemarch* coincided with the initiation of occasional musical entertainment, and events at the Priory, like a number of the settings and some of the action in *Daniel Deronda,* had much to do with drawing room recitals. Meanwhile, the added numbers of guests included a substantial gay and lesbian component whose members help connect George Eliot's interactions with her gay and lesbian friends, especially on the topic of marriage, with the creation of characters such as Priscilla Lammeter, Mr. Brooke, and Gwendolen Harleth.[25] Finally, the Leweses' travels abroad and Sundays at the Priory combined to yield material for the story of Gwendolen and her mother in *Daniel Deronda.*

Although Lewes's death in 1878 put an end to the salons as they went forth on Sundays, not only did George Eliot depend on the help of some of her former guests as she undertook to publish the final volume of Lewes's *Problems of Life and Mind,* but a number of the guests' activities afterward took them in surprising directions sometimes prepared for by the time they had spent at the Priory. On the travels side, the final events of George Eliot's life included the disaster of her 1880 honeymoon with John Walter Cross, which resulted in her last substantial period at a Black Forest spa that attracted many British visitors, Bad Wildbad.

Although Lewes's journals contain few descriptions of the events of the afternoons, combining his entries with the accounts of other visitors reveals that neither scandal nor dullness dominated the parties. Instead, intellectual, artistic, scientific, political, philosophical, wealthy, sometimes titled guests contributed not only to a lively social atmosphere but also to the workings of George Eliot's creative imagination and the marketing of her books. If the traditional image of nearly all-male groups of guests

---

[25] Dennis Gouws and Nancy Henry have added to this list of possibly non-heteronormative George Eliot characters. Gouws argues that Seth Bede and Dino de' Bardi "exemplify an enthusiasm-enabled, potentially transgressive manhood" and consequently "challenge the integrity of her moral realism" (1). In "The *Romola* Code," Henry describes another *Romola* character, Nello, as a man who shows repeated interest in Tito as a love object.

standing as stiff as statues, conversing in subdued tones, and reverently approaching the sibyl does not account for the range of activities at the Priory—the music, the rose-filled garden in the summer, the buzz of continuous anecdotes, the richly philosophical conversation, and the romantic interests of the guests—nor does it, or other more familiar accounts, suggest the more business-oriented activities of the afternoons. Together with the travels abroad, Sundays at the Priory placed George Eliot among people similar in many ways to the characters in her poetry, her last two novels, and *Theophrastus Such*. George Eliot's participation in Society—with the big S—resulted partly from carefully contrived Sunday salons in London and led to fiction and poetry peopled by other members of Society, as she and Lewes pursued their social activities both abroad and at home in London, at the Priory.

CHAPTER 2

Travels Abroad
Taking the Waters

Our routine is this. Up a little before six and after tub and toilet out on the promenade. There drink the sparkling water and lounge in the sun listening to the tolerable band performing overtures, movements from Beethoven, and Haydn's symphonies, pot-pourris and waltzes. Nine-thirty we start for our ramble often with our books, oftener not. We walk and talk, sit and muse or read, listen to the birds and watch the mystery of light and shade in beech and fir woods.
—George Henry Lewes, *George Eliot Letters*, 1 July 1866

Between 1866 and 1868 George Eliot and George Henry Lewes were, quite deliberately, building a social circle that eventually matured into the guest list for Sundays at the Priory. In several cases, their annual travels had already resulted in new or enhanced friendships. In 1860 they had become acquainted with the T. A. Trollopes in Florence, and the following year journeyed with Tom Trollope to the remote monasteries of Camaldoli and LaVerna where George Eliot had the opportunity to talk about monasticism with an actual Catholic monk and to see an entire building fitted out with every religious subject (Annunciations, Crucifixions, Nativities) all done by the Della Robbias in the same medium of ceramics. In 1864, they shared their Italian time with Frederic Burton, depending on his taste as an artist to enhance their enjoyment of Luini, Titian, Veronese, and the Bellinis, especially in Venice.

During 1866, the Leweses established their routine of visiting European spas, always with the primary goal of better health for one or both of them. At the same time, such venues lured many well-off English travelers to a non-English environment likely to encourage the loosening of social prohibitions. In 1867 they made their daring journey through Spain, a project that depended on encouragement and advice from friends who had gone before. Their route helped fortify their relationship with Robert Browning since choosing Biarritz as one of their stops followed his recommendation.

After Biarritz, on their way to Spain, they solidified their acquaintance with the Frederic Lehmanns by detouring to Pau, a Pyrenees mountain spa, where Nina Lehmann was seeking therapy. In 1868, the couple visited Baden Baden, their first highly fashionable spa stop, and, afterward, even the journey to the small and remote Sankt Märgen yielded a new titled acquaintance, the Countess Ida Von Baudissin, who attended a Sunday on 19 June when she visited London in 1870.

During all their travels abroad, the Leweses were likely to encounter both old and new friends, but the health-seeking habits of the Victorians meant that the spas provided especially frequent points of intersection. By the end of 1868, George Eliot was expressing satisfaction with the success of their effort: "We have made some new friendships that cheer us with the sense of new admiration of actual living beings whom we know in the flesh, and who are kindly disposed toward us " (H&J 134). The following January 1869 brought the serious launch of Sundays at the Priory.[1]

Spas

The couple began their systematic routine of hydropathy at European spas in 1866, a routine that ultimately resulted in *Daniel Deronda*'s opening setting and also in details in several poems along the way. But both George Eliot and Lewes were long used to seeking health at watering places: at seasides and the towns surrounding inland springs in England, and at mountain spas abroad. The couple began resorting to watering places for health improvement at the same time they began their courtship. The summer of 1853 began with an interval at Tunbridge Wells for Evans but concluded with a period at St. Leonard's during which Lewes most likely joined her, partly to participate in the therapies available at the facilities of Spa Cottage, supervised by Dr. Emil Grosslob.[2] But Lewes's health did not improve in St. Leonard's, and, after their return to London, he again departed for a watering place, this time to Malvern, a visit which provided him with material for two periodical pieces written in his Vivian persona,

---

[1] Nancy Henry (*Life of George Eliot*) concurs that the salons began in the "late sixties" (154).

[2] See McCormack, *George Eliot's English Travels*, 44–47.

Figure 9
Baden Baden. Author's collection

"Douche the First" and "Douche the Second." In 1854 their momentous elopement, which included their quest for material for Lewes's biography of Goethe, took them to German destinations, notably their first home together in lodgings in Weimar. Excursions from their headquarters there on the Kaufstrasse included destinations, notably Ilmenau and Bad Bercka, that offered hydrotherapy, providing an incidental but desirable occupation with which to vary Lewes's Goethe research.

Despite the brevity of the couple's side trip to Ilmenau, it formed one of the most memorable interludes of the couple's early life together, so much so that they returned thirteen years later for a sentimental revival. By 1867, the train had reached the town. Nevertheless, on that occasion they switched to an open carriage at Arnstadt, a transfer that permitted them to reminisce in fuller detail, "so that at particular turns in the road we could say—Here we plucked the plumes from the roadside trees—Here I saw such a dog, or told such an anecdote—Here we rested & had coffee &c" (*GHLL* 2:122). At the same time, the railways, along with the expanded bathing facilities, meant that Ilmenau had lost a good deal of the quiet isolation they had enjoyed on the earlier visit.

In September of 1854, the lovers spent five happy days in this out-of-the-way spot.[3] They launched this phase of their continued pursuit of Lewes's subject on the twentieth, traveling by railway and post-wagon. Later they blamed their headaches and upset stomachs on the long, jolting journey. But the headaches faded, and they soon found themselves wandering in the pleasant meadows by the River Ilm.

In Ilmenau, they climbed the mild hills extending to the south and west, sometimes as pure refreshment, at other times with specific Goethe-related destinations in mind. Their excursion to the rustic Goethehäuschen auf dem Kickelhahn, despite a long period of fruitless wandering until set on the right path, they nevertheless called "a merry walk!" (H&J 232). The impressive bathhouse, including "a douche lofty and tremendous enough to invigorate the giant Cormoran" (Pinney 122); the fresh food; the beeches and the pines; the rich eggy colors of the buildings in the valley all contributed to the memorable joys that the illicit honeymooners shared during their watering-place experience in Ilmenau.

Meanwhile, their travels in Germany in 1854 brought them new friends and also confirmed relationships with some old ones. Haight's account of George Eliot's elopement includes a long list of both the Weimar and the Berlin acquaintances whose visits constituted the apparent social normalcy of their first months together, emphasizing the importance of its members and their acceptance of the unmarried couple. Gerlinde Röder-Bolton provides a wealth of material to demonstrate that in Weimar the couple suffered little or no ostracism, indeed moved in a stimulating artistic milieu.

Only one domestic circle from their German trip did not appear to welcome Evans. On Thursday, 7 December, in Berlin, Lewes set out with "Magnus the chemist" (as opposed to his brother "Magnus the painter" [H&J 424]) for a Sitz bath, when a spontaneous invitation from Ignaz Olfers, director of the Neues Museum, diverted him from his purpose. Evans reports the event in a generous tone. Lewes returned to Dorotheenstrasse to dress "having wisely given up the Sitz in favour of a party at Prof Olfers" (37). His partner settled down for an evening alone in Berlin.[4]

---

[3] Ashton, erroneously, reduces the holiday to a single afternoon (*George Eliot: A Life* 71).

[4] According to Röder-Bolton, also puzzled by this single social exclusion, Evans wrote about her evening alone "claiming that it was the first night she spent *alone* [her italics] in Berlin . . . though Lewes had been out on his own alone" (159).

Two weeks later, Lewes again went to Olfers', while she worked on her Spinoza translation and again on 25 January, while she read Adolf Stahr. On the other hand, Hedwig Olfers attended Henriette Solmar's salon on Friday, 9 March, where she apparently had no objection to meeting Evans. It was a small foretaste of the routine but variable and sometimes unpredictable ostracism awaiting them in England, where Lewes frequently responded to dinner invitations addressed solely to him. Their relationships in Weimar included the Adolf Schölls, a happy family of five; the Sauppes, who, with the Schölls, joined them on an excursion out of town to the Tiefurt Schloss; and the French ambassador, the Marquis de Ferrière, no less. English friends in town included S. D. Williams, "an agreeable, unaffected young man" (H&J 25), Thomas Wilson who was in Weimar as an English teacher (H&J 446), and James Marshall who was serving as secretary to a Duchess (425). As in the months at Berlin that followed, their social relations in Weimar had an ease that they had to surrender entirely when they returned to England early the following spring. Without question, Franz Liszt issued the most important social invitation of their stay. The breakfast party in the vine-covered garden adjoining his lofty house, the Altenburg, initiated friendly relations that persisted until the end of the Leweses' stay.

A few days after returning from Ilmenau, the Leweses received an important English visitor, Arthur Helps, future Clerk of the Privy Council. He would remain Lewes's friend through the troublesome days to come. After they returned home to England, Helps facilitated Lewes's writing projects and invited him down to Hampshire over Christmas. Until 1857, when they finally announced their situation to the Evans family back in Warwickshire, Lewes left Evans home on Christmas day to go to Vernon Hill. Afterward, he waited until Boxing Day to leave her on her own in Richmond.

In Weimar, things went well with Helps. Evans reports that he and Lewes talked together all morning long, after which the three met for coffee, and the conversation concerned travels abroad: "In the evening we drove to Ettersburg, and he entertained us with charming stories about his Spanish travels" (H&J 23). The morning-long talks could not, however, have settled all the issues relevant to the couple's circumstances. In the middle of October, Lewes sent out two letters "explaining his position" (27), one to Helps and one to Thomas Carlyle. The importance of Carlyle stemmed from the people Lewes expected to meet at his next stop, Berlin, people who also knew the Sage of Chelsea: Varnhagen Von Ense, Otto Gruppe, Christian Rauch. He did not want his anomalous living arrangements to disqualify him from the company of the Berlin residents he needed to interview about Goethe. And, in the end, they did not. He dedicated the biography to Carlyle. During the 1870s, Helps's daughter Alice eventually became a regular Sunday guest at the Priory.

Meanwhile, the Leweses found a nearby watering place to which they returned several times. Bad Bercka lay only a few miles from Weimar, but it offered in miniature the usual spa amenities: comforts for the body such as garden walks and restaurants, as well as the baths and the waters in which they placed their hopes of health. George Eliot, in "Recollections of Weimar," catches the spirit of joy they found there: "One of our visits to Bercka is individualized in my memory. . . . We set off in a high wind which was very perturbing to G. It softened a little as we went on, but was still violent enough to blow G's hat off. He ran in pursuit of it and so entirely lost the sense of annoyance in that of the comic, that he began to run with squared legs and arms, making a perfect Töffer sketch of himself. When we set out home a shower came on to which we were indebted for the said rainbow. We had neither of us before seen a rainbow thus springing from the ground, and we eagerly watched it till it faded away" (H&J 229). When the time came to move on to Berlin, their social acquaintances would become even more important, especially to Lewes's Goethe biography. But, although walks in the Tiergarten and along the Unter den Linden pleased them very well, they had left their watering-place joys behind. The honeymoon, though by no means over, had changed.

Setting the Pattern

After returning from Berlin to Britain in 1855 the Leweses did not travel beyond its borders for several years. Their journeys took them to seaside resorts to accommodate research for Lewes's *Sea-side Studies* project, which required waterfront destinations: Ilfracombe, Tenby, and the Scilly and Channel Islands. They then returned to Germany, although not to a watering place per se. Instead George Eliot chose Munich and Dresden as the main locations to write the later chapters of *Adam Bede*. After the publication of George Eliot's first full-length novel, they remained at home in England until the completion of *The Mill on the Floss,* whose publication called for a celebration. The Leweses chose Italy and mounted a three-month simulation of a Grand Tour that reached as far south as Paestum. *Romola* kept them visiting Italy as George Eliot pursued her research both on-site and in the Maglibecchian Library. Only after publication of another

English novel, *Felix Holt,* did the Leweses initiate the series of interludes at mountain spas that they continued till their dying days.[5]

At Schwalbach and Schlangenbad in 1866, the couple established the mountain-spa routine they followed ever after. They drank the waters at the various springs and had their showers and wraps and baths. They listened to the music that often played all day long, from the first glass of water before breakfast through the evening coffee. They drank chocolate at outdoor cafés while reading the London *Times,* and they strolled the promenades and parks, as well as pursuing more active walking excursions or, later, drives, into the nearby hills. They generally retired for the night at 9:00 or 10:00 P.M.

The layouts of the various spas the Lewses visited most often contained similar components that helped govern and cater to the activities favored by the guests. The Kursaals housed spaces for gambling, eating, drinking, reading, writing, smoking, and conversing, all usually contained within a lavish or at least eager display of architecture and ornament. The tree-lined promenades offered shady walks and the diversion of encountering acquaintances. Some Kurpark walks followed the boskiest paths along shallow swift-running little rivers such as the Oos at Baden Baden and the Ilm at Bad Bercka, while paths taking other directions reached the various springs. The hotels, broad low buildings limited by the absence of lifts to a manageable height of four or five stories, provided comfort and often elegance, as well as food for the body. And there was always a chance of improved health from drinking the waters and taking the baths.

Despite the sameness of the facilities among the many German spas, they differed in the treatments they advised, the composition and temperature of their waters, and the theories of hydropathy held by the individual physicians practicing there. Thomas Madden lists the possible varieties of spring: "Chalybeate, sulphurous, salines (simple alkaline, muriated, and acidulous), bitter waters, iodated, earthy, and chemically indifferent mineral spring" (6). Differences in the chemical composition of the waters meant that the various spas addressed differing maladies. According to Madden, the waters of Schlangenbad "are employed in rheuma-

---

[5] Otherwise, as the Leweses proceeded to the main destinations, they stopped at such places as Plombière, Chaudfontaine, and Bonn for brief periods of taking the waters for just a day or so. They also availed themselves of the baths situated in places on itineraries composed without particularly health-seeking motives in mind. In Rome, for example, in 1869, they enjoyed their baths on the Via Barberino (GHLJ 7 April), and in 1870 George Eliot remedied an attack of unwellness with a visit to Charlottenburg, on the edge of Berlin. See the Appendix, a chronology of "The Leweses' Travels Abroad," which includes the longer stays at European spas.

tism, rheumatic arthritis, impeded menstruation, and neuralgia," while in Schwalbach, "three quarters of visitors have anemia, also dyspepsia and constipation" (13). Although Madden attributes efficacy with chronic indigestion and "cartarrh of the respiratory organs" (140) to Baden Baden, he qualifies these with his own opinion of the Baden Baden waters in general, which he finds rendered ineffective by the area's climate. On the subject of the effectiveness of drinking and bathing, authors often warn against excess. According to Madden, the thermal baths can kill as well as cure.[6]

Mary Ann Evans's experience with spas began as a young woman in Warwickshire with Leamington, where she hoped to remove from Coventry during the 1842 quarrel with her father she called the Holy War. It went on until after her 1880 marriage to John Cross, when the newlywed Mary Ann Cross hoped that the therapy at Bad Wildbad would help her new husband recover after his sudden onset of mental illness in Venice. In between, although she sometimes sent Lewes off alone to try his luck at English spas, from the time they began their regular visits in the 1860s, they generally traveled together to or through the Schwarzwald.

In addition to the hope of health that served as the primary attraction for the sickly couple, the beauty of the mountainous scenery surrounding the Black Forest spas vastly appealed to the Leweses. Although the gambling put them off, they also enjoyed the sociability, the concerts, and the availability of long walks. Regarding the medical care, they had uneven experiences that yielded uneven opinions. In an 1861 letter to Theodosia Trollope, who was considering trying the regimen at Malvern, George Eliot describes James Gully, one of the most famous spa physicians, as "a quack" (*GEL* 3:472). On the other hand, George Eliot so admired the St. Leonard's spa physician, Emil Grosslob, during the summer of 1853, that the Leweses called on him on their return south-coast visit in 1861. In general, the Leweses' frequent returns to watering places at home and abroad suggest a confidence that could not have entirely excluded the men who practiced there.

The spas of both England and the Continent reached many of the works George Eliot produced after she began her visits, including "Agatha," *Middlemarch,* and *Daniel Deronda.* A side trip from a mainly spa journey in 1868 yielded the first, a poem about an aged woman intending a religious pilgrimage. Although George Eliot set her long poetic drama *Armgart* in Berlin (with a side reference to the spa at Charlottenburg), she conceived the idea as she and Lewes pursued one of their lengthy walks toward the

---

[6] See *George Eliot and Intoxication* about the ambiguity of drugs that can either kill or cure, presented in the context of Jacques Derrida's deconstruction of the Platonic Pharmakon.

soaring viaduct outside of Harrogate Spa in 1870.[7] George Eliot made some use of her growing experience in such venues subtly in *Middlemarch,* primarily in the Finale's description of Lydgate's fate as watering place physician. But the major impact reached *Daniel Deronda,* and it all began, not in Bad Homburg in 1872, where George Eliot famously wrote home about her impressions of Byron's gambling grandniece, but four years earlier when Lewes first introduced George Eliot to the action at the roulette table at Baden Baden during their 1868 summer visit.

Schwalbach and Schlangenbad

The Leweses' first large-scale period at a Black Forest spa began in 1866 with Schwalbach and Schlangenbad, followed by more bathing in Bonn, Louvain, and Chaudfontaine. The journey started and ended with strenuous touring of Belgium and the Netherlands, including stops in Rotterdam, The Hague, Leyden, Amsterdam, Cologne, and Coblenz on the way out and Bonn, Aix, Liège, Chaudfontaine, Louvain, Ghent, Bruges, and Ostend on the return. Along the way they had to avoid a troublesome war, which crowded the cities disagreeably with soldiers, but they took a certain pride in their ability to do so.

At first, the experience in Schwalbach delighted them. They had privacy, superb walks, their work, their reading, and the satisfaction of at least taking action against their physical ills. From their hotel, the Duc de Nassau, they could step right outside the door onto the hillside promenade. Picturesque half-timbered houses lined the principle street, while gift shops displayed Schwalbach souvenirs: "pretty trifles in Bohemian glass; carvings in horn, wood, and ivory; jewellry; prints and books; and children's bravery" (Wilson 111). Because of the hilliness of the town itself, more challenging excursions than the promenade also began at the doorstep of their rooms (*GHLL* 2:96). They found the water "delicious" (2:96), the music "tolerable" (2:98), and the regime strengthening.

Three springs feed the baths at Schwalbach, which in the 1850s immersed or sprinkled 350 people a day (Madden 137). Once Madden found his visit coincided with that of the Empress Eugénie and contrasted the sumptuous baths reserved for royalty with the "lofty and airy [but] in no wise handsome" facility for ordinary people (137). Schwalbach's physician was Dr. Gentpath, who treated the majority of the visitors primarily for anemia but also for dyspepsia and constipation.

---

[7] Bodenheimer overlooks Dr. Grahn's reference to Charlottenburg when she identifies the setting of *Armgart* as "an unnamed European capital" (179), rather than Berlin.

Authors suspicious of the effectiveness of hydropathy conclude that regardless of its efficacy the spa routine often facilitated recovery not only through its walking and water drinking components, but also in interrupting harmful habits maintained at home. Madden, for example, believed in the superiority of hydropathy to drastic draughts of strong drugs. But authors also warned of the importance of the correct length of treatment. Too long, they believed, could render the treatment deadly.

While the Leweses took the waters conscientiously, the crown to their joy in Schwalbach was the privacy they found in the walks among the pinewood-covered hills that crowded closely around the town. According to Lewes, their fellow guests, the majority of them women, made "expeditions in carriages & on donkey to distant spots & points de vue, but the varied and indescribable beauties lying immediately within reach are left unvisited" (*GHLL* 2:98). The Leweses took full advantage of the forest solitude. In a letter to his son, Lewes compares himself and the "mutter" to Adam and Eve: "I wonder whether they stopped to kiss as often?" he asks (2:98) about their own walks. Within the privacy of the empty woods, in a post-Eden Eden, they liked to take interludes of rest lying supine under the trees while gazing upward at the filtered, leafy light.

In Schwalbach, the couple discovered that they could shape their days to insure the desired proportions of work, exercise, privacy, therapy, and company when they wanted it. They took particular pleasure in their freedom to dine independently. Ever since the gustatory tyranny of the table d'hôtel in Berlin in 1855, with its financially obligatory attendance and its call for participation in polite conversation, they tried to avoid this dining arrangement, and they did so successfully in Schwalbach.

Driving through the Rhine valley on the way to this satisfactory destination, the coach had passed through the nearby spa town of Schlangenbad. From his perch on top of the omnibus, Lewes made a mental note of its attractive appearance. This came in handy when several factors prompted them to move on from Schwalbach. Laughing at the slapstick fears of other visitors who ran here and there to escape the threat of a Prussian invasion of the militarily irrelevant mountain spa town, they became caught in their own snare and developed their own anxieties on the subject. Their pleasure in Schwalbach also diminished partly because of a rainstorm. Since Lewes had liked the look of Schlangenbad when he viewed it from the omnibus, they followed their original intention to move there after Schwalbach.

Despite the proximity of the two spas, Schwalbach and Schlangenbad differ in their size, their styles, and the composition of their waters. According to Madden, "From Schwalbach to Schlangenbad, the transition is easy and natural, for only five short miles separate them and yet how different are these Spas" (142). For one thing, Schlangenbad had a milder climate: "Being situated on the southwestern slope of the Taunus range, and well protected from harsh wind by the hills, it enjoys a much milder and more genial climate than Schwalbach" (142). This author finds additional advantages in its quietness, despite his positive evaluation of its band (143).

Despite Schlangenbad's comparative plainness, the Leweses secured luxurious accommodations at the Hotel Palntz, in a suite complete with a balcony. Madden describes a typical evening in Schlangenbad: "As usual the band was playing after dinner, and all the visitors were assembled, the ladies plying their never-ending embroidery, the children playing around them, and the men all sending up volumes of dense smoke, like so many ambulant factory chimneys" (143). This cozy family scene emphasizes the less fashionable small-spa atmosphere, so different from Baden Baden or Bad Homburg, and different, as well, from Schwalbach just down the road.

The waters at Schlangenbad, which rise from thermal springs, receive praise from both the guide books and from Lewes. According to Madden, the Schlangenbad waters "afford peculiarly agreeable sensations to the bather and render the skin soft and white" (143). Lewes concludes that "we like this place better than Schwalbach, partly because of the Schwimm Baths which are incomparable luxuries—water as clear as crystal and soft as milk" (*GEL* 4:284). When they moved on by boat, they had reason to regret it because of a "bad dinner on the Rhine" (GHLJ 22 July 1866). Lewes "was violently sick on arriving at Bonn," and the sulphur waters there pleased him only when he was fully immersed: "the most luxurious and soothing of baths" (22 July). On getting out, however, he found the evil sulfur smell unpleasant.

Both Schwalbach and Schlangenbad turn up in *Daniel Deronda* in a single character name: the shared surname of the Baron and Baroness von Langen, Gwendolen's companions in Leubronn. Frequently prefaced in the guide books with the description "Langen" (long), Schwalbach suits the adjective because of the shape created by its location in a deeply carved mountain valley. Schlangenbad encloses the same word within three-letter sets at either end of the name. The Von Langens in *Daniel Deronda* have hardly any identity beyond their existence at Leubronn and their unanticipated and highly fortuitous invitation that provides Gwendolen her opportunity, after meeting Grandcourt's former mistress at the Whispering Stones, to find escape from England and her problematic suitor's attentions at a distant spa. Reduced to little other than their convenient association with this setting, they carry a name adapted from two of the Black Forest watering places George Eliot visited in 1866: Schwalbach and Schlangenbad.

The stays at Schwalbach and Schlangenbad set a lifelong pattern. The Leweses continued to frequent the spas of Germany, varying them with English, French, Belgian, and Swiss watering places, for the rest of their lives. They believed in the effectiveness of change of air and experimented with the various bath and shower possibilities. They drank the waters, which sometimes seemed to help. They enjoyed the concerts and some of the luxury. Consistently, at the Kursaals and along the walks, they met people and went to places that contributed to George Eliot's creativity.

"Agatha"

Two years after Schwalbach, the Leweses were back in the Schwarzwald, again seeking health and relaxation, and, as it turned out, finding more material to encourage a creative imagination, if not permanent good health. They made a substantial stop in Baden Baden and then headed for the more remote Bad Peterstal where they lingered three weeks, before beginning a quicker itinerary through Switzerland. The journey included two stops that stimulated George Eliot: the village of Sankt Märgen, the setting for "Agatha," and its neighboring town of Freiburg, which George Eliot mentions in widely scattered but always positive connections in several of her works.

In July of 1868 the Leweses had a ten-day stay in Freiburg, made "memorable" by much "lionizing" (*GEL* 4:458) of George Eliot. Then they drove out from Freiburg to seek refuge, health, and solitude in a village to the east of the town. One of George Eliot's most direct adaptations of a European site as a setting occurs in "Agatha," where all the topographical and architectural details of this small hilly and remote location match the setting in the poem. Advancing toward Sankt Märgen, George Eliot expressed her hopes of wrapping herself warmly and sitting out of doors where the best views look southward toward Switzerland and France.

George Eliot wrote enthusiastically of Sankt Märgen. The scenery pleased her: "A region of grass, corn, and pine woods, so beautifully varied that we seem to be walking in a great park laid out for our special delight" (*GEL* 4:457). In a letter to John Blackwood, she creates an evening scene at their hotel: "Last night as we were having supper in the common room of the inn we suddenly heard sounds that seemed to me like those of an accordian [*sic*]. 'Is that a zittern?' said Mr Lewes to the German lady by his side. 'No, it is prayer.' The servants, by themselves—the host and hostess were in the same room with us—were saying their evening prayers, men's and women's voices blending in unusually correct harmony. The same loud prayer is heard at morning noon and evening from the shepherds and workers in the fields" (*GEL* 4:457). The pretty music at dinner promised well for their stay.

But the inn itself, despite its charming introduction to local religious life, offered the Leweses only inadequate shelter against the mountain weather. One day they did brave the temperature and attempted to make themselves comfortable in the sun. But the following day they gave up. Meanwhile, in the company of another guest, the Grafin Ida von Baudissin and her eighteen-year-old daughter, Agnes, George Eliot made the visit on which she based her 1868 poem, "Agatha." The voice of the poem describes her character Linda as a young noblewoman whose philanthropies include keeping a school. This figure probably combines the Grafin and her daughter, who eventually, like Linda, came to head a school in Freiburg (*GEL* 4:459).

In "Agatha," the details of Sankt Märgen, which George Eliot selects for attention, help establish the merits of the pious Catholicism practiced by Agatha and her neighbors, a religion that brings together members of the community in loving mutual concern. The poem renders Catholicism in almost exclusively female terms. In the first hundred lines, George Eliot merges characters and settings in maternal/Madonna images, including the earth, Agatha, the cows, and the visitor from Freiburg, Countess Linda. The action occurs "where the earth spreads soft and rounded breasts / To feed her children" (11.3-4). The Madonna image on the cottage wall is made diminutive and domestic, smiling on "home things" (1.24). Pictures of mostly female saints associated with marriage and maternity, Ursula and Ann (supplemented by the mild St. Francis of Assisi), ornament the walls of Agatha's cottage. The water of the tiny brook running past the cottage is like laughing children. Agatha's stream turns a sawmill and also "feeds the pasture" (1.58) for the "matron" cows (1.60), named individually: Blanchi, Nägli, and Veilchen.

Even the Augustinian monastery on the other side of the hollow participates in a feminized, domesticated community religious ritual. Its bells unite the people dispersed among the mountains, hollows, and valleys by calling them to pray the Angelus at the same intervals several times a day. As they all respond together to the ringing by participating in the same act of devotion, the people unite themselves to one another.

But though the monastery bells ring out a command responded to throughout the area, the poem's voice points out that they no longer issue from a community of monks whose "shadows fall no more / Tall-frocked and cowled athwart the evening fields" (11.34–35). As at the monastery in the nineteenth century, working families have replaced the holy brothers in the cloisters: "Their silent corridors / Are turned to home of bare-armed, aproned men, / Who toil for wife and children" (1.37). The peasants also honor a highly domesticated Mary "dear / As all the sweet home things she smiles upon" who "puts her crown away / And with her little Boy wears common clothes" (11.29–30).

As anchorite, mystic, and pilgrim, the central character, Agatha, like the religion she practices, in turn unites the community members, who all recognize her virtue in caring for her dim-witted cousin. They also appreciate her willingness to pray for them when needed. For their part, the villagers provide the inhabitants of the one-room cottage with food and clothing. At the cottage, the garden gate and the front door stand open because, like Mary (as depicted in ubiquitous paintings of the Annunciation), Agatha receives visits not only from needy neighbors but from a specific angelic character: "One long summer's day / An angel entered at the rose-hung gate, / With skirts pale blue" (11.87–89). The voice, embodied as another visitor to the cottage, introduces Countess Linda, who, clad in blue, holy in her saintly philanthropy, has hair like Rosamond Vincy's, "soft and blonde as infants'" (1.90), but appears as a "mamma" to the orphan children she patronizes in Freiburg.

With Linda's arrival, dialogue between her and Agatha replaces the observations of the narrative voice (so vaguely drawn as to lack even an identifiable gender), who participates in the poem's action by going along on the cottage visit. The dialogue reveals another community function of the devout cottager. By herself making a pilgrimage to Einsiedeln, the massive Benedictine abbey south of Zurich, Agatha will represent all the villagers, whose agricultural tasks keep them from doing it themselves. Hence, Agatha, among the most impoverished of George Eliot's characters, is nevertheless herself a traveler. She has already made one pilgrimage to the Benedictine shrine; she anticipates a return in the future.

Agatha's pilgrimage destination could not form a more dramatic contrast with her surroundings in Sankt Märgen. The monastery at Einsiedeln is of enormous size, with high towers flanking its entrance and interlocking quadrangles housing the church, the monks' residences, and the lodgings for pilgrims. A pilgrimage site since the fourteenth century, its central location in Switzerland made it an attraction for Swiss Catholics both before and since the Reformation.

The monastery attracts devotions to two figures, its founder, the Benedictine hermit St. Meinrad, and the Black Madonna, so called because of the coal-darkened visage on her ornately dressed statue in the chapel. The construction of the Abbey celebrates both of these objects of devotion because the shrine to the virgin stands on the location of the saint's first refuge, a small chapel, complete with door and windows, enclosed within the abbey church itself.

Despite the distance of geography and circumstance, when Agatha draws near her goal, the tiny chapel housed within the massively frescoed larger building, she sees a structure not very different in its proportions from her own cottage in the hollow. Though the black marble of the chapel and its ornament are more sumptuous, both are small in scale, just one room. Both, in addition, are full of devotional iconography: Agatha's pictures of her favorite saints and the chapel's frescoed walls. The chapel extends George Eliot's comparison between Agatha and the Madonna she worships. Indeed, the similarity between the two one-room buildings, one the residence of Agatha, the other of the Black Madonna, suggests that George Eliot was including in her poem a little reward of recognition for the well-traveled reader, the possibly rare reader who would appreciate the improbable similarities between cottage and chapel.

But for all the celebration of Agatha's Catholicism, nearing the action at the end of the poem, the persona reintroduces peasant superstition into the plot. Returning home drunk after a celebration, a group of peasants sings the song that concludes the poem. The singers concede that when they reach Agatha's cottage they "go and shake the latch," but accompany this with a wish that the three residents "sleep on till morning beams, Mothers ye who help us all" (11.56–57). In this concluding song, Agatha, the epitome of Catholicism, shares attention with Toni, a neighbor crushed to death by a wagon. The villagers believe that Toni lingers in Sankt Märgen in the shape of a ghostly white cow that wanders about the village in the mist, and, like Agatha, contributes to its neighborliness. The conclusion of the poem thus presents an unanticipated, rawly superstitious, male-dominated scene that contrasts with the female saintliness gone before in Agatha's cottage.

The experience in Sankt Märgen, for the Leweses, however, was both too rustic and insufficiently independent. Lewes tired of making conversation with the other guests, whether saints or sinners, including the mother/daughter models combined in the Countess Linda. And so the couple moved on, back to Freiburg, and then on to Switzerland.

Journeying in Switzerland George Eliot was revisiting a country which formed one of her destinations when, in 1849, she undertook her first European travel in the company of her Coventry friends, the Charles Brays. After wintering in Geneva at the home of the family of François d'Albert-Durade, she returned to Warwickshire, and the head of the family traveled with her, thus giving her brother Isaac, universally accepted as the model for Tom Tulliver, the opportunity to see and judge their relationship. D'Albert-Durade became first (and forever) her friend, then her portraitist, then, years later, her translator, as well as an often-mentioned model for Philip Wakem in *The Mill on the Floss*.

George Eliot's second journey to Switzerland (1859) centered on two goals: rendezvousing with the Richard Congreves in Lucerne and the revelation to Lewes's sons of his new familial relationships.

George Eliot's friendship with Maria Congreve revived an acquaintance from her girlhood, for in 1849, as a young Coventry resident, Maria Bury accompanied her father, Dr. John Bury, on a professional call on Robert Evans. She and the novelist met again when they became neighbors in Wandsworth in 1859. The relationship survived after the Leweses moved to their series of residences in the Marylebone/St John's Wood area through shared meals and exchanges of overnight visits. When George Eliot married John Cross in 1880, one of the few announcements to friends that she wrote herself, rather than entrusting to Charles Lewes, required braving the Congreves' Positivist belief in permanent widowhood and/or the suspicions that she was either defying or trivializing what she had required others to acknowledge as her own marriage to Lewes.

In 1859, the Congreves supplied valuable companionship for George Eliot during Lewes's delicate journey to visit his sons at school. While he was away she passed the days at the comfortable and "charming" (H&J 78) lakeside Schweizerhof, strolling and chatting and waiting for Lewes to return with news of how his sons had welcomed his news. The delicacy of his mission as he advanced from Zollikoffen to Hofwyl called on him to equip himself with gifts, tact, and support as he approached the pleasantly situated school which provided benches overlooking a gentle valley, benches that Lewes took advantage of in his serious talks with his sons. Evans remained in Lucerne near the Congreves, not venturing even as far as a hotel in Berne, lingering instead in the harborside hotel that commanded a view of all the nautical traffic on the busy lake.

Lewes's satisfaction with his completed mission in Zollikoffen called for celebration when he returned to George Eliot in Lucerne. Accordingly, the following day they embarked on a river steamer for a cruise all the way down the lake and back again. The scenery edging Lake Lucerne, like a neat narrative, begins gently with a series of pleasant villages and rises to an impressive climax supplied by the spectacular Alps rising at its distant southernmost point. Generally, the sightseeing boats zigzag from one village to another: Bauen with its small, white-sided churches; Rutli, where greenery reaches all the way down to the lake; Treib with its colorful chalet and boats docked ready for use below the landing. The view gathers impact as the lakeside altitudes increase, with the Massif rising off to the right. The trip also included poetic resonances from the story of William Tell and from the monument to Goethe situated on a tip of land off to the starboard side of the southbound steamer.

This lake route brought the Leweses closer to Einsiedeln than they had ever reached before or since. But to visit the monastery as a detour from the cruise in 1859 would have required a circuitous land journey physically impossible on a day with hours occupied by the length of the lake and a leisurely lunch at the town, Fluellen, where the steamer turned back toward Lucerne. Nor did their 1868 Swiss journey provide the opportunity to duplicate Agatha's pilgrimage. To be sure, they started out as she does with a stop in Freiburg before they proceeded from Sankt Märgen to Basel, which would lie along Agatha's planned route south on the way to Einsiedeln. But, although they were following Agatha's projected route to start, no evidence indicates that the Leweses completed the journey to Einsiedeln. Instead, they turned south toward Thun and Interlaken (H&J 132). Meanwhile, the guide books on Switzerland describe all the details included in the poem, in particular the custom of sending just one villager on pilgrimage for the spiritual benefit of his or her neighbors unable to travel themselves. George Eliot's nineteenth-century guide books, with all the abundant background and detail they contained, provided her more than tips on traveling well and cheaply. She was not above depending on them for descriptions, anecdotes, and ideas she gathered from the ample narratives that accompanied information on hotels, railways, and sights.

Leubronn

The two most fashionable nineteenth-century German watering places, Baden Baden and Bad Homburg, both contribute to the settings and characters for the key chapters in *Daniel Deronda,* which establish and carry forth the novel's important gambling motif. Although the incident usually described as the "germ" of George Eliot's last novel, the view of Lord Byron's grandniece gambling recklessly at roulette, occurred in Bad Homburg in 1872 (Haight, *Biography* 457), it was at Baden Baden four years earlier that Lewes first drew George Eliot's attention to the activities in the casino.

The Leweses arrived to sample the luxury of Baden Baden in June 1868. They stopped at the Hotel de Russie, which provided "everything we could wish except in price" (GHLJ 3 June). In Baden Baden, life centered on the Kursaal, the nearby trinkhalle, the gardens behind, and the promenade in front. Their first two days, the rain prevented their usual walks, so Lewes found himself lounging in the Reading Room sampling the latest *Pall Mall Gazette*. Then, momentously for George Eliot's fiction, "at two-o'clock I looked into the Conversation Haus & watched the gambling" (GHLJ 4 June 1868). Impressed in spite of himself, he immediately "fetched Polly to see." They stood observing the action under the cherubs and scrolls of the ceiling decoration, horrified and fascinated by the greed and compulsiveness shown by the afternoon rainy-day crowd. They remained watching until the "excellent" orchestra began its performance and lured them outside to listen, despite the chilly wind sweeping across the lawns and promenades in front of the Kurhaus.

The next two days of sunshine permitted the Leweses to pursue their more usual out-of-doors activities. On Friday they drank their water, heard the band, and "looked in at the Reading Room" (GHLJ 5 June 1868) yet again. On Saturday, they had a lengthy and healthful day climbing the hills toward the Altes Schloss. During their periodic rests, they read William Morris's *The Earthly Paradise* in the woods along the way. Altogether, they spent nearly five hours out of doors on the hill. The contrast between nature's and society's haunts could not have been stronger when they revisited the Kursaal after dinner to have another look at the roulette. By the time they left Baden Baden, George Eliot had had her first encounter with serious gambling, an activity that she develops as one of her metaphors for disruptions to causality, fellow-feeling, and narrative itself, to a slight degree in *Middlemarch* in Fred Vincy's plot, and as the dominant metaphor, as well as an important plot element, in *Daniel Deronda*. The aversion to gambling embodied in both plot and metaphor in *Deronda* had already begun to grow four years before the 1872 Bad Homburg trip usually regarded as pivotal to the composition of George Eliot's last novel because of the casino visit on which they watched with sorrow the gambling of young Geraldine Leigh.[8]

After Baden Baden, the Leweses found their Paradise in Bad Peterstal, little more than twenty kilometers south of Baden Baden but situated in very different terrain. Indeed, the move there from Baden Baden has the aspect of a retreat. Lewes mentions both high prices and "stupid" gambling as reasons for their departure (*GEL* 4:450). But the Leweses also enjoyed the remoteness because it distanced them from the reviews of *The Spanish Gypsy* currently appearing in London, and about which they both had some nervousness.

---

[8] See chapter 5 concerning the 1872 Bad Homburg journey.

Baden Baden and Bad Peterstal could not contrast more vividly. Baden Baden's fancy buildings, broad promenades, active spielbank, and busy shops hosted well-heeled visitors and provided them the usual spa therapies. Bad Peterstal provided similar therapies, primarily baths, showers, and drinking waters, but in a far different setting: simpler and more dramatically mountainous. While Baden Baden sits on the edge of the increasingly high hills that rise from the Rhine plain, Peterstal lies deep within one of the twisting valleys that penetrate these ever steepening hills.

The couple made their approach along the road that begins at the railway station at Appenweier and rises in altitude from village to village as the range itself gets higher. Among the Peterstal hills that plummet so steeply down from their heights into the valley, the couple found themselves nestled almost face to face with walls of green grass or shoulders of dipping and swirling, nearly vertical meadows reaching upward toward the patches of mountain forest. The chalet architecture of its homes and gasthauses, with their sloping roofs and flower-filled balconies, made Peterstal appear more like an Alpine village than an overdecorated spa town.

Like the scenery, the small scale, the excellent food, and the preservation of anonymity, the waters again seemed to offer comfort to the health-seeking couple. According to George Eliot, they drank "diligently," and they bathed "at due intervals" (*GEL* 4:454). She describes the water as "nectar-pearly with carbonic acid, and rich in iron and palatable salts" and concludes, "We are both wonderfully stronger, but poor little Pater still pays tribute to his enemy King Liver in the form of headaches that linger on to the second day" (4:454). On the other hand, palpitations such as Lewes had experienced during a climb at Bonn, had disappeared.

Bad Peterstal also had the remoteness desirable to a nervous poet awaiting the reception of her daring departure from writing the novels that, even before *Middlemarch* and *Daniel Deronda,* had already made her famous and beloved. The most important news from home, news of the reception of George Eliot's major venture into poetry, *The Spanish Gypsy,* came as if swirling up the deep valley of the River Rench as Lewes and Blackwood corresponded about the questionable reviews. The reviews were indeed mixed, but the remoteness of the town "unknown to Murray" helped dilute their effects. George Eliot wrote to Blackwood on 24 June that "I think we have hardly ever, except in Spain, so long ignorant of home sayings and doings, for we have been chiefly in regions innocent even of Galignani" (*GEL* 4:459-60). The distance between London and the watering place where they had a "life all peace and poetic suggestion" distanced them as well from professional critics of poetry as penned by one of the public's favorite novelists.

As usual they bragged about their superiority to the more pedestrian visitors who are "almost without exception lingering the live-long day about the precincts of the 'Bad'" (*GEL* 4:454). They sustained a nodding acquaintance with the British community, from which they successfully hid their identities until the very end of their stay, one explanation for its unusual duration. When queried at the table d'hôtel, Lewes pretended to be his own brother, and he deflected curiosity effectively for three weeks before one exceptionally "pretty" and "cultivated" guest beguiled him out of his incognito. The news spread through the hotel, and provided them a departure suitable for a Corinne at the Capitol: "The Landlord seemed overwhelmed with the 'honor his establishment had received'; several gentlemen and ladies came to express their enthusiasm and to beg my card; and all the guests assembled to see us off, waving handkerchiefs and bowing. It was very pleasant" (*GEL* 4:458).

Just as their joy in Bad Peterstal did not abate for a full three weeks, the mixed reviews of *The Spanish Gypsy* did not deter George Eliot from continuing to write poetry. At their next mountain stop, Sankt Märgen, she did not find the surroundings as beguiling as at Bad Peterstal. But she did gather material for her most direct adaptation of the mountain village as the setting for "Agatha." Meanwhile, George Eliot, poet, with her editor/consort, undertook to stabilize Sundays at the Priory into an arena where Lewes could tout her poetry and further his studies of physiological psychology. When Sunday at the Priory became a regularly mounted, numerously attended institution starting in 1869, poetry absorbed much interest.

CHAPTER 3

Months of Sundays

That trick is, the artificer melts up wax
With honey, so to speak; he mingles gold
With gold's alloy, and, duly tempering both,
Effects a manageable mass, then works.
But his work ended, once the thing a ring,
Oh, there's repristination! Just a spirt
O' the proper fiery acid o'er its face,
And forth the alloy unfastened flies in fume;
While, self-sufficient now, the shape remains,
The rondure brave, the lilied loveliness,
Gold as it was, is, shall be evermore:
Prime nature with an added artistry.
—Robert Browning, Priory Guest, *The Ring and the Book*

Valentine's Day, 1869, fell on a Sunday and brought to London a short interlude of faux spring weather that coaxed the foliage in the Priory garden into premature budding. This uncommon February sun and warmth, added to the usual prospect of fascinating, and possibly useful, conversation, helped bring many callers to the Leweses' home in St John's Wood that day. As guests gathered in the drawing room before the long windows, for once occluded by neither rain nor fog nor the earliest of the early winter dusks, the occasion demonstrated the success of the couple's attempts to regularize their contribution to the season of London salonizing. Robert Browning had recently brought out *The Ring and the Book,* as much a metatext about writing poetry as the story of an Italian murder. He led the conversation about versification, and several of the guests noted the high points of the afternoon in diaries, memoirs, and letters to friends.

The Leweses had been moving toward such a goal since the mid-sixties period that formed a transition between social isolation for George

Eliot and the institution of Sundays at the Priory. Having found their new home in St John's Wood in late 1863, the couple began welcoming friends in various ways and numbers during 1864 without yet establishing a regular day for receiving. Callers that year included the perennials Bodichon and Burton, the Theodore Martins (she was Helen Faucit), and the Richard Congreves. During the early months of 1864, they met several times with the Martins on various days of the week, while weekend visits to and from the Congreves in Wandsworth, which occupied all of Sunday, indicate that there were as yet no regularly scheduled salon afternoons. On Sunday, 10 April 1864, Lewes's mother, Elizabeth Willim, dined with them, another arrangement that suggests they were not anticipating other visitors.

The year 1865 began with small Sunday dinners and a visitor or two afterward. Then in February they threw a Saturday night gathering George Eliot describes with an exclamation point as "our first Evening party since last winter!" (H&J 123). Since Lewes was at this time involved in the launch of the *Fortnightly Review,* such occasions facilitated his reentry into the world of journalism on the editorial side. Meanwhile, George Eliot was briefly reviving her journalistic publications with the four small pieces, including the two Saccharissa essays, for the *Pall Mall Gazette,* plus a review of William Lecky's *History of the Rise and Influence of the Spirit of Rationalism in Europe,* written to contribute to the success of the new *Review.*

Socializing and journalizing continued to mix at the Priory and elsewhere through 1865. On 24 June, Lewes "dined at Greenwich with the multitude of so-called writers for the Saturday" (H&J 124) at which the conversation concerned current contributors and touched on George Eliot's recent essays. The following day, a Sunday afternoon occurred that in a small way anticipated the ones to follow in later years. Seven people came to the Priory: "Barbara and the Doctor, Maestro, Colonel Pelly and his friend Mr Jeffrey the Conchologist, and Mr Neuberg. Later Danby Seymour." Two weeks afterward, an "agreeable gathering" (H&J 125) of eight, together with a group of five on 9 July and a "good group" on the twenty-third included more repeat visitors and soon-to-be regulars, notably Herbert Spencer, Robert Browning, Henry Crompton, and the Alexander Bains. Still mostly men, however, the group at this point meets Haight's description of an assemblage of journalists and positivists.

The Leweses' extensive travels of the mid to late sixties included not only the Black Forest trips of 1866 and 1867 but also the Spanish journey from January through March of 1867. But by May Lewes was at home and referring to "Our usual gathering[s]" (GHLJ 26 May 1868).

After a September 1868 interlude in Harrogate, the couple returned to London in October, where their first Sunday at home consisted of her work on *The Spanish Gypsy* and his dogged plugging away at his science, as well as another routine visit to Lewes's mother. On Sunday, 20 November, Lewes left George Eliot alone at the Priory while he went "to consult with the people concerned in the management of the Reader" (H&J 121). They finished up their social year with December dinners with Anthony Trollope and Frederick Chapman, then with Ned Pigott, one of Lewes's oldest and most constant friends. Christmas fell on a Sunday that year, and they welcomed Bessie Parkes and Isa Craig, but otherwise entertained only a "long call" (H&J 122) from Dr. Juda Stummer, the German physician who had recently treated Lewes at Malvern, but who never resurfaces on their guest lists.

Dinners at the home of the wealthy and social Ernst Benzons and concerts at St. James's Hall augmented their social life that year, as did Lewes's attendance at the 1868 British Medical Association meeting at Oxford, supposedly an occasion for increasing his status among scientists, but also an opportunity for recruiting future guests for Sundays at the Priory. In 1868, in preparation for Lewes's role at the meeting, the couple spent March and part of April at Torquay, then had an interlude in Germany before Lewes made his journey to Oxford. In addition to validating and enhancing his scientific interests at the heavily attended Oxford meeting, Lewes gathered a group of potential guests, notably Charles Eliot Norton, Haight's main source for the description of Sundays at the Priory. Other Oxford trophies included Dr. Clifford Allbutt, Dr. Joseph Frank Payne, and physiologist George Rolleston.

Indeed the afternoons Norton describes in Haight's excerpt provided the January 1869 launch of the Sundays in the form they would take for the next decade: a small lunch followed by callers, an ongoing increase in the number of women in the group, the occasional pursuit of a worthy charitable cause, and conversation that often concerned what this group would regard as business as well as pleasure, since the business of so many of them concerned some kind of published writing on topics of frequent common interests. Their travels abroad, Lewes's attendance at the 1868 BMA meeting, joining the audiences at London concerts, and introductions from friend to friend allowed them to assemble groups of respectable size most Sundays during the spring of 1869 and with a new regularity that established Sunday afternoon as the Leweses' day.[1]

---

[1] Not that the Leweses had London Sundays all to themselves, the most notable competitor being G. F. Watts's salon at Little Holland House, which had an overlapping guest list with the Priory, particularly among the at that point loosely defined and delineated

Poetry at the Priory

The arrival of the Nortons in St John's Wood in January of 1869 coincided with the beginning of a Priory season whose visitors and activities had much to do with poetry, for George Eliot, as U. C. Knoepflmacher first noted, spent much of her time between *Felix Holt* and *Middlemarch* writing poems rather than prose ("Fusing" 47). Not only was George Eliot herself writing poetry, but she penned her own theoretical essay "Notes on Form in Art" in 1868, followed by "On Versification" in 1869. She was also reading widely in literary history. Knoepflmacher mentions Thomas Warton's *The History of English Poetry* and Edwin Guest's *History of English Rhythms* as part of her autumn reading in 1868. Indeed Knoepflmacher's tour de force contribution to Ian Adam's classic *This Particular Web* (1975) has George Eliot deciding at this point between a second long poem (about Timoleon) and the prose project that became *Middlemarch*. He argues that GeorgeEliot's immersion in poetry creates in her later fiction a realism that differs from the simpler representation she practices and advances in her early fiction.[2] The saturation of *Middlemarch* with a mass of literary, historical, and artistic allusions demonstrates how "[b]y fusing history and fiction, the prosaic and the poetic, the factual and the mythological, George Eliot blurs through the superiority of her own 'sugared invention' the fixities which her main characters [Casaubon and Lydgate, for example] adopt" (50).[3] He quotes "Notes on Form in Art" to support his point that in *Middlemarch* her allusiveness allows her to "integrate smaller and smaller parts, all carefully differentiated by creating new 'conditions of common likeness or mutual dependence'" (51). Indeed, he describes the novel as "that poem in prose called *Middlemarch*" (68). What Knoepflmacher calls George Eliot's "replacement" of a planned poem about Timoleon with *Middlemarch* causes Haight to celebrate (fervently) the abandonment of the grandiose poetry project in favor of the greatest novel she ever wrote (413).

At the Priory afternoons, the guests participated in differing ways in George Eliot's temporarily overwhelming interest in writing poetry. Nor-

---

Pre-Raphaelites. Other regularly held Sunday gatherings would include the likes of Henry Huth's assembly of bibliophiles to sample their host's collection of seventeenth-century volumes. The sanctity of Huth's Sunday afternoons allowed, in fact probably encouraged, his wife and daughter to spend their own Sunday afternoons at the Priory. Georgiana Burne-Jones and Lucy Clifford mention that they conducted Sunday salons themselves, though both spent so many Sundays with the Leweses that it is difficult to see where they fit them in.

[2] See *The Limits of Realism* as well.

[3] *Middlemarch* allusions include Isaac Casaubon, Meric Casaubon, Francis Meres, Sidney, Dante, Wordsworth, Byron, Samuel Daniels, and, of course, Shakespeare.

ton himself was promoting Walt Whitman (whom George Eliot mentioned in a mixed tone in an 1856 number of the *Westminster Review*) among others, and his wife Susan Norton delivered to George Eliot a much appreciated volume by the Nortons' friend from Massachusetts, James Russell Lowell. Lewes was still promoting *The Spanish Gypsy,* which had finally reached publication the previous year, and most of the visitors had read it.[4] Meanwhile, George Eliot was composing poems eventually published in 1874 in a volume titled *The Legend of Jubal and Other Poems.* The individual poems themselves began appearing in periodicals one by one in 1869.[5]

Occupied with poetry, George Eliot gathered its practitioners, theorists, and historians about her at the Priory in 1869, the height of her poetic career. The habit sustained by educated Victorians of bringing out a volume of poetry during their early twenties afflicted most of the people likely to turn up at Sundays at the Priory. But that season the Priory also entertained some of the more aspiring among professional poets of the time. Harry Buxton Forman, a friend of Charles Lewes's from the Post Office and a devoted critic of the Romantics, built on his fortuitous acquaintance with Lewes's son to extend his interests to the poetry of George Eliot, through the invitation from his co-worker to Sundays at the Priory. His visits continued from 1869 to 1873.[6]

Valentine's Day brought the faux spring Sunday when the garden outside the Priory showed early leaves, "budding beyond the permission of the calendar" (*GEL* 5:16). Thirteen guests, at that time considered by the hosts a "numerous" party, gathered in the neo-Gothic house on the Regent's Canal (H&J 135). In a group that included, besides Robert Browning, the *Golden Treasury* anthologist Francis Palgrave; Mark Pattison, the future biographer of John Milton (for the *English Men of Letters* series in

---

[4] So had the "Boston Set," as Lewes called it, whose members, he claimed in 1869 in a letter to his son Charles (*GEL* 5:37), could quote long passages from *The Spanish Gypsy.*

[5] Contributors to the September 2011 number of *George Eliot–George Henry Lewes Studies,* devoted entirely to George Eliot's poetry, speculate on what prompted her attempts in the unfamiliar genre. Herbert Tucker attributes the shift to a desire for the playful experiments possible in form, prosody, and content (20). Linda Peterson, drawing on Haight, mentions certain "events of 1864" as well as "professional motives" resulting from "the disappointing critical and commercial response to *Romola*" (31). Kimberly J. Stern, writing heroically of *A College Breakfast-Party,* believes that George Eliot chose poetry because of its usefulness as a vehicle for philosophical debate (93). Alexis Easley points out that publishing "The Legend of Jubal" and "Armgart" in *Macmillan's* reveals George Eliot's eagerness for celebrity (107). Others, La Porte, too, poses the question and argues that she was consciously placing herself within a nineteenth-century tradition that attributed gender-specific subjects and techniques to verses written by the "poetess" rather than the "poet" (172).

[6] Haight attributes to Forman "Dithyrambic praise of *Agatha* in an essay in his book about *Our Living Poets* (1871)," but also names him as a participant in a bizarre forgery of the poem as well (*GEL* 5:36–7, n. 2).

1879); Alexandra Orr, who specialized in Browning and his poetry; and George Eliot, who had just that day finished "How Lisa Loved the King," poetry dominated the conversation. Along with this solid poetic contingent, lifelong regulars Bodichon and Burton, as well as the Theodore Martins, completed the group of eager listeners for Browning and the others.

One of the Priory's most overlooked guests, Browning created the most memorable sensation of the day. As the group gathered around the famous figure, Browning, according to George Eliot, "talked and quoted admirably apropos of versification" (H&J 135). Mark Pattison offered the opinion that "the French have the most perfect system of versification in these modern times" (H&J 135), a comment George Eliot seemed to respond to as remarkable since she emphasizes it with an exclamation point. Faucit, who had found *The Spanish Gypsy* so touching that she cried while reading it (T. Martin 299), was in the middle of Browning's recently published *The Ring and the Book* and delighted to discuss it with the eminent poet. "How pleasant," she gushed, "to pop upon him thus while reading his poem! If possible it gave greater zest to it." Browning received her admiration gracefully and returned it by making a proposal that impressed the woman actor already very used to being sought out to perform, including by the Leweses. According to her diary, Browning exclaimed to her, "Ah, if I could have had you to *act* my Pompilia." The potential for acting Pompilia enriched her reading: "As I proceed with this book this speech fills me with grateful happy thoughts. How kind of him to say so!" (T. Martin 301–2). Even Dr. Joesph Frank Payne, a lifelong but infrequent visitor from the medical contingent, contributed to the poetic discussion by bringing along his brother John Burnell Payne, who had a professional interest in *The Spanish Gypsy*. Everyone involved seems to have regarded Valentine's Day in 1869 at the Priory as a triumphant afternoon in the service of poetry and a supreme experience in London literary salonizing.

The poetry-related discussions lingered in George Eliot's thoughts through the following Monday when the previous afternoon's conversation with Dr. Payne's brother brought forth one of her hastiest post-salon notes. After her guests departed, she penned an invitation to Payne for the following Wednesday, commenting that "Mr Lewes tells me that I shrink from a duty in being unwilling to talk to you on the subject you mention [*The Spanish Gypsy*], so I am compunctious" (*GEL* 5:12). When the nervous young man arrived at the Priory, she responded to his timid critique by narrating the composition process of the poem, a narration Haight summarizes in notes leant him by Payne's niece. He concludes that the version Payne heard corresponds with the creative process Cross includes in the *Life in Letters,* in the passage he calls "Notes on the Spanish Gypsy."

On the Wednesday afternoon when Payne had George Eliot all to himself, he was not seeking casual conversation, but rather taking advantage of a Priory visit by projecting a periodical publication of his own. When he met George Eliot tête-à-tête, he began the conversation by launching a narrative of his spiritual concerns. Like many Priory guests who had reason to expect a sympathetic response to conscientious struggles of doubt and faith, he had gone through the process of preparing for the Church and later turning from orders to a writing career. With his literary goals in mind, Payne was hoping to write an "elaborate article" (*GEL* 5:16) on George Eliot's dramatic poem.

Lewes's encouragement of George Eliot's invitation to tea provides another illustration of their use of the Priory as an arena for self-promotion among likely reviewers of her work.[7] Although George Eliot knew nothing of Payne's own writing, she knew he contributed to prestigious periodicals. In her letters, she enumerates "the Pall Mall Gazette, Macmillan's, Vanity Fair" (*GEL* 5:12, n.7) as venues for Payne's publications. At this poetic tea party, she also learned they had friends in common in Warwickshire, for the Paynes were related by marriage to her old Coventry schoolmistresses, the Miss Franklins.

Payne's writing career produced critical essays on both literature and art. By 1869 he had published a three-part series on Pre-Raphaelite painting, the first part, according to William Michael Rossetti, a small history of *The Germ*. His piece on "English Art" came out in June of 1869 in *Macmillan's*. But sad reasons intervened to prevent completion of the "elaborate" article for which he was gathering material during his post-salon interview with George Eliot at the Priory, for Payne died later that year at the age of thirty.

Meanwhile, a tense little note to her old Coventry friend Sara Hennell reveals how seriously George Eliot was taking both her poetry writing and the opinions of the circle that gathered at her salons. Together with Spencer, Hennell lunched at the Priory the week before Valentine's Day, and the talk concerned Browning's poetry. Without any of her usual graceful introductory personal remarks, the letter George Eliot hastened to write after the luncheon moves directly to a discussion of *The Ring and the Book*, which pivoted on Browning's assertion (to the best of George Eliot's memory) that "Man cannot create, but he can restore" (*GEL* 5:13), as illustrated by allusions to *Faust* and then the biblical Elisha in Part I of *The Ring and the Book* (5:13). George Eliot does not restate Hennell's point of view, though the latter's interests in faith and piety may have called

---

[7] See Easley regarding George Eliot's poetry and her abilities at "self-marketing" (107).

forth a spiritual interpretation of the biblical allusion. But she corrects her friend's interpretation of the two allusions which, in apparent contradiction of Hennell's interpretation, she calls "manifestly symbolical" (5:14). She then hastens to account for Hennell's error by theorizing that her old Coventry friend read the lines out of their context, or that they were possibly "pointed out or quoted to you by your friends" (5:14). With little tact, she laments how misinterpretations of literature afflict authors (linking herself with Hennell, whose work on *Thoughts in Aid of Faith* drew mixed responses) and abjures Hennell "to set any one right, when you can, about this quotation from Browning" (5:14). The crispness of the note indicates how, as George Eliot was developing a star-studded social life in London, she was withdrawing slowly but steadily from the friends of her youth in Warwickshire, a withdrawal abetted by Lewes, who found the lot of them, especially Charles Bray, intellectually inadequate. The Coventry friends did not appear at Sundays at the Priory, although the correspondence with Hennell continued for a good while with some regularity before dwindling to annual birthday notes.

The Sundays of early 1869 also marked the first occasions on which George Eliot read from her works in progress to guests at the Priory. Lewes clarifies how this practice began with the private readings in which they engaged during her entire creative life. On 14 February 1869, he notes, "Polly read her poem of Lisa *to me*" (my italics). On the twenty-first, he follows his guest list with the notation that she read "Lisa aloud," though he does not specify the audience. But on the twenty-eighth, he clarifies his assertion when he names their post-salon dinner guests: "*Dr Ward* [his italics], Gertrude and Charles to dinner. Polly read them Lisa and Armgart." Reading aloud to her guests, a practice rarely if ever associated with George Eliot, but which she carried on with her subsequent works, began with the poetic endeavors that coincided with the commencement of the regular Sundays in 1869.

The Big "S"

Society with a capital "S" was represented in those early days by members of the titled Stanley family. Lyulph Stanley became the first to visit, in January 1869, and he continued coming, although infrequently, through 1880. Just turning thirty at the time of his first visit, he belonged to a family of passionate social activists and, like Payne, followed the common Victorian pattern of losing his religion, in his case followed by a leaning toward Comtism (Jones 14). Afterward, he dedicated himself to reform from a secular perspective. He eventually found his main endeavor in educational improvements. When he married Mary Bell in 1873, he did not hesitate to bring her to the Priory.

Stanley's sisters, Kate and Rosalind, contributed the respectability of titled woman guests to the early Sundays. Kate, Lady Amberley, came with her husband once or twice a year until her early death in 1874, while Rosalind, married to George Howard, the ninth earl of Carlisle, made year-round and regular appearances, often together with her husband, but sometimes individually, through 1877. Like the Pattisons, the Howards had a reputation for carrying on in an unhappy marriage. Biographer Virginia Surtees Michael catches the sense of turbulence in her title, *The Artist and the Autocrat*. She describes George Howard as mild and "uxorious" (18), a patient Pre-Raphaelite watercolorist, and Rosalind as an aggressive suffragist whose temperance activities eventually resulted in her closing all the pubs around Castle Howard where, by the 1880s, she was living apart from her husband. Meanwhile, she had borne eleven children, many of them during the 1870s, the decade during which she participated in the salons at the Priory. George Eliot welcomed her partly for her decorativeness; she describes her later as "pretty Mrs. G. Howard," one of several visitors (Edmund Gurney, William Allingham, Kate Field, and the golden-haired Emilia Pattison) whose comeliness balanced the appearance of the famously plain-looking Priory hosts.

As a friend of the Burne-Joneses, Rosalind Howard found Georgiana Burne-Jones's socializing with the Leweses helped pave the way for her to follow her friend to the Priory despite the Leweses' scandalous circumstances. The two couples spent Christmas together in 1868 and talked about George Eliot's lack of beauty and about *The Spanish Gypsy*, which George Howard liked, while the Burne-Joneses, who had not yet read it, remained apprehensive about their friend's ability to handle poetry (Michael 64). Indeed the Howards preceded the Burne-Joneses to the Sundays, although not to the Priory where the more famous artist and his wife had lunched the previous March. The George Howards made their first visit on 7 February: he in his long Victorian beard, she with her short and temporarily un-pregnant figure clothed in the usual Pre-Raphaelite dress, sans crinolines. Two weeks later, despite the return of winter in the form of intermittent snow showers, the Amberleys followed the Howards, making the unusual move of bringing their three-year-old son, Frank, sent to play in the garden until the sporadic storms drove him inside to the care of the maids (children appeared very rarely at the Priory). In the *Amberley Papers* Kate Amberley concludes, "I liked my visit . . . I talked entirely to Mrs Lewes, and like her very much" (38). The two women touched on the education-related topics that absorbed nearly all the Stanleys, including the mother Henrietta, involved in the founding of Girton College. They also, in what had become a set topic, talked about poetry.

The Summer of '69 and the Illness of Thornie

Although the Leweses had made a long European tour in the spring, they remained at home through the summer of 1869, and the Sundays at the Priory continued. At some points during the summer, however, they survived only barely.[8] Lewes's second son, Thornie, had arrived home from Africa gravely ill, and, although the couple looked forward to receiving guests as a welcome respite from daily involvement with serious illness, sometimes the numbers dwindled. On the Sunday in May that Haight describes as a "devastating" (514) first visit to the Priory by Henry James, the eager young novelist found himself rushing out for a doctor to attend to Thornie. Though attendance remained strong through May and June, with between eight or nine and sometimes as many as fifteen guests, it fell off in July, and on the twenty-second Lewes wailed in his diary, "No one called!" The following Sunday, only John Walter Cross appeared, for his first visit. Meanwhile Bodichon was not waiting for Sundays to form a particularly close day-to-day relationship with the invalid, though she sustained her attendance on Sundays throughout the summer as she did throughout her life.

At the same time, the summer brought some important new faces to the group, including Nikolaus Trübner, responsible for publication of many of the authors he met there; Richard Monkton Milnes (Lord Houghton) whose own gatherings attracted such fearful gossip; Emanuel Deutsch, widely accepted as the model for Mordecai in *Daniel Deronda;* and Sidney Colvin, who in 1873 became Slade Professor of Art History at Cambridge and Director of the Fitzwilliam Museum. Nannie Smith, Bodichon's sister, was in town and occasionally brought her companion, Isabella Blythe, while Eliza Lynn Linton did not give up on the Priory until the following year.[9] Another addition resulted from the engagement of ultra-Positivist

---

[8] Rosemary Ashton declares that, after the return of Thornie they did not resume Sundays at the Priory until 1870: "After ceasing to entertain or go out while they had been nursing Thornie, they now resumed their Sunday afternoons at The Priory" (*George Henry Lewes: A Life* 250). Lewes's journals, however, prove that the Sundays went on that summer despite the need to nurse Thornie.

[9] Linton's resentful review of Cross's *Life in Letters,* which complains that George Eliot had some inordinate power over men, most probably draws on her observations as the guests crowded around George Eliot at Sundays at the Priory.

Edward S. Beesly, who proudly introduced his fiancée, Emily Crompton, on 5 December 1869. George Eliot found marital engagements among her guests delightful and romantic. She wrote to Maria Congreve that Beesly was "one of a group of prospective marriages which we have had announced to us since we came home. Besides Mr. Harrison's there is Dr. Allbutt's, our charming friend from Leeds" (*GEL* 5:40). Sister to Henry Crompton, another regular, Emily Crompton helped keep the Positivism in the family.

Bodichon's record at the Priory confirms her position as George Eliot's closest friend. Not only did she visit nearly every Sunday when she was in London, but she brought important people with her. In the earliest years, the notations of Lewes, since they often place her early arrival side by side with one of her friends, suggest her responsibility for the appearance of, in particular, artists, educators, and feminists, some of whom became long-time stalwarts. While Bessie Parkes's friendship with George Eliot went back as far as Bodichon's (that is, to the early fifties), and she would have arrived without needing an introduction from anyone, Nannie Leigh Smith and Isabella Blythe, for example, would hardly have turned up at the gate in St John's Wood without Bodichon's instigation.

Indeed Bodichon's friendships provided some of the most persistent Priory visitors. The Priory acquired another woman regular when on 23 May Bodichon introduced a co-worker in the cause of women's education, Anne Jemima Clough.[10] The two had met during the early fifties, indeed shortly after Clough's flight to Florence to the deathbed of her beloved poet/brother, Arthur Hugh. At that time, according to Hirsch, "In conversations about the higher education of women the two women grew to have great respect for each other" (181). Her name appears in Lewes's diary linked with her friend's, and Clough soon became a Priory regular.

George Eliot's well-known connections with the founding of Girton College resulted from her lifelong intimacy with Bodichon, the institution's co-founder (with Emily Davies). George Eliot's monetary support, her suggestions for a suitable curriculum, and her 1877 visit prove that she made her most important contributions to higher education for women to her dearest friend's institution at Girton rather than the Sidgwicks' at Newnham. But Newnham's advocates also attended Sundays at the Priory, including Henry Sidgwick, F. W. H. Myers, and Clough herself, whom Sidgwick chose in 1871 to supervise lodgings in Cambridge for women come to town to attend the university lectures then open to them. In the

---

[10] In addition to Clough, Bodichon's friends included the Allinghams and Betham-Edwards and, later, fellow artist Emily Greatorex as well as Bodichon's Girton protégée, Phoebe (Hertha) Marks.

beginning, these lodgings moved from one location to another, but Clough continued in her position after the construction of the building that forms the heart of Newnham College today.

Clough turned up at the Priory regularly but not frequently. Her occupations in the late sixties and early seventies took her all over England. At that time she was serving on the North of England Council, an organization devoted to offering university-level lectures to women locally in cities such as Leeds, Liverpool, and Manchester. At the same time, she often stayed in or near London. The widow of her beloved brother, Arthur Hugh, welcomed her in the city, as she did to the household at Combe Hurst, just outside London. She came to the Priory three times during the summer months of 1869, usually on days when Bodichon was also visiting. Thereafter she attended about once or twice a year.

Although the Priory crowd would have offered Clough a pool of talented, expert speakers for the lectures she was organizing, it is unlikely that she made any great contribution to the day's conversation. Clough's niece, Blanche Clough, who authored a memoir of her aunt in 1897, describes Clough's dedication to improving education for girls and women at all levels and in numerous locations. But she also describes her aunt's speaking ability and social skills less positively. In public, "she did not come forward as one who had many ideas to communicate" (138). In society, she "used to take but little part in general conversation, and kept rather in the background, but that there was a serenity in her manner and a suggestion of power about her which impressed people. Mr. Symonds remarked of her about this time that it was difficult to talk to her, because she usually seemed to slip out of the conversation, but if the talk was turned on educational matters, it was at once clear that she was on her own ground" (Clough 106). Clough's portraits show a wide mouth under a no-nonsense, eagle brow, and if she rarely made the sort of comments that led Lewes to crow about "capital talk," she did help make up the numbers during the terrible summer of Thornie's illness, and she also evened the balance between the Girton and the Newnham crowds, both of which visited at the Priory. Other guests who joined the committees formed to promote Newnham, Frederic Myers and W. K. Clifford, did not begin their own attendance at Sundays until 1872 and 1873, respectively.

Finally, just before Thornie's death prompted them to cease all social life and retreat to a farmhouse in Limpsfield Surrey to mourn, George Eliot wrote enthusiastically to Oscar Browning of the visit of a Russian couple, the Kovalevkys, who arrived at the Priory via the good offices of William Shedden-Ralston of the British Museum who published collections of Russian fairy tales. Miriam Haskell Berlin, who translated and introduced Madame Kovalevsky's reminiscences of George Eliot in the 1984 *Yale Review,* suggests that the couple's marriage, entered into to remedy the wife's inability to obtain a passport without her parents' consent, did not bring them together in a familial union (533).[11] The wife's ambition to study mathematics, which at home had suffered repeated obstacles because of her gender, benefitted from the independence she achieved by marrying geologist Vladimir O. Kovalevsky, a circumstance that enabled her to flee to Heidelberg to pursue her studies. The couple seldom lived together; indeed he soon departed for Vienna while his wife returned to Heidelberg. In her journal, George Eliot records her reaction to these plans with an admiring exclamation point (H&J 138).

The Russian couple did, however, arrive at the Priory together on 3 October 1869. According to the wife's colorful account, her presence at the Priory, and George Eliot's discovery of her ambitions, delighted the novelist. George Eliot reported in her journals that so did young Madam Kovalevsky's appearance and demeanor: "a pretty creature with charming modest voice and speech" (H&J 138). Although Lewes notes only eight guests on 3 October 1869, Kovalevsky remembers a group of twelve that included "a young lord just returned from a long journey in a little-known country, several musicians and painters, two or three people without a definite specialty" (544). Nevertheless, Kovalevsky insists that the events she narrates took place on her first meeting with Herbert Spencer, and Lewes and she agree on his presence on 3 October. Writing sixteen years after the event, Kovalevsky reports George Eliot's conversation word for word:

> I had already been there some time when an elderly man with grey whiskers and a typical English face entered. No one spoke his name, but George Eliot went to him immediately saying, 'How glad I am that you have come today, I can present to you the living refutation of your theory—a woman mathematician. Permit me to present my friend. I must warn you,' she said to me, still not uttering his name, 'that he denies the very possibility of the existence of a woman mathematician. He admits that from time to time a woman might appear who equals the average level of men in intellectual capacity, but he argues that an equal woman always directs her intellect and insight to the analysis of her friends' lives and never would chain herself to pure abstraction. Try to dissuade him.[12]

[11] Although Haight gives her first name as Sonya (*GEL* 5: 59, n. 6), Berlin reproduces the name as Soph'ia Kovalevskaia (533).

[12] See Nancy Paxton's *George Eliot and Herbert Spencer,* which argues that each of George Eliot's novels engages a favorite theory of Spencer's and, one by one, demonstrates their inadequacies. K. K. Collins also quotes Kovalevsky's account of meeting with Spencer (99–100), as well as two other passages from the Berlin version.

Kovalevsky, still unaware of his identity, gave Spencer forty-five minutes of women's rights "with the enthusiastic fervor of a neophyte" (545). After which, she remembers George Eliot saying "you have defended our common concern with such courage . . . and if my friend Herbert Spencer is not yet persuaded, then I am afraid that he must be judged incorrigible" (545). Only then did the nineteen-year-old, according to George Eliot, a "perfect Hebe in face" (*GEL:* 5:59), identify the old man with whiskers to whom she had been speaking with such confidence. Kovalevsky returned to the Continent soon after the October encounter with Spencer to continue her studies. She went on to a remarkable career. Having earned a doctorate, she became professor of mathematics at Stockholm University.[13]

1870

In 1870 the Leweses sustained a grueling six full months of salons throughout January, February, March, September, October, and November. While in 1869 they hosted a guest list of around sixty-five, in 1870 the total number of individuals who showed up at the salons was climbing towards a hundred. Some of the most regular visitors began coming in 1870, among them members of the Cross family; William Allingham and, eventually, his wife; and Thomas Sanderson, later the bookbinder Cobden-Sanderson. A heavily underlined entry in Lewes's journal notes an isolated visit, but one of extreme importance on 6 March: "*Dickens* to lunch." Willy nilly, the lunch was his last visit, for within three months (9 June) Dickens died. Having contributed to the lunch a spooky anecdote concerning Abraham Lincoln's anticipation of his own death, Dickens soon followed the American president to the grave.

William Allingham, on the other hand, another fresh face introduced by Bodichon, joined the core group and remained a faithful visitor for the duration. Born in Donegal, he began collecting Irish ballads while working as a customs official in Ireland. Moving to England in the mid-sixties, he sought to remedy his susceptibility to depression in Lymington on the Hampshire coast where he made the acquaintance of Tennyson, who was

---

[13] In addition to the 1869 visit, Kovalevsky claims she met George Eliot in London just days before the novelist's death in 1880. Even Berlin expresses some doubt about this claim, pointing out that "George Eliot rarely talked about her work," as Kovalevsky claimed she did that afternoon, but concedes that a letter from Charles Darwin at Down proves that both Kovalevskys were in England in December 1880 (535). Their discussion about death in George Eliot's novels gives Kovalevsky a neat ending to her memoir, for George Eliot's own death followed within days of the supposed meeting.

living nearby at Ferringford in Freshwater, Isle of Wight. While collecting and composing ballads, Allingham continued to enlarge his English acquaintance in the Pre-Raphaelite circle as well, including D. G. Rossetti, the Burne-Joneses, and John Everett Millais, and also cultivated one of his most treasured relationships: with Thomas Carlyle. As John Norwich concludes, "A lion hunter he may have been, but his lions loved him" (*Diary,* Introduction 15). Tennyson took to him for his wit and his reverent manner toward the Laureate (Welch, *ODNB* 1:865).

Allingham visited George Eliot on Sundays from the autumn of 1870 to as late as 15 February 1880. His *ODNB* entry describes a vibrant Irish charm: "To his contemporaries in England, Allingham seemed to carry an atmosphere of Irish open space and vitality. They relished his ready wit and appreciative presence; and his reserve and dark good looks were remarked upon by Georgiana Burne-Jones" (1:865). In his creative imagination, he inhabited the world of the fairy tales and Irish ballads he collected and himself penned the well-known fairy poem that begins "Up the airy mountain," always mentioned as an important detail in even the shortest biographical snippets. Pam Hirsch asserts that editing *Fraser's* not only changed Allingham's life for the better, it also introduced him to his future wife, who produced illustrations for his periodical (279).

Allingham was forty-nine when he first began coming to the Priory where George Eliot made him feel welcome with friendly compliments. He attended with regularity for several years until 1874 when he presented to George Eliot a copy of *Lawrence Bloomfield,* his 1864 rhymed-couplet narrative poem about Ireland's sorrows and conflicts, as full of spies, intrigue, and stereotypes as anything produced about Italy during the 1860s. George Eliot thanked Allingham for the poem and concluded that "its wisdom and fine sympathies have cheered me greatly" (*GEL* 6:33). Shortly later, he married and immediately brought his wife to Sunday at the Priory, a meeting that took off brilliantly. When George Eliot saw Helen Allingham's delicate watercolors of country cottages, renderings that stop just this side of pastoral sentimentality, she conceived the idea of a new set of illustration for *Romola.*[14] Although this series never materialized, Helen Allingham produced a frontispiece for her brother Arthur Paterson's *George Eliot's Family Life and Letters,* published in 1928.[15] The watercolor represents George Eliot's country house at Witley from the

---

[14] The suggestion, however, could not have come from dissatisfaction with Frederic Leighton's original illustrations in the *Cornhill* as their exchanges of letters on the subject convey her general satisfaction, and the artist became a perennial guest at the Priory.

[15] According to Baker and Ross, an engraving "signed WHYMPER" (496) adapted her watercolor as an illustration for the third volume of Cross's *Life in Letters.*

sunny, south-facing rear, abundant with delicate green foliage climbing the walls toward the red roof. A stone stairway on the left leads to a curving pathway flanked by flower beds of red, yellow, and purple, while two white birds of undistinguishable species peck their ways across the path. On a later page, Paterson also includes a watercolor of George Eliot herself, possibly also contributed by Helen Allingham.

The Allinghams remained visitors to George Eliot even after Lewes's death. On 15 February 1880, they joined a group in the drawing room at the Heights near which they had bought a home of their own, Sandhills. The afternoon, on which six guests attended, made a depleted but plausible imitation of Sundays at the Priory just three months before George Eliot married John Cross and departed for a summer honeymoon on the Continent.

Another new guest noted, like Allingham, for his sensitivity, Thomas Sanderson began his visits in 1869 but continued them in 1870 and beyond. Sanderson did not find his niche in life until after Sundays at the Priory had ceased forever, for he did not begin learning the bookbinding craft until 1883. The introduction to *Credo,* his autobiography, published of course by his own Doves Press, describes him as "Master Bookbinder, ardent Socialist, advocate of the Arts & Crafts Movement, proprietor of the most personal of the great English private presses: Cobden-Sanderson was a passionate idealist. He believed in the value of craftsmanship as an aid toward the ideal. His mystical gift was most evident when he contemplated the universe in the world around him. His extraordinary sensitivity and his pantheistic spirituality are remarkable. The Doves press was established to reflect C-S's [sic] spiritual vision" (n.p.). According to E. L. DeCoverly, "He had many influential friends; he seemed to know everyone in the literary and artistic world." The frequency of his Priory visits throughout their existence brought him into the very world DeCoverly describes as contributing to the success of the eventual Cobden-Sanderson press.

After a single Sunday during the summer of '69, the day on which he made the only guest, John Cross returned in January of 1870, and, as the months went by, one or more of his surviving sisters (Anna, Mary, Emily, Eleanor, and Florence), or his brother William, might join him in varying combinations. In *George Eliot's Life in Letters,* Cross claims that the intimacy between the families sprang up full blown in August of 1869 when the Leweses visited the Crosses at Weybridge and heard the eldest sister, soon to die after childbirth, sing some verses from *The Spanish Gypsy.* Nevertheless, it took half a year more before the sisters joined their brother John at the Priory.

An 1870 addition to the titled guests was Lady Colvile, born Frances Elinor Grant in 1838 and married to Sir James Colvile, who gained his experience in Bengal, beginning as Advocate General of the East India Company of Calcutta. Born in 1810, he was twenty-eight years older than his wife whom he married in the incongruously Neo-Gothic Calcutta Cathedral. Eventually Lady Colvile brought along her sister, Jane Strachey, also married to an older man, General Richard Strachey, who occasionally joined his wife and sister-in-law at the Priory. Strachey also gained his fortune and experience in Bengal, in his case as an engineer. Jane Strachey's life took her from the Earl of Hardwick, on which she was born as the ship was rounding the Cape of Good Hope in 1840, through intense activities on behalf of women's suffrage, to Gordon Square where she joined the Bloomsbury Group in 1919 at the age of nearly seventy. She wrote children's books and a volume called *Poets on Poets,* which came out in 1894. Together with the wealthy Irish, such as Lord and Lady Castletown, who owned miles of land in Ireland, veterans of service to the empire in India made up a group of Priory guests who, like George Eliot herself, profited from the expansion of the British Empire.[16] From 1872 through 1880, the sisters remained friends with the Leweses; indeed, the last pen stroke of George Eliot's life addressed Jane Strachey concerning Sir James's death. Fittingly, the letter was a gesture prompted by a friendship carried forth at the Priory Sundays since 1869.

"Poetry Halts"

Meanwhile, for all the attention to poetry in the Priory conversation during 1869–70—discussions of its theoretical underpinnings and techniques, the presence of eminent practitioners such as Browning, and George Eliot's own output—prose was also occupying the creative energies of the novelist, for all along she was engaged in the combination of two planned stories into her masterpiece, *Middlemarch.*

By October 1869 George Eliot had written some three chapters of her new novel (Haight 421). On the twenty-eighth, Lewes's diary records a family lunch that included his son Charles and a visit from his nephew

[16] Nancy Henry's thorough description of George Eliot's familial and financial involvements with empire mentions friends of the Leweses, such as Trollope, whose children, like Thornie and Bertie Lewes, ventured out to the colonies, but omits their friends who themselves had returned from India to England where they become visitors at the Priory. In interview, Caroline Daker has noticed the immense wealth of some of the guests at the Priory, who, like the colonials, had amassed great wealth, noticing particularly the Alfred Morrisons, another pair of lifelong visitors.

Vivian. He reports that "Polly read aloud Jubal and Middlemarch." Haight proposes that, afterward, when she stalled on her story of provincial life, she "turned again to poetry" (421), not to resume her novel until she completed her "Brother and Sister" sonnets and some other pieces. Then, more than a year later, on 4 December 1870, George Eliot did something which signaled the final waning of her foray into poetry. She read aloud to a Sunday group, not from her poetry in progress but from the portion of her narrative not yet included in *Middlemarch,* the narrative about "Miss Brooke."[17] The presence of John Blackwood, its potential publisher, assured the ardent interest of at least one of the small group present. Others who may or may not have stayed long enough to listen included Eleanor and Emily Cross, as well as Sir Henry Maine and Elphinstone Montstuart Grant Duff who generally arrived at the Priory together.

Henry Maine, at the time Professor of Jurisprudence at Oxford (H&J 424) and Grant Duff, Under-Secretary for India (H&J 404), were fast friends, and Grant Duff authored Maine's memoir when the time came in 1892. Maine gained fame for his book *Ancient Law* (1861) and did articles for the *Saturday Review,* several of whose authors the Leweses welcomed despite their ridicule of the periodical itself. Avrom Fleischman's list of George Eliot's reading notes that she read several of his articles.[18] Indeed, of all Maine's various topics, Fleischmann singles out his sociology as having much in common with ideas George Eliot embodies in *Middlemarch:* "The organic unity of traditional societies and their tendency to break down and become something else is the realm in which his thought and Eliot's although not identical, meet" (*Intellectual Life* 173). He would have made a most sympathetic listener for "Miss Brooke."[19]

---

[17] A tiny trace of ambiguity, however, occurs in Lewes's notation ("Polly read what she has of 'Miss Brooke' aloud") because the pair often spent Sunday evenings, after everyone had gone, reading aloud to each other, and he notes the texts in his journal entries directly after listing the guests. However, the diary for 28 February 1869 noting the guests and that "Polly read *them* [my italics] Lisa and Agatha" confirms that she had already begun including Priory visitors in her creative process. In the case of "Miss Brooke," the presence of Blackwood and the small size of the group suggest that she carried forth the reading at some point during the afternoon. In addition, Lewes notes subsequent Sunday readings of what they by then were calling *Middlemarch:* on 22 October 1871, then on the third and thirty-first of March and the twenty-eighth of April, 1872. If Lewes alone heard these readings from *Middlemarch* then it would be odd that they occurred only on Sundays.

[18] Surprisingly, Fleischmann's useful list of George Eliot's reading does not bulge with Priory names. She read Spencer, of course, as well as Turgenev and Trollope and the articles of Frederic Harrison, whom she consulted about legal matters while writing *Felix Holt*. Among biographies, she read Leslie Stephen's *Samuel Johnson* and C. Kegan Paul's *William Godwin* and selected some of the lighter literature including Mary Cross's short story "Marie of Villefranche," Alllingham's "Songs, Ballads and Stories," William R. Shedden-Ralston's *The Songs of the Russian People,* and Frederick Locker[-Lampson]'s *London Lyrics* (1–106).

[19] Elsewhere, in connection with her participation in the conduct of Charles Appleton's

Meanwhile his friend Grant Duff found none of the awkwardness sometimes attributed to George Eliot in her Priory manners. In his diary he notes: "To see Mr. and Mrs. Lewes (George Eliot) at the Priory, St John's Wood. She receives every Sunday afternoon, and has a good deal of skill in managing a *salon,* in addition to her other gifts" (*Notes from a Diary* 139). His diary repeats several of Lewes's anecdotes that he found amusing, but omits any mention of the reading of "Miss Brooke." Grant Duff, too, would have made a good audience for an anecdote or a reading, as his obituary describes him as at once "inarticulate" and opinionated because "[h]is habit of considering questions from various points of view did not prevent him from forming strong opinions." The multi-perspective narrative of *Middlemarch* could just suit a tendency to shift points of view. They both remained callers even after Lewes's death.

For their part, Emily and Eleanor Cross not only continued as guests at the Priory; they and their brothers and sisters were developing into a quasi-family of Crosses and Leweses that became ever more intimate. They celebrated Christmases together, made plans, eventually, to move their main residence from Weybridge Heath west of London to some location closer to Cheyne Walk where George Eliot and brother John intended to spend their married days, and indeed welcomed George Eliot as their new sister when the couple married in 1880. However, much of their contact still took place at Sundays at the Priory where they augmented the family closeness of the relationship with more formal meetings that nevertheless helped sustain the most important friendship of the Leweses' later years.

Whichever members of this small group had the first taste of *Middlemarch,* hearing George Eliot read of Dorothea's religiosity and her meeting with Mr. Casaubon, they participated in a historic occasion and one that began the contribution of the Priory salon to the publication history of *Middlemarch.* While many biographers and scholars (notably Carol Martin) credit Lewes's innovative plan of publishing *Middlemarch* in its own volumes issued serially during 1871 and 1872 as a revolutionary and pivotal publishing strategy that helped weaken the dominance of the officious lending libraries, the ongoing campaign Lewes sustained of stirring up interest at the Priory also belongs to the publication history of this particular book as one of his marketing tactics. Martin's list of reviews of *Middle-*

---

periodical, the *Academy,* Fleischman overestimates the importance of George Eliot's visits to Oxford where, he believes, George Eliot, Appleton, and Mark Pattison conversed and made plans for the *Academy.* At the time, Pattison and Appleton were both among the most regular Priory visitors and need not have waited for the rare Oxford visits for their exchanges of (according to Fleischman, neo-Hegelian) ideas.

march reveals that about half the periodicals waited until the entire eight volumes appeared in print, while the rest noticed it part by part. For marketing purposes, Lewes far preferred the latter approach. He took Charles Appleton of the *Academy* to task for delaying his notice until January 1873.[20]

Originally, Lewes complained about Appleton's decision to review the parts not one by one as they appeared but only after the final segment came out, which not only delayed the publicity (thus failing to stir up more interest) but also minimized the final product which could hardly deal in the detail possible in a series of eight essays, each reviewing just one of the eight parts. Even a very long review could not devote as much space to the novel as segment-by-segment reviews. But the editor had been attending the Priory sessions since January 1869, and whatever Lewes said to Appleton about reviewing *Middlemarch* in the most productive way resulted in an invitation for the reviewer the editor had selected, Edith Simcox, to the Priory before the publication of her review. Simcox called on 13 December 1872. Not until three weeks after her first visit did the *Academy* publish an almost outrageously positive review. These events all helped initiate her desperate passion for George Eliot, and she became a frequent Sunday visitor for the rest of George Eliot's life.

Sundays at the Priory thus joined the published reviews of individual volumes as part of the marketing and indeed the composition of *Middlemarch*. Martin corrects the notion that, unlike Dickens, for example, George Eliot took no account of responses to the earlier parts of her novel in composing the later parts. She argues that "Eliot's and Lewes's journals, as well as other correspondence, modify these assertions by showing how Eliot valued and needed positive responses" (190). She concludes of George Eliot that "she might not have *read* reviews but she knew what they said" (her italics, 191). Martin goes on to describe how critical responses impelled George Eliot to make sure that favorite characters appeared side by side in all the volumes, rather than alternating the Dorothea and the Vincy/Featherstone plots from one part to another.

Lewes sometimes also tantalized his guests with bits of *Middlemarch* plot events that they could anticipate. He colluded with Blackwood, who attended the salons when in town from Edinburgh, to publish Alexander Main's *Wise Witty and Tender Sayings* in January 1872 in between the appearance of Book 1 in December and Book 2 the following February.

---

[20] He also took Blackwood to task as a result of a journey to Weybridge in 1872 when, checking availability at Waterloo Station, he found no copies of *Middlemarch* in stock at Smith's. Sarcastically, he inquired whether "one couldn't stir Smith up to look after his stalls" (*GEL* 5:232).

He encouraged intimate Priory guests, notably Sidney Colvin and Lord Houghton, to write reviews of the novel despite their personal association with the author. So that, during 1871 and 1872, the salons provided a series of opportunities by which Lewes (and the less energetic but equally conspicuous participant George Eliot) worked to guarantee the success of *Middlemarch*.

After the initial foray in December 1870, no reading from the masterpiece-in-progress occurred until the following October 1871. The guests then included three of the Cross sisters, Mary, Emily, and Eleanor, as well as Burton, Robertson, Payne, and Beesly, who heard the "closing scene of Middlemarch Part III" (GHLJ 22 October), the scene of Mary's refusal to open Featherstone's iron chest so that he can burn one of his wills, which appeared in print the following April. With the first part due out in December of that year, George Eliot was giving her guests quite an advance. The following March, she read again to groups as many as thirteen or so guests, and on 28 April, "Polly finished reading Part V of *Middlemarch*," the confrontation between Raffles and Bulstrode at Stone Court which came out in volume form the following August.

The privileged folk who visited on those Sundays participated in Lewes's most ferocious attempts at promoting interest in George Eliot's writing to date. Colvin, for one, found one of Lewes's strategically tantalizing interest provokers a bit contrived: "During the serial publication of *Middlemarch* I particularly remember his taking me apart one day as I came in, and holding me by the button as he announced to me in confidence concerning one of its chief characters, 'Celia is going to have a baby!' This with an air at once gratified and mysterious, like that of some female gossip of a young bride in real life" (91–92). He nevertheless produced a frequently anthologized and highly positive review.

Sundays at the Priory not only allowed the Leweses to stimulate interest in *Middlemarch*, its successful publication swelled attendance at Sundays at the Priory. It clinched George Eliot's celebrity and brought increasingly large parties of guests to St. John's Wood, so that the years between *Middlemarch* and *Daniel Deronda* became the heyday of the Leweses' Sunday salons. George Eliot's notation on New Year's Eve of 1870 that "poetry halts right now" (H&J 142), in favor of her work on *Middlemarch*, marks the reduction of her preoccupation with poetry.

No matter how thrilling Helen Faucit, Mark Pattison, George Eliot, and Browning himself may have found Valentine's Day of 1869, now that George Eliot had switched from poetry back to fiction her salons grew larger, more socially elevated, and more stimulating to her creative imagination as she composed *Daniel Deronda*. The salons had come a long way from the mostly male gatherings of journalists and positivists, and in the years between *Middlemarch* and *Daniel Deronda* they flourished. New additions included people of the same social rank as the *Deronda* characters, and their interactions within the Priory's salon culture supply events and people similar to plot elements and characters in *Daniel Deronda*.

CHAPTER 4

Between *Middlemarch* and *Daniel Deronda*
Singers, Lovers, and Others

Nothing but first-rate music will go down with Miss Arrowpoint.
—*Daniel Deronda*

Alas! Alas! He was no demon foul;
But a poor mortal sprighted with a soul
Bisexual, conflicted
   —"Dweller," Roden Noel

The characters of *Middlemarch* include many gentlefolk who share the social rank of Priory guests, if not their intense intellectualism. The novel's remote Midlands market-town physical setting, as well as its 1828–32 temporal setting, have helped to preserve the notion that George Eliot drew her characters only from her girlhood acquaintances in Warwickshire (her father Robert Evans as the model for Caleb Garth the most generally accepted among them) and to deflect attention from Priory Sunday guests as models for George Eliot's composite characters.[1] Nevertheless, the famous identification of Emilia and Mark Pattison as the Casaubons, to which Haight takes such fierce exception despite the more general acceptance, suggests that George Eliot was already turning to her guests for inspiration. Georgiana Burne-Jones (McCormack) and Jane Senior (B. Hardy, Sybil Oldfield) have much in common with Dorothea, as does Mary Cross with Mary Garth (McCormack). Richard Ellman produces the most daring Priory-connected

---

[1] See McCormack, *George Eliot's English Travels: Composite Characters and Coded Communications,* as well as Henry's *The Life of George Eliot.*

suggestion: that Johnny Cross supplied George Eliot with a model for Will Ladislaw.

But *Daniel Deronda*'s later temporal setting, its greater number of socially elite characters, and its London settings combine to suggest an ever stronger reliance on the Leweses' flourishing social life as creative inspiration for the "widely sundered elements" combined in George Eliot's characters. After the publication of *Middlemarch,* the numbers of guests at the Leweses' Sunday salons peaked, as did the number of titled guests and of women. Meanwhile, subtractions did not necessarily suggest any rift with old friends, despite some cruel cutoffs such as those described by Walter Sichel and Eliza Lynn Linton. Sometimes, as with Anthony Trollope, other reasons accounted for disappearances from Lewes's lists, in his case his worldwide travel, after which he returned to pick up friendly relations where he had left them off.

Among *Daniel Deronda* plot elements, the scenes of drawing room musical performances and the mysterious indifference of Gwendolen Harleth toward the men she allures have some relation to events at the Priory during the years between *Middlemarch* and *Daniel Deronda* when singing became more usual, and gay and lesbian guests made up a group of significant size.[2]

Music, Music, Music

Lewes contrived a splendiferous launch of musical performances at the Sunday salons on 23 April 1871. At the time, the Franco-Prussian War had affected both aspects of the Leweses' social lives, their salons and their travels abroad. With both German and French friends to concern them and favorite destinations in both countries, they worried on their own and on their friends' accounts as European travel became difficult.

On the French side, Bodichon brought to the Priory Charles Francois Daubigny whom she had known since 1864: "through working with Corot" (Hirsch 211). He attracted Bodichon's admiration for "his efforts in trying to record transient effects of cloud and sky, working quickly to catch effects before the weather changed" (211). At the time of his visit in January, he too was in distress, a fugitive who had left his home in France including all the artistic treasures by his own hand that it housed. George Eliot's heart went out to Daubigny, "a grave, amiable, simple-mannered

---

[2] See chapter 5 regarding the effects of the Leweses' travels abroad on the composition of *Daniel Deronda.*

man," whose "house on the Loire, full of his own painting on such objects as his daughter's bedstead and all such family memorials, has been completely destroyed. He is now living with his family in small lodgings in Kensington" (*GEL:* 9:9). The tranquil landscapes in so many of Daubigny's paintings contrast with George Eliot's pained description of the artist cruelly exiled by war and trying to divert himself at the Priory.

On the other side, a ménage obliged by the war to move away from Germany, where they were enjoying the facilities at Baden Baden, consisted of an unusual group of three: the opera singer Pauline Viardot, her husband Louis, and Ivan Turgenev, the man whom for decades the Viardots had included in their family circle on a long-lasting if mysterious basis. According to Rebecca West, for Pauline Viardot, "Nothing in her life was more prodigious than the public and persistent way that Tourgenev settled down in the home of her and her husband, creating a scandal, never paying them a sou for his extensive quarters and his luxurious living, and leaving his money at his death to a distant relative to whom he owed nothing" (n.p.). Meanwhile, the musical Viardots, together with their musical son and daughter, traveled about presenting performances of highly praised singing, composing operettas, and giving music lessons, and Turgenev traveled along with them in some undefined status that most people believed included tolerance on Louis Viardot's part for a romantic attachment between his wife and the author.

Rediscovering Turgenev in London overjoyed Lewes because it renewed a friendship formed decades before when the two young men shared student days in Berlin. Viardot's biographer, Michael Steen, describes Turgenev's youthful enjoyments in a city "almost overwhelmingly rich in culture," which "provided a wonderful opportunity for a young man who had an entree to the salons, where artists, musicians, scholars and statesmen met" (127). Turgenev, he further reports, became caught up in love affairs and fathered a child (128). Barely twenty years old at the time, Lewes, presumably a companion in Turgenev's rollicking exploits, mentions their 1838 period of companionship in a letter to Robert Lytton in 1871 describing Turgenev as "a superb creature and a real genius" (*GEL* 9:15). When the Viardot/Tugenev ménage began entertaining widely in London, Lewes, though not George Eliot, enthusiastically attended their musical Saturday nights, which offered a variety of performances by the soprano, her husband, and enough friends to fill out choruses, quartets, and scenes from operas.

Viardot, described by West as "the celebrated sallow, long-mouthed Spanish Primadonna," was at the time entering her fifties and, despite the lack of beauty in her plainly styled dome of hair and unprepossessing features, had herself conducted successful salons in Paris. Her London soirées succeeded just as well, at least with Lewes, who lamented to his hostess that George Eliot's reluctance to "go out" (*GEL* 9:15) prevented her being there. Finally, Viardot volunteered to sing at the Priory, and she bravely placed no time limits on her performance; she would sing, she told Lewes, for as long as George Eliot would like to listen.

Sixteen people came out the April day that Viardot sang at the Priory.[3] Lewes exulted that Lady Castletown was making her third visit (*GEL* 5:143), and she pleased him further by taking her place next to him to draw his attention to the luminaries making up the audience, awed by the "variety of genius there was standing in a small circle on that occasion—Touguéneff, Viardot, Browning, Trollope, Burne-Jones, and Polly" (9:15). William Sheddon-Ralston added another friend of Turgenev to the group.[4]

The performance succeeded admirably. George Eliot reported that Viardot "sang divinely and entranced everyone, some of them to positive tears" (*GEL* 5:143), while Lewes's journal notes that Viardot "sang superbly" (23 April 1871). In his letter to Robert Lytton he adds an exclamation point: "a splendid exhibition it was!" (*GEL* 9:15). He singles out Edward Burne-Jones as particularly impressed by the performance of the plain-looking but expert soprano.[5] Even the singer, whose performance lasted all afternoon, looked back on the occasion with pleasure. Three years later, Turgenev, in a note of thanks to George Eliot for her praise of his writing, conveys Viardot's satisfaction at having pleased "one whose novel and sure talent she most admires" (9:119). In 1878, Viardot asked Turgenev to forward a photograph of herself as a gift to George Eliot (9:243).

Nor did the day end there. Indeed it had begun early with a visit to the Benzons from which the Leweses returned to entertain Trollope, Turgenev, William Henry Bullock, and Emily Cross for lunch. After the

---

[3] Catherine Brown, in "Why Does Daniel Deronda's Mother Live in Russia," proposes Viardot as a model for the Alcharisi (37) and mentions some of the other guests with connections to Russia.

[4] According to Fleischman's list, George Eliot read Ralston's article on "The Modern Russian Drama" in 1868 (50) and his book of *Songs of the Russian People* in 1872 (60). Another guest who may have contributed answers to the question Brown's title poses would include Olga Novikoff.

[5] In the *Memorials,* Georgiana Burne-Jones separates the visits of Turgenev and Viardot, placing the latter on "another Sunday" (17) from the one on which she met Turgenev. During this period of the Burne-Jones marriage, the problem of her husband's mistress, Maria Zambaco, lurks in the subtext of all the events the *Memorials* narrate. Dividing the visits of Viardot and Turgenev into separate Sundays, at least momentarily, dissolves and separates another pair of lovers involved in an anomalous and ongoing relationship.

musical afternoon, they joined a dinner party at Alexandra Orr's that kept them out until quarter to twelve, making for, as Lewes's journal concludes, "twelve hours of incessant talking!" (GHLJ 23 April). Although he could scarcely have carried on his incessant chatter while Viardot was singing, again the Leweses were demonstrating the stamina required by their life in Society.

Neither the Viardots nor Turgenev remained long in London. By July 1871 Europe had settled down, and they left for Paris and then returned to Baden Baden. Despite the mutual admiration between the two fiction writers, the Leweses did not encounter Turgenev again until 1878 when they met at Six Mile Bottom at one of the Bullock-Halls' house parties. Nor did the singing Sundays continue at the Priory. Viardot made a special exception; she did not set a pattern, for not until nearly a year later, in May of 1872, does Lewes again mention music as part of the afternoon. This time, various of the guests performed repeatedly if not inevitably. Sundays at the Priory remained primarily a literary, rather than a musical salon.

Among the most frequent performers, George Du Maurier had numerous qualifications for contributing to the pleasures of a Sunday afternoon. His granddaughter Daphne remembers, "His talk was most delightful, but above all the delight caused me by his charming singing is a thing I shall never forget" (xx). Her introduction to her grandfather's biography compares him to Orpheus (xxi). T. Martin Wood, a 1913 biographer, claims that Du Maurier could have sung professionally and that he was a good conversationalist with "considerable interest in the progress of Science" (150), a most useful interest among the other Priory guests. At staff meetings of authors and illustrators for *Punch,* where he placed his satiric cartoons, Wood reports that Du Maurier smoked silently through the business portion, but "[w]hen that was over he entered into his own, regaling his comrades with droll stories" (148–49). Frederic Locker mentions his singing as one of the events that enlivened Sundays that might otherwise have succumbed to dullness (310).

Like many of the guests, Du Maurier gained more than a good time at the Priory; he also gained material for his work for *Punch.* As Wood points out, "We have in the portfolio of Du Maurier the epic of the drawing-room" (1), and he could hardly have ignored the resources he encountered in George Eliot's drawing room on his frequent Sunday afternoons. One of the steadiest in attendance, both with and without his socialite wife, Emma Wightwick, he specialized in caricatures of high life and aesthetes in which his images appear above captions consisting of exchanges between the people pictured. Although Du Maurier's figures often wear evening

Figure 10
George Du Maurier. Courtesy of the National Portrait Gallery London

dress and converse in deviant spellings designed to reproduce the speech of the aristocracy, much of their conversation would fit in well among the kinds of topics and interactions that occupied guests at the Priory.

Lewes shows some awareness of how he, for one, helped Du Maurier's work by saving up anecdotes for his friend's possible use. In an 1872 letter to his son Charles, Lewes recounts a recent visit to the Crystal Palace at Sydenham: "a drearier day's pleasure I never spent. It is the last visit I shall pay that Cockney Paradise" (*GEL* 5:278). He then repeats a conversation he overheard in the Aquarium between "two young ladies, dressed in the extravagance of fashion" (5:278) who fault the octopus on display for its ugliness. With his comment "Wouldn't this do for du Maurier?" (5:278) he shows his awareness of his friend's methods of gathering material from his own social life, including the heavily anecdotal Sundays.

One late Du Maurier drawing-room cartoon, which appeared in *Punch* 22 May 1880, exemplifies those to which Priory exchanges might have contributed. Entitled "The Mutual Admirationists" and subtitled "Fragment over heard by Grigsby and the Colonel at one of Grigsby's Afternoon Teas," its accompanying dialogue reads: "*Young Maudle (to Mrs. Lyon Hunter and her Daughters):* 'In the supremest Poetry, Shakespeare's for instance, or Postlethwaite's, or Shelley's one always feels that,' &c, &c." Beneath the same group occurs as well: "Young Postlethwaite (to the three Miss Bilderbogies), The greatest Painters of ALL, such as Velasquez, or Maudle, or even Titian, invariably suggest to one,' &c, &c."

Such bracketing of the transcendent artist with members of the present company would repeat topics and combinations often encountered at the Priory. On 7 June 1879, his contribution, "Two Thrones," pictures a group of eager men directing all their attention to a modestly dressed woman performer seated at the piano while a society woman, elaborately clothed, looks on enviously, thus recapitulating part of the Gwendolen-Mirah plot. Mutual enrichment resulted from Du Maurier's regular attendance: good conversation and welcome singing for guests and hosts and useful material for drawing-room satire for Du Maurier.[6]

Richard Liebreich, a German ophthalmologist who lived in France, also fled the war of 1870 by moving to London, where he headed the ophthalmology department of St. Thomas Hospital. By 1872 he had found his

---

[6] Resentment over Du Maurier's direct, though amusing, jabs at the aesthetes won him some animosity among their numbers. Burne-Jones, for example, found him too severe on D. G. Rossetti and remained distant until Du Maurier's publication of *Peter Ibbetson* in 1892 so pleased him that it brought forth a reconciliatory letter (*Memorials* 229). Du Maurier made a reply that brims with admiration for Burne-Jones's work and memories of their shared youthful efforts.

Figure 11. "The Two Thrones." *Punch*, 7 June 1879

way to the Priory, singing there for the first time on 12 May. Thereafter, often accompanied by his wife, he continued to come three or four times a year, usually singing about once per season. His glees with Du Maurier brought together the eye patient and the ophthalmologist in harmony.

The Lehmann family, together with Ernst and Elizabeth Benzon (née Lehmann), occupied a significant portion of the Leweses' social life, not only for their appearances at the Priory in numbers but also because they hosted dinner parties that George Eliot sometimes (as in May 1876) attended along with Lewes. The Chambers sisters of Edinburgh (Nina and Amelia) had married the Lehmann brothers (Frederic and Rudolph). Daughters to Robert Chambers of the *Edinburgh Review,* they had their girlhood roots in the world of journalism; indeed Nina Chambers Lehmann remembered seeing Lewes at her father's home as a child (Litzinfer 8). John Lehmann, in 1962, detailed these visits: "Excitement among the children grew steadily on the evenings when Lewes was expected. Shortly after he appeared, he would collect them round him, some on his knees, others sitting on the floor, and start telling them stories, on one evening weird and macabre, on another fairy-tale romances with happy endings. But they were puzzled, and a little frightened, when they were taken to see him act Shylock" (127). These events would end with "hilarious sing-songs" (127). The Leweses renewed these acquaintanceships enthusiastically partly by inviting all the Lehmann family members to the Priory.

Indeed the entire complex of Lewes/Lehmann friendships flourished in musical environments. The Leweses encountered the F. Lehmanns at the opera, they attended the Benzon dinners when lured there by the promise of wonderful music, and they welcomed the singing of Amelia Lehmann at Sundays at the Priory. Frederic Lehmann played the violin, and, although he never played at the Priory Sundays, he did accompany George Eliot's piano playing on other evenings (Collins 76). The story George Eliot heard at Pau from Nina Lehmann concerned a courtship, hers and Frederic's, taking place largely through musical communication and mutual admiration—as does the Klesmer marriage to Catherine Arrowpoint in *Daniel Deronda.*

In May of 1874, Charles Hamilton Aidé, who had made his first Priory visit in 1872, joined Beatrice Trollope, Amelia Lehmann, and Du Maurier in singing for the company. Described in most sources as both multi-talented and lightweight, Aidé wrote novels, plays, and songs with considerable success. In 1868 Charles Dickens accepted a story, "The Mystery of the Moated Schloss," for *All the Year Round,* saying he was "very happy indeed" to publish the "thoroughly well told story" (*Letters* 205). The following year Dickens showed still more confidence in Aidé by accepting after some revision a full-length novel, *In That State of Life,* and publishing it in sixteen serial installments. In all, Aidé published a total of nineteen novels, several of them still available. Henry Irving produced one of his plays.

In addition to his published songs, whether he was writing fiction or drama, Aidé frequently called on his musical talents. His 1875 play, *A Nine Day's Wonder* (which features a character named Christian Douglas, who, like Aidé, inherits from his parents a legacy involving a scandalous duel and later joins the army) includes as a leitmotif a song of Aidé's composition. Sheldon Novick and Jeffrey Richards agree on the success of Aidé's own salon, which Novick further describes as "musical evenings" (5). He sang at the Priory intermittently, generally in a group rather than solo.

The third singer, Beatrice Trollope, known as Bice, made another Priory guest whose presence resulted partly from the Leweses' travels abroad. The Thomas Trollopes welcomed the illicit couple when they stopped in Florence in 1861 at a time when the Brownings were still standoffish. Since then, Theodosia Trollope had died, and the widower had married Frances Eleanor Ternan, the novelist.

But little Bice, twelve years old at the time of her mother's death, had difficulty accepting it. Trollope took her into seclusion on a broken-down farm in the Oltrarno. Unable to bear the vacant beauties of their beloved house in the Piazza d'Indepenza, he moved the two of them across the river: "And so I and my motherless Bice went to live among the vines at Ricoboli" (13). The loss of her mother had also deprived Bice of singing instruction formerly carried forth by Theodosia Trollope, but supplemented by Italian masters. At Ricoboli, Trollope not only found a family of girls nearby as companions for his daughter, he eventually engaged an English governess (Ternan, whom he later married). In Florence, Bice remained popular where her talent resulted in her being "besieged with invitations" (63). Befriended by Isa Blagden, she visited England and had a year at a school at Brighton in 1867 (63). She came to the Priory primarily during the spring of 1874, singing several times.[7]

Bice Trollope shares with Mirah Lapidoth her stature, her mild manner, and her accomplished singing: "Petite in her person, though thoroughly well and elegantly formed," she showed herself "gentle and affectionate" (Trollope 17). She also had from her earliest years ample supplementary

---

[7] She also sang at Lady Castletown's, thereby again bringing the Gwendolen-like Cecilia Wingfield into the same musical drawing room as one of the models for Mirah (*GEL* 6:51, n. 7). Three days earlier, she had performed at the Priory, another of several occasions placing the two women side by side.

training with Italian masters and the ability to tackle Italian music. On 11 May 1874, George Eliot, apologizing to Mary Cross for the discomfort of the "long, cold journey" (*GEL* 6:48) from Weybridge to the Priory, takes comfort that she had the opportunity to enjoy Bice's singing.

But if Bice Trollope's stature, artistry, and Italian material link her with Mirah, vetted by Klesmer specifically for drawing-room venues, she joins another Priory performer much more frequently mentioned as a model for the diminutive singer, Phoebe Sarah Marks, beloved protégée of Barbara Bodichon. Bodichon befriended the young woman when she aspired to enter Girton College, and Pam Hirsch regards the relationship as one that brought deep satisfaction to Bodichon in her later years and helped compensate for her own childlessness. Bodichon devoted a good deal of energy getting Marks (nicknamed Hertha) into Girton College, and George Eliot not only donated ten pounds to the effort (Hirsch 282) but offered verbal encouragement as well.

Specifically connecting her with the musical scenes in *Daniel Deronda*, many readers have suggested Marks as a model for Mirah, both for her ability and her ethnicity.[8] Although the young woman herself read *Daniel Deronda* and could detect no resemblance, she shared Mirah's masses of irrepressible dark curly hair and in fact did concede that one of the personal comments George Eliot made to her found its way into the voice of the narrator in the novel: that "her utterance sounds foreign from its distinctness" (quoted in Hirsch 282). Bodichon brought her to the Priory on 3 January 1875 and thereafter she attended with regularity, usually in the company of Bodichon, through 1877. Bodichon's French-born husband, Eugène Bodichon, had taught Marks French songs for a capella singing that may have had their place at the Priory, material that would distinguish her from Bice Trollope (and from Mirah). But although she entertained the group with her "lovely, rather low-pitched singing voice" (Hirsch 279), she never, according to Lewes's journals, became a regular singer as did Bice, Richard Liebreich, Amelia Lehmann, Hamilton Aidé, or George Du Maurier.

On 5 May 1872, the Leweses were finishing up the Priory season and in the process of preparing for their summer let. During May, in an unusually frantic search, they consulted agents and inspected at least five houses, in Red Hill, Watford, and Chislehurst, before settling on Elversley, set high on the hill just south of the North Downs overlooking the town of Red Hill. Here George Eliot worked through the summer on *Middlemarch* in the quiet retirement the couple preserved when in Surrey.

---

[8] See Rochelson, *A Jew in the Public Arena*, 233, n. 9.

But before they left, their Sundays had come to average between eleven and seventeen guests, and singing was about to become more usual. On 5 May the hosts permitted two of the women guests to join Du Maurier in performing. Gertrude Smyth, wife of Colonel Edward Skeffington Randal Smyth, and her sister Cecilia Wingfield, ventured to entertain. Wingfield generally arrived with her mother, Lady Castletown, and the relationship they developed with the Leweses later in the year when they all shared time in Bad Homburg together suggests Cecilia Wingfield and Lady Castletown as plausible models for Gwendolen and her mother in *Daniel Deronda*.[9] The singing incident on the fifth reinforces the suggestion.

As in *Daniel Deronda,* the performances of the untried amateurs did not go well. Matilda Betham-Edwards, who otherwise was having a most satisfying afternoon, was there to comment. Lewes had begun by introducing her to Liebreich, perhaps bringing Edwards, whose nickname, she reports, stemmed from her French inclinations, together with the German as a peacemaking gesture. Edwards commented on Liebreich, whom Lewes introduced as "the inventor of Chloral," specifically as a German. She expected, she writes, to meet Germans socially at the home of the biographer of Goethe.[10]

Betham-Edwards had her little individual talk by the fireplace with her hostess, which, she remembered, turned on their shared experiences of growing up on a farm.[11] Afterward, she yielded her place: "our brief chat over, I fell back" (44). She found a vacant chair next to an old acquaintance, Frederic Leighton: "On this Sunday afternoon he seemed oblivious of everything around him, his eyes fixed on the priestess-like, rather Sybil-like figure opposite. After a mechanically uttered phrase or two he burst out—a lover's voice could hardly have been more impassioned: 'How beautiful she is!' After all, was not the artist right? What is physical perfection compared to spiritual beauty?" (44).

But Betham-Edwards objected to what happened next as the guests drank their tea. She quotes Lewes as saying, "We have a singing bird

---

[9] See chapter 5 for a detailed account of the Bad Homburg holiday and additional connections between the Castletowns and *Daniel Deronda*.

[10] By 1874, Betham-Edwards may have had reason to deplore her meeting with Liebreich, the "inventor of chloral." In a July 1874 letter to Bodichon, George Eliot implies that her friend has reported news of Edwards's addiction and impoverishment: "Your picture of poor Miss E[dwards] is deplorable. I cannot help thinking it is a misfortune that she took to writing. But it seems that the only chance of her finding dignity and independence is that she should be left to extricate herself. That chorale is a very pernicious thing to begin taking: the doctors say that women who begin with it never leave it off" (*GEL* 6:69).

[11] In this passage, Betham-Edwards again refers to George Eliot's dark eyes (45).

here. . . . She must charm us before departure." Betham-Edwards reports, "The fashionably dressed young lady in question, some Lady Clara Vere de Vere, did not deny the delicate imputation, and true enough, before the party broke up, those almost solemn precincts were ringing with just such a song as might divert the guests of any Belgravian drawing-room." Betham-Edward's "Lady Clara" could only have been one of the two young Irish women, that is, either Smyth or Wingfield, both of whom sang that day.

The scene in *Daniel Deronda* when Gwendolen's singing fails in the drawing-room setting climaxes the chapter concerning the entertainment at Brackenshaw Castle, after which Klesmer delivers the blow to Gwendolen's confidence and vanity: "it is always acceptable to see you sing" (ch. 5). But neither of the usually suggested models for Klesmer (most often Franz Liszt and Anton Rubenstein) was in attendance at the Priory either 5 May or indeed at any other time. Moreover, Klesmer's harshness toward amateur singing (especially by pretty young women), does not repeat the practices of the hosts at the Priory. None of the favorite performers, Amelia Lehmann, Du Maurier, or Liebreich, sang professionally.

According to Lewes's guest lists, Gertrude Smyth did not reappear at the Priory, though Cecilia Wingfield remained a steady visitor. However, she never sang again. By whatever process she learned that she (and/or her sister) had not met the standard required by the hosts and the rest of the audience, she responded with some pluck by continuing her attendance as a (non-singing) guest.

Betham-Edwards regarded the mediocre singing as a turning point: "Belgravia, indeed, had forced an entrance into the Priory, and, as we might expect, that intrusion was followed by an exodus. More than one old friend and habitué, more than one distinguished guest dropped off" (45). The "gathering place of souls" gradually changed its character. Its doors had been thrown too wide and "fools rushed in where angels feared to tread" (45–46). At the same time, Betham-Edwards herself continued coming to the Priory through 1873, often sharing the afternoon with the Belgravians. Given her faulty chronology long after events, she could be anticipating the most conspicuous of Belgravians, who began their visits in 1875, two members of the Grosvenor family, Richard and Norman.

The Leweses never permitted a mediocre musical entertainment at their salon again. The following Sunday they presented singing by one professional woman and two tried-and-trues of their male singers, Liebreich and Du Maurier. Friends from the Berlin days, the Adolf Stahrs, had sent along Madame Marianne Brandt, a pupil of Madame Viardot. (Suhn-Binder; *GEL* 5:272–73, n. 2). For some reason omitting Brandt, George

Eliot comments in a letter to Kate Field about her regret not only that Emilia Pattison had failed to appear as hoped for on the twelfth but also that Field herself had missed "some pleasant singing of men's voices" that day (5:272). The pleasure provided by the welcome performers was prolonged. As Lewes notes, the music continued until quarter to seven, as the afternoon turned into evening, an exception he made sure of noting in his records.

The dynamics of tactfully presenting only good music to one's guests, specifically the scene in which Gwendolen tries and fails, make *Daniel Deronda* resonate with the results of 5 May 1872 at the Priory. But after one more Sunday afternoon, the Priory season ended, and the Leweses retired to Surrey, where George Eliot was still working on *Middlemarch*.

Gay and Lesbian Guests: "Unknown Struggles of the Soul"

Sundays at the Priory occurred just before the fracturing of the homosocial continuum that Eve Sedgwick locates at the end of the 19th century.[12] According to Sedgwick, this fracturing created perceptions of gay men as threats to the power of men in general and to domestic order, at the same time establishing a homophobic antagonism based on the creation of a new category for gay men that resulted in a heterosexual/homosexual dichotomy. As Foucault asserts, the adoption of the term "homosexual" at the time led to a perception of gay men as a separate "species" (quoted in Sedgwick 5). According to Sedgwick's timetable, the Leweses had less homophobic motivation to inspect their guests for sexual orientation than would have been the case had their salons occurred two decades later.

Throughout their existence, Sundays at the Priory welcomed guests whose biographers' declarations, sustained relationships with same-sex partners, long avoidance of marriage, and/or comments of contemporaries concerning effeminacy in men or mannishness in women suggest manifestations of same-sex desire. Haight, not unusually for the time in which he wrote, considers same-sex love abnormal, perverted, and unnatural. He takes a defensive stance determined to quash suggestions about sexuality he regards as unusual. He applies the word "bachelor" to single men and invests it with an overlay of man-about-town independence, rather than the sexual interest in men it often blurred.[13] Haight completed his work

---

[12] Elizabeth Dell and Jay Fosey agree with Sedgwick's timetable, noting passage of the Criminal Law Act that outlawed "same sex" relations in 1885 (10).

[13] See Dennis S. Gouws's "George Eliot's enthusiastic bachelors: topical fictional accounts

just before the sexual revolution of the 1960s, indeed on the very eve of the Stonewall resistance, at a time when attainment of gay rights still lay in the future. Haight acknowledges only Edith Simcox (and, on the basis of Simcox's assertion, Maria Congreve) as women who loved George Eliot with sexual passion.[14] Having repeatedly consulted Simcox's *Autobiography of a Shirtmaker* as one of his most important sources for his subject's later life, he could not possibly deny the sexual component of her love for George Eliot.

Meanwhile, several women personally involved with other women came to Sundays at the Priory. Nannie Smith and Isabella Blythe, both journalists who had contributed to *The English Woman's Journal,* maintained a house in Algiers next door to the Bodichons' home. Eliza Lynn Linton's biographer, Nancy Fix Anderson, in *Women Against Women in Victorian England* (1987), describes Linton as a lesbian, partly on the basis of the *Autobiography of Christopher Kirkland,* written in a male voice.

Mary Ponsonby, after a single visit in 1873, made a series of more closely spaced Priory visits during a spiritual crisis she suffered in 1876. In *Henry and Mary Ponsonby: Life at the Court of Queen Victoria,* William Kuhn devotes considerable space to discussions of Mary Ponsonby's sexuality. He describes her carpentry as part of her "delight in pastimes usually favored by men" (20), pastimes in which "the masculine element keeps occurring" (21). For all her typically women's accomplishments in dancing and watercolors, she also, in Canada, "went with her husband into the woods and took target practice with a rifle" (21). To clinch his argument, he mentions that she liked to play billiards.

On the subject of the "faint element of ambiguity about Mary Ponsonby" Kuhn also mentions some of the friendships she sustained with women, specifically naming "Ethel Smyth and Violet Paget (Vernon Lee) both of whom would be regarded as lesbians or bisexuals today" (22). He continues that she preferred the company of women to that of men, although his sections on friends also name a number of men. Early in the biography, he notes that, at twenty-eight, Ponsonby married later than most Victorian women and that her passion during the courtship did not match that of her husband who produced the more ardent marital letters.

---

of nineteenth-century homoerotic Christian masculinities and the manhood question" for a discussion of bachelorhood and its troubling implications in the highly domestic Victorian culture. "Located on the frontier of a successful, reproductive domestic world and its marginalized alternative" (3) he asserts, bachelors' "transgressive potential situated them in a topical political and moral public discourse about effeminacy, selfishness, masturbation, and same-sex eroticism" (4).

[14] He does call Emily Faithful a "decidedly queer" young woman (243).

Simcox's *Autobiography* contributes accurate knowledge of other women like herself. John Walter Cross's two sisters, Eleanor and Mary, participated in a painful same-sex love triangle whose interactions went forth at the Priory. While Simcox considered the elder, Mary, as a possible confidante regarding her love for George Eliot, Eleanor, the younger, had a crush on Simcox, who did not take her interest seriously. Of all the sisters, Eleanor Cross kept Simcox informed about George Eliot during the difficult aftermath of the marriage to John Cross, a period during which the novelist ignored Simcox and her devotion. When urgency compelled Simcox to seek information about George Eliot (as when she heard news of the groom's illness during the Venice portion of the honeymoon) she took the railway out to Weybridge Heath to the Cross home, where she found in Eleanor her most reliable informant.

Meanwhile, several of the male Priory guests, including Oscar Browning, F. W. H. Myers, Arthur Sidgwick, Henry Sidgwick, Alexander Kinglake, Roden Noel, George Romanes, Edmund Gurney, Charles Hamilton Aidé, and others, made up a group whose sexuality could well have united them in mutual interests and understandings unshared by many of the other guests. Several of these men, members of the Cambridge Apostles, belonged to the set whom Myers, though not himself an Apostle, invited to meet George Eliot at his Trinity College rooms in 1873. The visit prompted Myers to produce the most tedious and wearisome of George Eliot anecdotes, generally known among specialists as the sibyl-in-the-gloom story, reporting her ponderous reflections about God, Immortality, and Duty (in capital letters). Although the Cambridge men who attended Myers's party formed the most cohesive group of gay men at the Priory, their central personality, J. A. Symonds, did not come along with them. Instead, their circle included Myers, the Sidgwick brothers, Noel, Romanes, and Gurney, some of whom launched their seasons at the Priory after Myers introduced them to George Eliot at his Cambridge party in 1873.

The interests shared among the Cambridge men included an interweaving of traditional philosophy, physiology, psychology, and parapsychology, the latter a curious set of beliefs that did not accord with the rational skepticism that prevailed at the Priory. Henry Sidgwick, for one, with his academic position at Cambridge, combined serious philosophical inquiry with his interest in spiritualism. Lewes expresses his scorn for séances and spirit rappings on several occasions, and he makes fun of Myers for his predilections in a letter that Haight dates 11 January 1875, which issues an invitation to lunch for the following Sunday. Lewes claims that he intended the invitation to occur the previous day, but "[t]he discussion of Spiritualism drove it out of my head; probably by mediums of unknown powers?" (*GEL* 9:142). He resisted the psychical paraphernalia proceeding from concentration on a possible all-spirit alternate sphere even more strenuously and disrupted the single séance the couple agreed to attend with Sidgwick and Myers. But the Cambridge group took its spiritualism seriously and sustained this interest through the 1880s, institutionalizing their preoccupation in founding their Society for Psychical Research.

In *Providence and Love,* John Beer frames his narration of George Eliot's friendships with Sidgwick and Myers within a discussion of the beliefs she by and large did not share with them. While they speculated and argued about multiple personalities, second sight, clairvoyance, and the afterlife, she had all her writing life, or at least since her essay on "Worldliness and Otherworldliness The Poet Young" appeared in the *Westminster* in 1857, argued that motivating morality by the promise of an ultimate reward misascribes human virtue to fears of a miserable punishment hereafter. Good acts more usually proceed from human considerations rather than an egoistic fear for the fate of one's own soul. She planned her unwritten book-length "Idea of a Future Life" to examine the moral effects in the here and now of a belief in future happiness.

Daniel Deronda shows no departure from the beliefs about immortality that George Eliot expresses in her 1867 poem "Choir Invisible": that the best moral effect possible lies in the legacy of a positive influence on living souls. Even Mordecai's happy death depends not on his anticipation of heavenly rewards but in his faith in national memory and Daniel's share in his commitment. The novel does, however, contain dialogue and incidents that involve clairvoyance, séances, and the possible presence of departed souls moving unseen among the living, all drastic contrasts with George Eliot's previous fiction. In one important incident, Mirah senses her father's presence in her immediate area without any physical evidence as she walks down a London street. The accuracy of her intuition validates her non-rational conclusion.

The more important event occurs earlier in a chapter George Eliot opens with the declaration, "Second sight is a flag over disputed ground" (ch. 38). Standing on Blackfriars Bridge one evening, Mordecai intuits Daniel's imminent arrival, and the fulfillment of this vision validates the process represented as a "flag over disputed ground." Finally, Mirah shows more belief in spiritualism than any other character because she constantly feels her dead mother's presence: "She has been just as really with me as all the other people about me—often more really with me" (ch. 37). When Mirah and Mordecai have their first meeting since Mirah's childhood, as arranged by Daniel, the mother's spirit also participates: "It was less their own presence that they felt than another's [i.e., their mother's]" (ch. 47). The ultra-realist George Eliot, in her last novel, retreats from the hard reliance on the necessity of rationalism and demonstrable physical facts to the achievement of reliable conclusions.

Indeed George Eliot's "second-sight" passage accounts for the "matter of knowledge that there are persons whose yearnings, conception—nay travelled conclusions—continually take the form of images which have a foreshadowing power" (ch. 38). She regards such yearnings as a possible super-sensitivity to an accumulation of small impressions that seem to predict a feared or desired event. She concludes that people who have confidence in their prophetic ability "are not always the less capable of the argumentative process" (ch. 38), a remark that would apply to Priory visitors such as Henry Sidgwick, a professor of philosophy and a parapsychologist at the same time.

Meanwhile, *Daniel Deronda* characters make remarks that suggest the prevalence of such topics in mid-century Victorian culture, rather than indicating or advancing the narrator's or the author's beliefs. In the scene during the Offendene charades, when the suddenly opening panel terrifies Gwendolen, members of her audience attempt to explain the embarrassing incident. When someone suggests that the absence of a medium in the audience precludes supernatural agency, the narrator goes on to identify that human agency: little Isabel, one of Gwendolen's superfluous sisters. But members of the audience for the charades have shown their familiarity with the procedures of the séance. Gwendolen herself applies the word *clairvoyante* (ch. 7) to her cousin Anna's suspicions on the day that Gwendolen has secret intentions of running off with the hunt. At dinner at Topping Abbey over the Christmas party, the company in general speculates on the resurgence of the medieval monks as spirits moving around the rooms of Topping Abbey, their former home.

Finally, George Eliot's laconic diary entries during her last years contain an indication that she was not impervious to the parapsychological theories of her Priory guests. The snippets she enters during spring of 1879 include such entries as "lovely mild day" (22 May 1879; H&J 174) and "Ill" (17 May 1879; H&J 174). Then, on 28 May 1879, between a notation on driving to Godalming to open a bank account and one recording receipt of a letter from Emilia Pattison, the former skeptic writes: "*His presence came again*" (7:152). In addition to the emphasis of italics, what distinguishes this apparent reference to Lewes's spirit is its indication that he has come before in some sort of spiritual manifestation at least once without her mentioning it in her journal.

During this period of her mourning George Eliot was associating more with Henry Sidgwick than with any others of the old Priory crowd (except Michael Foster, also involved with her project) as she worked to establish the George Henry Lewes Studentship at Cambridge. She met with Sidgwick throughout April, and on the sixth noted visits by Cross, Charles Lewes, and Trübner, "and finally when I was alone Mr. H. Sidgwick with whom I had a long and important conversation about the Studentship and *other interesting subjects*" (9:127, my italics). Just six weeks later she writes about a repeat visitation from Lewes's spirit that would accord with events Sidgwick considered possible. If George Eliot's discussions with Sidgwick prepared her to receive a visitation from the spirit of her departed beloved, it also brought her closer to the Victorian belief that departed souls might intermingle with the living. Not impervious to the spiritualism of Victorian culture, the Leweses discussed such matters during their salons, and she, at least, shows this sign of susceptibility to spiritualism as embraced by the Society, many of whose members had visited at the Priory.

In *Henry Sidgwick: Eye of the Universe,* Bart Schultz details additional interests that bound his subject's group together, mentioning the writing of John Stuart Mill, Walt Whitman, Wordsworth, Arthur Clough, the Tennyson of "In Memoriam," and the Greek revival underway at the universities.[15] He remarks that "nearly all of Sidgwick's closest friends were champions of male love" (17). After giving up his Cambridge position in 1869 because of his inability to subscribe to the Thirty-Nine Articles, Sidgwick returned to the university as Knightsbridge Professor of Moral Philosophy in 1883 (Schultz 22). Indeed, he "spent his entire adult life in the academic setting of Cambridge" (22) where Newnham College stands as the most conspicuous monument to the Cambridge reforms he accomplished. His publication of *The Methods of Ethics* in 1874 made for a timely increase in his reputation just when the Cambridge men added themselves to the guest list at the Priory. His friends describe him as a brilliant conversationalist. Schultz quotes Frank Podmore about talk "alive with sympathy and humor" (quoted, 22). Another reaction, from F. W. Maitland, goes even further: "a wonderful talker; a better I have never heard" (Schultz 24). Such glorious fluidity guarantees his place among the "capital" talkers valued at the Priory.

Sidgwick's serious university scholarship on "Moral Philosophy" makes an incongruous combination with the spiritualism that increasingly absorbed the Sidgwick/Symonds clique. Trevor Hall, writing on

---

[15] See Frank Turner's *The Greek Heritage in Victorian Britain,* especially regarding the effects of Benjamin Jowett's translation of Plato.

The Strange Case of Edmund Gurney in the mid-1960s, employs strategies similar to the ones Haight uses in his 1968 biography of George Eliot: specifically, defensiveness about sexuality embodied in assertions of "normality," especially regarding Gurney himself. Hall describes F. W. H. Myers as a bad influence on Gurney on the basis of his sexual orientation (xxviii) and points out that "Arthur Sidgwick, Frederic Myers and John Addington Symonds were all linked by homosexual relationships, according to the biography of the last-named by Phyllis Grosskurth (1904)" (xxviii). As with Haight's noting relationships with women to dismiss similar suggestions about John Walter Cross, Hall cites Gurney's marriage and his attractiveness to women to support his conclusion that "I believe Gurney himself to have been perfectly normal" (xxix). He adds that Myers accompanied the newly married couple on their honeymoon, a not unusual Victorian practice, though Schultz reports that the bride did not welcome the extra man.[16]

Several members of this circle of gay men, ten years after Sundays at the Priory ceased, became involved in the incidents of the "Strange History" evoked in Hall's title. Hall's book attempts to sort out the suggestions of suicide in the circumstances surrounding Edmund Gurney's death.[17] He hypothesizes that, before decamping to Brighton where he died in a hotel room, Gurney had discovered that the mesmerism and séance exhibitions celebrated in the 1886 book *Phantasms of the Living*, published by the Society for Psychical Research, included examples of contacts with spirits, clairvoyance, and hypnotism fraudulently contrived and engineered by members of the Society. Attributed on the title page to Gurney, Myers, and Podmore, the book contains examples of contacts with spirits, clairvoyance, and hypnotism conducted by the Society, which also names Noel and Romanes among its practitioners. The activities Hall describes include the exhibition of episodes in which the hypnotic subjects were the "Brighton Boys," working-class youths recruited for the purpose.

Hall attributes suggestions that George Eliot modeled Daniel Deronda on Gurney to the young man's extraordinary good looks. For the rest, he regards him as a "saintly" dupe of his two fellow authors, Myers and Podmore. In all, besides his appearance, everything else about Deronda fails to apply to Gurney: the character's aspirations toward a life of historical significance, the weighty moralizing intellectualism, and the discovery of his Jewish heritage.

---

[16] Schultz quotes Richard Deacon's *The Cambridge Apostles*.
[17] See Schultz's note on the suicide (765, n. 42), which cites Gordon Epperson, whose *The Mind of Edmund Gurney* dismisses Hall's suggestion about suicide.

Some members of the Cambridge contingent at the Priory did little to conceal their sexual activities and desires. Schultz describes Roden Noel as "one of Sidgwick's most licentious bisexual friends, one who was once photographed naked as Bacchus" (76). According to Grosskurth, he even led Symonds astray: "The Hon Roden B. W. Noel, handsome, feminine in manner, and inordinately vain," frequently tempted Symonds "to succumb to homosexuality" (11). It was when Noel came to stay with him that Symonds "abandoned himself to sex" (11). According to Brian Reade, Noel maintained an "uninhibited" (21) manner and believed that he inherited his sexual orientation (22). Reade concludes that Noel's poetry contains manifestations of his sexuality: "In Noel's 'Water-Nymph' of 1872, pederastic images were presented through the fictional thoughts of a mermaid. . . . In a large part of his published work there seems to be a consistent ambivalent glow, suggesting that here was a man, happily married and with a family, who throughout adult life was beset strongly by both homosexual and heterosexual feelings" (23). He adds that Noel very much liked the poetry of Walt Whitman.

According to Henry James biographer Sheldon Novick, though not a member of the Cambridge group, Priory guest (and singer) Charles Hamilton Aidé participated, along with many of these men, in "an overlapping, vaguely defined circle that a later generation—not entirely accurately or fairly—would call aristocratic and homosexual and that the middle-class press satirized as 'aesthetes'" (5). Novick describes Aidé as a slight, bearded but uneffeminate-looking man. Aidé sported a "youthful appearance" (5) and dressed "perhaps too carefully" (5). Both Richards and Novick describe him as fond of mentoring younger men, including Henry James. Novick believes that James modeled Hyacinth Robinson of *The Princess Casamassima* on Aidé. He concludes by describing Aidé's own salons in Queen Anne's Gate as unique because they were led by a man, unlike Paris salons conducted by women, where the "dynamics were driven by heterosexual attractions" (6). At the Priory, however, the London Sunday salon that welcomed both men and women, the substantial number of gay and lesbian guests assured that "heterosexual attractions" were far from monopolizing or governing the sexual dynamics.

Meanwhile, three examples from among Priory guests help clarify the attitudes of the Leweses to all this: Oscar Browning, Frederic Myers, and Edith Simcox.[18]

---

[18] Henry's investigation of encoded same-sex eroticism in *Romola* depends partly on recognizing allusions to texts from or about fifteenth-century Florence that leave no doubt of George Eliot's awareness of the nature and prevalence of such relationships. She concludes, "Eliot's knowledge of homosexuality—and boldness in representing it (however coded)—should not surprise us" (329).

Browning's delicate professional situation at Eton elicited from the Leweses their firm, if belated, support. Many sources praise Browning's pedagogy. According to Noel Annan, he downplayed class differences among his students so that a beneficial social equality prevailed in his house at Eton. At the same time, for leisure entertainment, he toyed with the piano at all-male gatherings that included soldiers and sailors: "Browning left behind him 10,000 letters, of which 2,000 were from soldiers or sailors and some from a few shady characters. He never concealed his interest in young men and wrote an ode in alcaics to the penis" (quoted in Schultz 411). He was dismissed from Eton College in 1875 during a long wrangle with headmaster J. J. Hornby ostensibly based on the number of students Browning admitted to the house he, with his mother supplying the maternal touch, supervised. Although both historians and contemporaries express doubt as to whether Browning ever engaged sexually with the Eton boys, the scandal also concerned suspicions of excessive intimacy. The tussle went on with considerable publicity, including Parliamentary debates, newspaper commentary, and several attempts to support Browning with "memorials" (Wortham 111). He gained some of his strongest support from Priory visitors Fitzjames Stephen and Charles [Kegan] Paul.

A less regular visitor than his biography of George Eliot implies, Browning appeared occasionally at the Priory between 1866 and 1878.[19] While away from London traveling with Simeon Solomon, sometimes identified as his lover, he corresponded occasionally with George Eliot and brought her small souvenirs as gifts. Early in the crisis, George Eliot wrote to him concerning the difficulties of the decision he faced: to leave Eton or to stay and fight, a letter full of sympathy and advice. Meanwhile, at the peak of his professional problems, in December 1875, he called at the Priory. The week before, Lewes had penned a note of support from himself and George Eliot in the form of an expression of willingness to sign the supportive Memorial in Browning's favor. Lewes wrote in French, an odd choice if he were seeking discretion because most educated Victorians, that is, the people who would have anything to do with Browning's fate, could read French. He concludes,

> Nous ferons notre possible—même notre impossible! Envoyez-vous une liste des noms. Nous pensons signer de nos deux noms le même testimonial. Est çe que cela serait convenable? (*GEL* 9:168)

---

[19] Although Lewes starts out using the name "Browning" to refer to the poet, at some point the Browning in question changes to Oscar. In any event Oscar Browning was abroad during the early days of the Priory. When the latter appears on the guest lists, Lewes, to prevent misidentification, often mentions his first name.

[We will make our possible the same as our impossible! Send me a list of the names. We think to sign our two names on the same testimonial. Will that be suitable?]

Lewes's opening, as well as his writing in French, shows some anxiety about Browning's situation. It implies a previous strong refusal to sign: the "impossible" that turns into the possible. But in the end, he emphasizes, both their names will appear. Whatever the Leweses knew or believed about Browning and the boys at Eton, they agreed in supporting him against Hornby. At the same time, the initial refusal and the letter in French suggest their caution. The 19 December 1875 visit to the Priory made his last for several years, although contact never ceased entirely, and he came again at least once as late as 1878.

According to Browning's own *Memoirs,* George Eliot repeatedly advised him to marry. He repeats one of her playful injunctions: "She used often to tell me to get married; 'Never show your face here again without your wife,' and in that I disobeyed her. I told her that if she made her command more precise, and would tell me whom I was to marry, I would comply directly, but that I could not accept a general injunction. I felt that Lydgate's experience of marriage had not been so successful as to induce the man, from whom in some measure she had drawn the character of Lydgate, to try the same experiment" (193).[20]

Fred Myers, whom queer histories always mention as one of the Cambridge gay contingent, began coming to Sundays at the Priory in February 1872 and continued for the duration. His friendship with the Leweses intensified after May 1873 when they accepted his invitation to visit Cambridge and see the boat races (*GEL* 9:90, n. 1). Alongside the sibyl-in-the-gloom incident, which took place on this occasion in the Trinity gardens, Haight quotes the appalling Pindaric ode that conveyed Myers' invitation to meet the Leweses to his friend R. C. Jebb (464) and names Gurney as one of the young men whom Myers introduced and invited back on the second day of the visit.

George Eliot's thank-you note to Myers after the party emphasizes the joys of marital union. She expresses her hope that Myers himself will one day marry: "You will yourself some time know by experience, I trust, that happy husbands and wives can hear each other say the same thing over and over again without being tired" (*GEL* 9:95–96). Her observation demonstrates her belief in what Schultz calls "the marriage solution." She

---

[20] Haight regards Browning's belief in himself as a model for Lydgate utterly misplaced, although it appears both in his *Memoir* and in the *Bookman* for 1900: "It is difficult to explain the vanity of Oscar Browning.... Perhaps he was confusing him with Ladislaw" (448).

remained consistent in her belief that everyone should marry regardless of her awareness of impulses incompatible with normative marriage.

Myers confessed some version of his deepest fears and needs to George Eliot in the precarious privacy of Sunday at the Priory. In a follow-up letter, dated 31 May, concerning his visit on Sunday, 11 May 1873, he expresses himself elaborately to her: grateful for her "compassion for mankind, dwelling as they do in such forlorn darkness that what no doubt seems to you the feeble and smoky glow of your own presence and character should nevertheless be to so many of them the masterlight of all their days" (*GEL* 9:97–98). He goes on: "you seem to bring to everyone what he needs, to me your presence, like your writings, gives most of all the sense of example and companionship in the higher and unknown struggles of the soul" (9:98). His ponderous diction reveals that he regarded the fears and needs about which he confided in George Eliot most seriously.

Perhaps some hope of mitigating such struggles impelled the Leweses to invite Myers, together with Henry Sidgwick, to their summer home, where they rarely entertained the London crowd, that year. But when Myers proposed bringing Gurney with them to Blackbrook, in Kent, George Eliot demurred: "We shall be delighted to see Mr. Gurney in town (we shall be up again some time early in November). But just now we prefer having you and Mr. Sidgwick only" (*GEL* 9:103). She attempts to compensate for the refusal: "I should be sorry to think that I should *not* see more of Mr. Gurney, who greatly charmed me. I trust that I am only deferring a pleasure" (9:103). Her letter emphasizes that entertaining people in the country made an exception to their rule, as it did. Before they bought The Heights in 1876, a potential visitor pretty much had to be Barbara Bodichon to get an invitation to join the Leweses at one of their country retreats.

The refusal did not cause Gurney to falter in his Sunday visits. On 7 December of the same season he came to the Priory with Myers. On Sundays when they both attended, Lewes lists their names side by side, a usual indicator that the guests named before or after any particular entry may have arrived together. In the case of Myers and Gurney, Lewes sometimes more explicitly lists them as a pair, specifically on 5 April 1874 and 14 November 1875. Between April 1874 and December 1875, in a series of eight visits, Myers came to the Priory without his beauteous young friend just once, on 10 January 1875. Then, in May of 1876, Gurney married.

After the marriage, the visits of the two men coincided less frequently. Twice in May of 1876, Gurney arrived accompanied by his wife, both on days on which Myers did not attend. Indeed, after the marriage, Gurney and Myers shared only one afternoon in the same group of guests, 11

February 1877, an unusual day because John Addington Symonds also attended.

Myers's further correspondence with George Eliot reveals that he was continuing to find life an ordeal. Schultz points to the 1876 suicide of Annie Marshall, a married cousin with whom Myers had fallen hopelessly in love, as the motivation for his turn to spiritualism. He hoped to, and believed he did, receive messages from her during a séance (301). One Sunday afternoon, 16 November 1877, he unburdened himself on this or some other overwhelmingly serious matters to George Eliot. Steady, heavy rains reduced attendance that day to only five additional people: Simcox, who had a happy hour alone with the Leweses, then Myers, Amelia Lehmann, and Frederick Locker with his daughter, something of a celebrity on the eve of her marriage to Lionel Tennyson at a ceremony attended by the Leweses.

After the Lockers, Myers arrived, and, like Simcox, he, too, had a memorable and intimate discussion with George Eliot. Five days later, George Eliot wrote him a letter full of weighty thoughts. She expresses her happiness that he has confided in her as she takes an interest in the struggles of younger minds such as his. She quotes a doleful lament from Myers: "My own mournful present and solemn past seem sometimes to show me as it were, for a moment, by direct revelation the whole world's love and woe, and I seem to have drawn closer to other lives in that I have lost my own" (quoted, *GEL* 9:201). The increase of fellow-feeling resulting from some calamity found favor with George Eliot: "What you have disclosed to me affects me too deeply for me to say more about it just now than that my sympathy nullifies to my mind that difference which we were trying to explain on Sunday" (9:201). The mysterious vagueness does not clarify what justifies Myers's extreme language about having "lost his own" life (9:201) or the nature of the "difference" they discussed. She goes on encouragingly: "I gather a sort of strength from the certainly that there must be limits or negations in my own moral powers and life-experience which may screen from me many possibilities of blessedness for our suffering human nature" (*GEL* 9:201). The vagueness of both Myers's and George Eliot's words about Myers's self-described loss of his life, allows the possibility that he was speaking of a hopeless love for Annie Marshall, the suicide, or for Gurney, now married and drifting away.

Myers's own marriage in January 1880 to young Eveleen Tennant elicited a request for a visit to George Eliot and another celebration of the joys and opportunities of marriage. She rejoices "in this new blossoming of joy for you" (*GEL* 9:287) and wishes that "with this steady light of a *thoroughly sanctioned affection* you will do better and better things of the same sort as those you have already done so well" (her italics, 9:286). Fred Myers had finally taken the marriage solution.

The welcome publication of *Autobiography of a Shirtmaker* in 1998 leaves no doubt about the passionately sexual love Edith Simcox sustained for George Eliot. At the Priory, she far preferred the early parts of the afternoon, when she might have George Eliot more or less to herself, to the busy throngs that assembled later on, especially during the heydays of the seventies. If not invited to lunch, Simcox planned to arrive early, and she often appears in first or second place on Lewes's guest lists. As the afternoons advanced to early evening, from solitary adorations to thronged chat-fests, Simcox tended to fall into silence or to leave the Priory early. Indeed, she prided herself on her truncated visits. During Lewes's lifetime, the Sundays did not constitute the entire relationship with Simcox, for they often welcomed her on weekdays as well, encounters that satisfied Simcox better than the salons. She often notes in a tone of pride how she has controlled herself enough to restrict her Sunday visits at which, unlike Sidgwick or Du Maurier, she did not shine in conversation.

But on 16 November 1877, as the first arrival, Simcox saw George Eliot alone for a full hour, and she made the most of it. She finally elicited her host's response to her book on *Natural Law*. Dedicated to George Eliot, the book escaped her comment when first presented, and Simcox agonized over the omission. On the rainy day in February, however, the Leweses told her that the absence of other visitors meant that Simcox could "have the afternoon to myself" (Simcox 6). They talked about clothes (bonnets and trousers) and then about *Natural Law,* which George Eliot praised as "perfectly reverent" and "wholesome" (8). Finally, Locker's arrival interrupted one of Simcox's happiest days with her beloved. Simcox enjoyed her happiness all the way home through her walk in the rain, and was still drawing on it for pleasure-filled memories and energizing effects several days later.

At the same time, George Eliot often exasperated Simcox with her belief that marriage would answer all her emotional needs were she only to give it a chance. Near the end of 1877, Simcox paid a Monday call at the Priory by way of celebrating her original contact with George Eliot by letter five years earlier. The conversation wound about a bit before settling on a discussion of her employee Mary Harrison's marital chances. Simcox ventured her opinion that "at 27 there was not much times to lose" (13). George Eliot became "rather wroth with me for expressing a prejudice against late marriages; she thought that people who go on developing may have a much better chance of happiness in marrying after 30 than at 20" (13). Simcox, thirty-four at the time, forgives George Eliot's insensitivity to her own desires: "she was so beautiful and I was so fond of her that I wasn't angry when she proceeded to affirm that I had never been so fit to marry as now" (13). The call ended with George Eliot's admonition for Simcox not to come early to the following Sunday (on 16 December) as they would have lunch guests, and, finally, encouragement for Simcox to arrive in a mood "to make myself agreeable" (15). As with Browning and Myers, George Eliot was promoting the "marriage solution" for Simcox, too.

These three examples indicate that George Eliot refused to condemn the acts or inclinations of her gay and lesbian friends, but also that she did not acknowledge that same-sex physical relationships went forth between people she knew and entertained. She applied the word "bachelor" to some of her gay guests, notably Alexander Kinglake. But, most of all, she believed in marriage for the few people who had any likelihood of having confessed to her their same-sex desire. She encouraged both men and women, specifically Browning, Myers, and Simcox, to marry in order to achieve the highest moral possibilities of human life. And in the end, most of the Cambridge set, in particular, did marry. Symonds married Catherine North; Roden Noel married Alice de Broe; Fred Myers married Eveleen Tennant; Edmund Gurney married Kate Sibley; Henry Sidgwick married Eleanor Balfour.

Similarly, in George Eliot's fiction, the characters who show no interest in normative relationships also show no interest in same-sex love and live emotionally circumscribed lives. Priscilla Lammeter takes satisfaction in managing the Lammeter establishment, but has only her simple-minded father for companionship, a respectable, competent, but emotionally limited life that reduces her opportunities to enact fellow feeling. Mr. Brooke, too, has views that arise from a complete lack of respect for or interest in women as women, but he forms no close attachments with men either. Finally Gwendolen Harleth, who never responds emotionally to the men she captivates, takes no part in any romantic friendship with a woman, despite the depth of her daughterly affection for her mother.[21]

---

[21] Nancy Henry makes a persuasive case that in *Romola*, Nello the barber demonstrates a persistent sexual interest in Tito, while Gouws focuses on Dino de' Bardi from the same novel. Richard Dellamora asserts that "Gwendolen's friendship with her mother, with its incestuous tremors and components of masochism and androphobia, edges into decadent territory" (130). He believes that "Eliot was familiar with the standard features of female sexual inversion as it would be described in sexological literature of the late nineteenth century" (142). However, he bases this observation on George Eliot's reference to Lewes's psychological research in Berlin in 1870 as a "hideous branch" of study. Although Lewes did consult Carl Westphal, an authority on "desire between women" (142), George Eliot's comment does not specify this particular aspect of Lewes's work; hence her comment could concern his general

Indeed one arguably gay character in George Eliot's oeuvre appears long before she met the variety of sexualities she encountered in her own salon in London. In *The Mill on the Floss,* the hairdresser summoned from St. Ogg's to deal with Maggie's scissoring of her troublesome hair shows some unmistakably campy inclinations. He attends carefully to his own elaborate hairstyle: "his well-anointed coronal locks tending wavily upward, like the simulated pyramid of flame on a monumental urn" (Book 1, ch. 9). After "holding up one jagged lock after and saying, 'See here! Tut–tut–tut' in a tone of mingled disgust and pity" (Book 1, ch. 9), his manner makes Maggie resolve to avoid forever the St. Ogg's street where he keeps his shop. Even Mr. Brooke, the least interested of George Eliot's characters in women in any form, lacks the campy effeminacy of Mr. Rappit.

International Additions

During the *Middlemarch* years, the Priory guest list acquired a gaggle of newcomers who returned time and again over a period of years. One 1873 addition, Olga Novikoff, a well-known participant in the European spa/salon culture, found her way to the Priory through the offices of Oscar Browning, that is, as a friend of a friend. Lewes soon consulted Robert Lytton for his opinion as to her suitability, and Lytton responded with a vitriolic letter attributing great vulgarity to Novikoff and all her tribe: "the Bêtes Noires of Vienna" and "very underbred ridiculous people" (*GEL* 9:83). He repeatedly refers to her excessive weight and introduces two incidents of strange doings by Novikoff. Sister-in-law to the Russian consul, she came to Vienna because of her sister's involvement in a minor but unsalacious scandal, "a pushing, gushing, toadying, fulsome fat woman with the manners of a second rate adventuress" (9:83). A scrape of some kind arose from her sister-in-law's efforts to solicit the attendance of the Princess Metternich at her salons: "There was talk of half a dozen duels" (9:84). Olga Novikoff arrived in Vienna to smooth things over, but Lytton regards that mission as both ineffective and graceless. He introduces a second damaging rumor: that she and her sister staged a theft of their own jewelry but that "the matter was hushed up" (9:84). Haight acknowledges the importance of this exchange of letters concerning Novikoff by including on one of his chronology pages the note: "Lytton describes Mme. Olga Novikoff" (9:73).

---

involvement with mental disorders rather than with the sexual matters Dellamora specifies.

According to Lytton, Novikoff forwarded her social and political ambitions by claiming friendship on the flimsiest bases, in the case of his mother-in-law on a single meeting "in the streets at Ryde" (*GEL* 9:83). He goes on to report with glee that his wife decisively snubbed Novikoff, who was falsely claiming friendship with several Lytton relatives. Edith Lytton "who can be, when she pleases, a perfect refrigerator, iced the volcano at the first eruption" (9:84). He acknowledges that Novikoff carries on a correspondence with Prince Aleksandr Gortchakov, but quotes his own superior Sir Andrew Buchanan, who concludes that she "was in no sort of society at St. Petersburgh" (9:84). Lytton cuts short his own tirade with the simple statement: "I do not like Madame Olga" (9:84), then goes on to guess accurately that the Leweses wish to gratify a friend seeking her admission to their home. He concludes "I know of no reason whatever why you should refuse to having the pleasure of adding G. Elliot [*sic*] and yourself to the list of her 'distinguished acquaintances'" (9:85). Turgenev, too, did not like Novikoff (9:83, n.5).

Lytton ends his spiteful letter by putting off the Leweses who were looking for an invitation to Knebworth, the Lyttons' home in Hertfordshire, elaborately Gothicized by Robert Lytton's father, Bulwer Lytton, whom Lewes had visited there. Lytton declines the Leweses' company on the grounds of an insufficiency of bedrooms to accommodate a couple. Lewes may, however, come alone, concludes Lytton: "en garçon" (*GEL* 9:84). Although the Lyttons entertained the Leweses warmly in Vienna in 1870, and although Lytton couches his demurral within several declarations of affection, Lytton came to the Priory only rarely, did not bring Lady Lytton, and, indeed, his declining the Leweses' company at Knebworth perhaps shows a bit of the refrigerator side of himself.

Lewes's relations with Lytton merited no such coolness, for Lewes made repeated efforts to help Lytton with his literary efforts, giving Lytton's writing ambitions his invariable support. In 1871, just after the visit to Vienna, he recommended that Lytton submit a paper on Voltaire to the *Fortnightly Review,* which, however, did not publish it (*GEL* 9:6). In June, Lewes advised him to correct the "imperfections" of the fable Lytton had forwarded for his opinion and his help in placing it. In March 1872, Lewes was celebrating Blackwood's acceptance of Lytton's *Fables in Song* (9:45), although in June of the same year he was still struggling to improve the work: "Its chief want is unity of feeling" (9:54). By April 1874, Lytton was writing to express his gratitude to Lewes for finding a sympathetic reviewer for the poems. Edith Simcox's brother, George Augustus, who often came to the Priory with his sister, wrote a positive response to Lytton's work for the *Academy,* and Lytton showed some appropriate gratitude: "I am most obliged to you for sending me Mr. Simcox's valuable notice of them, and very grateful for the notice itself. It is not much to say that it is the best I have seen, for in fact it is the only good one" (9:123). Lewes's letters to Lytton show not only his willingness to help "Owen Meredith" along, but his eagerness to entertain the diplomat. Interspersed with anecdotes, his letters drop as many names as possible.

Haight tentatively dates the Lytton letter about Olga Novikoff as sent 21 March 1873. If so, it came a week too late. Novikoff "presented herself" (*GEL* 9:82) at the Priory on 16 March. If the Leweses found Novikoff as vulgar as did Lytton, they nevertheless put up with her patiently over a four-year period. Meanwhile, Russians appear but rarely in George Eliot's fiction, though Grandcourt spends time with "some Russians" in Baden Baden, thereby slowing his pursuit of Gwendolen to Leubronn. In *Daniel Deronda,* Grandcourt seldom shows good taste in people, and the Russians suffer guilt by association with him.

Novikoff, the Priory's Russian, like so many international authors, gathered her material at salons, including the Leweses'. Her *Is Russia Wrong? A Series of Letters by a Russian Lady* appeared from Hodder and Stoughton in 1878 and offered a preface by J. A. Froude. Her rhetoric often depends on prejudices expressed by hypothetical English friends in conversations of the kind that occurred at the Priory. She makes a rhetorical practice of attributing opinions to "a polite Englishman" or "my English friends." Letter VI complains that only ignorance accounts for British fears of Russia (81) and protests that at least Russians, unlike Britons, no longer whip their sailors. She dismisses many English people as "Turkophiles" (132) who "know but little about the causes of hereditary hatred of the Russian for the Turk. I venture, therefore, to state briefly the facts which my countrymen can never forget" (70). If similarly confrontational engagements with "English friends" occurred at the Priory, where she had the opportunity to meet "educated" and "polite" Englishmen, hers might not have been (as Lytton predicted) an uninterruptedly endearing presence.

But not everyone agreed with Lytton and Turgenev. Alexander Kinglake, whom George Eliot always described as a favorite of hers, befriended Novikoff and went to see her every day at her rooms at Claridge's. Kinglake, a sporadic guest of the Leweses, plays little part in the letters and memoirs that describe Sundays at the Priory. Indeed, Gerald De Gaury admits that Kinglake was "habitually reserved in society" (81), a possible result of hearing difficulties. The more intimate setting at Claridge's neutralizes the limitations created by poor hearing in a crowded drawing room like the Priory's. Far from regarding Novikoff as social poison at the embassies, De Gaury's biography of Kinglake reports: "She is described as being of keen intellect and warm sympathies. As god-daughter of the Tsar, and through her mother a friend of the popular Russian Ambassador in London before and after the Crimean War, the Baron Brunow, she was well received at the Russian embassy" (134). A veteran of the Crimea, Kinglake shared one of her major interests, Russo-Turkish relations.

Novikoff made several London salons into arenas for her pro-Russian proselytizing. Indeed she first met Kinglake at Little Holland House. But in general she evoked mixed opinions from the English people she was attempting to educate. According to De Gaury, a writer for the *Standard* expressed a negative opinion on her influence with Gladstone: "A serious statesman should know better than to catch contagion from the petulant enthusiasm of a Russian Apostle" (137). It described her as having "through her natural endowments and long familiarity with courts a capacity for controlling and entertaining social circles in a way which recalled the 'salons' of the past, the drawing-rooms of le Brun and Récamier. Others had likened her in influence to the Princess de Lieven" (xx). From 1873 through1876, she visited the Priory just a few times a year, usually clustering her afternoons within a single month.

Another woman of European origins, Mrs. Henry Huth, always accompanied by her daughter, visited during the same three-year period as Novikoff. According to her husband's biographer, W. C. Hazlitt, Henry Huth maintained a large book collection that included many seventeenth-century volumes. Hazlitt believes Huth invariable in his Sunday activities: "Mr Huth set aside Sunday afternoons, as I mention, for the visits of his bibliographical acquaintance, and he would make no exceptions to this rule" (275). Although not conducted by a woman, Huth's gatherings might themselves pass as salons, albeit highly specialized ones.

Hazlitt's comments on the Huths carry hints of marital incompatibility. According to Hazlitt, Huth had a delicate mental health, a "nervous debility" that sometimes left him "overcome by depression" (269). His Austrian wife arrived at the Priory without him, possibly because of Huth's shyness. Hazlitt thought Mrs. Huth materialistic: "poor soul!" she "laid greater stress . . . on her husband's wealth than he did, for of all the men whom I have known he was the most unassuming" (268–69). The Priory offered her a refuge from Huth's bibliographical gatherings, and she added to the ton of the parties. With international guests from America, Russia, Germany, France, and elsewhere, the Priory supplied a link in a loose chain of social venues frequented by members of overlapping international social circles.

In his biography, Haight comments that "[a]fter the publication of *Daniel Deronda* the Leweses' social life grew quieter. The Sunday afternoons—perhaps by design—were less crowded" (498). But Lewes's journal for 1877 not only shows many of the same names as before, but affirms that the months of Sundays ran from January through May and included November and December as well. On 27 May 1877 Lewes exulted in the number of guests: "27 people!" Moreover, they were receiving more visitors at their country home, including, that summer, the Henry Cromptons, Frederic Harrison, the Congreves, Gurney, Allingham, Benjamin Jowett, Spencer, Elma Stuart, and Alice Helps among them. But Haight also notes that "a few of the 'swells,' whose names Lewes delighted to note, disappeared from the lists" (498). Among the dropouts who deserve the name *swells,* members of the Castletown family failed to reappear. Having survived the snub to Cecilia Wingfield's singing, they did not survive the publication of the novel in which the daughter of a loving, dominated mother escapes to a spa as did the Castletowns and the Leweses two seasons in a row during the writing of *Daniel Deronda.*

CHAPTER 5

The Salons, The Spas, and *Daniel Deronda*

Last day and glad to leave!
—George Henry Lewes, Bad Homburg, 15 August 1873

After their Surrey summer at Red Hill and the completion of *Middlemarch*, George Eliot followed her usual pattern of taking a holiday as rest and reward for successfully bringing a novel to its conclusion. This time, she and Lewes decided on yet another spa visit, perhaps the most famous they ever made: to the fashionable precincts of Bad Homburg soon adapted by George Eliot as Leubronn in *Daniel Deronda*. From 21 September through 13 October 1872, probably by advance plan, the Leweses shared much time at Bad Homburg with frequent Priory guests Lady Castletown and Cecilia Wingfield.

Leubronn

Four years after their Baden Baden visit, the stay in Bad Homburg solidified George Eliot's intention to insert watering-place gambling metaphors, settings, and scenes in future fiction. On reaching the spa chosen for relaxation after having concluded *Middlemarch*, George Eliot still needed to write the novel's "Finale," a 2,800-word composition with a firm deadline, in which she assigns Lydgate his defeat in accepting a fate he has once ridiculed in others: a position (in season) as a prosperous Continental spa physician.[1] Meanwhile she found time to drink the waters, socialize, go

---

[1] It has seldom been noticed that Rosamond thus ends up at a European spa, quite happy, while Gwendolen starts out in one in the first chapter of *Daniel Deronda*.

Figure 12
Lady Castletown. Portrait by G. F. Watts

to the concerts, and observe the gambling in the Kursaal during the same period she was composing one of her firmest closures. She also wrote her famous letter to Anna Cross, describing a Gwendolen Harleth–like gambler who played in the casino during the first week she spent in Homburg. The "Finale" went off to Blackwood in the middle of the second. The Cross letter, with its acknowledged importance concerning the creation of Gwendolen, makes a neat transition point between the writing of *Middle-*

march and that of *Daniel Deronda*. (She repeats her description of the scene in a letter to Blackwood a few days later.) But in fact, as her notebooks reveal, George Eliot had been mentally or in writing gathering material for both novels for years.

The roulette scene from George Eliot's letter carries particular interest because of the identity of the fair young gambler, Lord Byron's grandniece, Geraldine Leigh.[2] Its placement in the *in medias res* opening guarantees its key position in the *Daniel Deronda* narrative. The spa provides the exclusive settings for chapters 1, 2, and 15, but gains reference at many other points in the narrative. Gwendolen and Deronda, in particular, refer to this setting frequently when they are elsewhere (Diplow, Topping, London) because of Deronda's voluntary assumption of a mentor's role toward Gwendolen there when he restores her pawned necklace. "As in Leubronn," repeats Gwendolen to Daniel on the rare occasions she can contrive a private conversation with him, a repetition that reasserts the spa's importance throughout the novel.

In Bad Homburg in 1872, the Leweses spent more of their three weeks among the Schwarzwald spa facilities and less out in the pine woods than they had done earlier, for example, at Schwalbach. This visit also contrasted with previous ones because of the serious increase in socializing. According to George Eliot, their social group in Bad Homburg in 1872 included both "grand" people and "others less grand" (*GEL* 5:312). They had their first encounter with Lady Castletown and her daughter Cecilia Wingfield on their second day there. Thereafter they seldom spent a day without meeting together in the Kursaal, attending the concerts, and, occasionally, driving out in Lady Castletown's vehicle. The rainy weather sometimes confined them to taking their exercise in the sheltered arcade rather than in the lovely Kurpark with its scatterings of wells and baths, but they resolved to stay on anyway because "the certainty that the weather is everywhere else bad will help our resolution to stay here" (5:315). Their conversations, described later by Lewes as "deeply interesting," created additional intimacy begun in the less intimate conditions at Sundays at the Priory.

By the time of the meeting in Bad Homburg, Lady Castletown and Cecilia Wingfield had become among the most faithful Sunday guests. An

---

[2] On the basis of this incident, Collins (citing Haight) singles out Leigh, whom George Eliot saw only from a distance, as the "origin" of Gwendolen (170, n. 4). Likewise, because of the same incident, Bad Homburg attracts most notice as George Eliot's model for Leubronn. But the briefness and remoteness of the sight of Geraldine Leigh allows attention to the spa visitors with whom the Leweses did spend time, the Castletowns, who share additional similarities with the characters in *Deronda*.

Figure 13. The Elisabethenbrunnen, Kurpark, Bad Homburg

introduction at a dinner at the Ernst Benzons led to their first Sunday on 2 April 1871, and for four years the mother/daughter pair appeared with great regularity, sometimes supplemented by one or another of Cecilia's many sisters. During the rest of April, Lady Castletown and Wingfield missed only one Sunday before the series of spring salons ended when the Leweses moved to summer in Surrey.

The Castletown pair skipped the following autumn Priory season but resumed regular visits in spring 1872, coming twice a month during March, April, and May. Then, after the singing incident described in chapter 4 and another summer in Surrey where George Eliot produced the final installments of *Middlemarch,* the Leweses shared with the Castletowns their interlude in Bad Homburg. Indeed from the spring of 1872 through the autumn of 1873, between Sundays and the Priory and a second season at the spa, the Castletowns were among the Leweses' most frequently encountered friends.

Born the daughter of the Reverend Archibald Douglas in Ireland in 1810, Augusta Mary Douglas married John Wilson in 1830. In 1869, when their daughter Cecilia was in her mid-thirties, indeed shortly after her marriage, Wilson became the First Baron and assumed the surname Fitzpatrick.

The Castletowns received their lands in Ireland, some 23,000 acres, as a result of the marital choices of Henry VIII and their family's compliant conversion to his Protestantism. The wife gave birth to a total of six disappointing daughters before producing the heir, Bernard, the future second baron of Upper Ossory, in 1848. At that point, free at last, Lady Castletown embarked on a mysterious relationship with a Brighton preacher.

Most of the egregiously numerous daughters married as successfully as any Mrs. Bennett might desire, into titles and/or wealth. Gertrude married Skeffington Smyth, and Augusta Fredrika (who was painted by Leighton) married twice. Her first husband, Vesey Dawson, a Coldstream Guardsman, died in the Crimean War in 1854, after which she married Charles Magniac, MP. Olivia Douglas Aimée became Lady to Sir John Gage Saunders Sebright; Edith Susan Esther married the Rt. Hon. Sir Charles Augustus Murray, and Florence Virginia Fox married General Sir George Wentworth Higginson (*Peerage*).[3]

The most noticeable exception to the pattern of apparently successful marriages among the sisters, the Honourable Cecilia waited until she was thirty-five before choosing the Honourable Lewis Strange Wingfield, nine years her junior, the third son of Viscount Wingfield and Lady Elizabeth Jocelyn. The *ODNB,* after mentioning his education at Eton and Bonn,

---

[3] The online *Peerage* grants the Fitzpatricks only four daughters.

and his stage debut in the London theater, summarizes a wealth of activities that would qualify Lewis Wingfield as unusually eccentric: going to the Derby as a "negro minstrel," spending nights in a workhouse and pauper-lodgings, and becoming an attendant in a madhouse. He traveled in various parts of the East and was one of the first Englishmen to journey in the interior of China.

In addition to these unusual pursuits, Wingfield reported on the Franco-Prussian War and wrote copiously: mainly fiction, travels, and theater reviews. Also a painter, he finally settled down as a costume and scene designer in the London theater during the mid-1870s. The *ODNB* concludes its entry with the statement: "Wingfield was slim and delicate-looking with a thin and feminine but musical voice."[4]

The *ODNB*'s description of Wingfield suggests that lack of mutual sexual interest may have kept the husband and wife apart. Cecilia Wingfield's intimate communications with the Leweses, if they included her responses to her husband's sexual indifference to women, would provide another demonstration of George Eliot's awareness of the predicaments of same-sex love.

The Castletowns arrived in force in London just as the seventies began. While Lord Castletown, Lord Lieutenant of Queen's County, had already had his place in the House of Lords, Charles Magniac took his in the Commons. The entire family quickly joined the most elite ranks of London society. With other titled masses (the hundreds invited to Queen Victoria's drawing rooms and levees), they accepted royal invitations. Their other pursuits suited them to the circles in which they moved. The couple shared their enthusiasm for hunting and shooting. Year after year Lord Castletown attended the Fox Club meetings, which took place at Brooks' or at the Trafalgar in Greenwich, and year after year he took office as Master of Hounds for Limerick or Kildare (*Times* 1872–79).

Lord Castletown's participation in the hunting offers one identifiable similarity to *Daniel Deronda*'s great fox hunter, Grandcourt. Otherwise,

---

[4] In the *Times* for 7 January 1871, "The Effect of a Bombardment" presents an anecdote featuring a more heroic Wingfield: "A little further on a infirmier hailed us and asked if we could do anything for a wounded man who on the Plateau d'Avron had received a ball through the foot. I was helpless, but fortunately my companion was Mr Lewis Wingfield, one of those Admirable Crichtons who have the secret of half a dozen professions at their fingers ends. He at once dressed the wound, and had the satisfaction of sending the wounded man away greatly relieved. We had not gone v much further when his surgical knowledge was a second time put into requisition. Our carriage was again stopped, and we found a crowd round a man whose hand had just been all but blown off by the bursting of a gun. Mr Wingfield bandaged up the wound, and we put the man in to the carriage to take him to an Ambulance and have amputations performed as soon as possible" (5, D).

Castletown regarded his position in the House of Lords most seriously while Mr. Gascoigne's suggestion that the languid Grandcourt might take an interest in politics evokes bitter mental irony from Gwendolen, who knows well how little Grandcourt cares to improve the condition of England. Lord Castletown receives little attention in the George Eliot/Lewes letters, journals, and diaries; hence the available information neither confirms nor denies additional similarities to Grandcourt.

Nevertheless, if the confidences Lady Castletown shared in Bad Homburg with Lewes concerned her time in Brighton in 1849, they well deserved his adjective "interesting" and suggest additional fuel for George Eliot's creative imagination. That year, still plain Augusta Wilson, she met Frederick William Robertson whose sermons earned him large congregations and the informal title "Robertson of Brighton" (Beardsley xvii). Because Robertson left a notebook in code, the record of his activities has unusual reliability. These activities included close friendships with the (then) Wilsons, who were visiting Brighton with two of their daughters, especially with the mother. Over and over, he records kissing her with excitement and delight. When she successfully persuaded Robertson to depart from his customary extemporaneous sermons by writing them down, she became his "muse" (306) and sustained control over the materials that would later form the basis for the posthumous biography his audience, in particular a most earnest admirer Lady Byron, desired as a memorial. It was Augusta who chose Stopford Brooke as editor, an editor whom she could count on for both accuracy and discretion.

Christina Beardsley confirms that the illicit couple ultimately consummated their love. An athletic Anglican in the muscular Christianity tradition, Robertson frequently went riding over the Downs with his equally athletic woman friend, and Beardsley quotes an agreement they made on one long ride: "She not to count life over, not give up happiness. I to shew [sic] her if God permit that her influence in this w[orld] [Beardsley's brackets] is for good, not evil, by striving to cultivate power and be true to myself and God" (135). Both of them unhappily married (as their compact indicates), the couple struggled conscientiously against the sin and the potential scandal of their love. Weekdays he showered kisses on his beloved; Sundays he delivered sermons about achieving Christian virtue. Meanwhile his diary records the ups and downs of their passion in simple code.

John Wilson Fitzpatrick manifested his jealousy of Robertson several times (Beardsley146, 148, 152); nevertheless, Robertson of Brighton, leaving his pregnant wife behind, accompanied the Fitzpatricks to their estates in Ireland in August 1849 and for several years afterward. At Lisduff in Queens (now Laois) County, Robertson made his most significant notation: "4 hours in bed with Augusta" (152). Beardsley concludes that despite suspicions, Stopford Brooke managed to cover up the affair. Nevertheless, when Robertson died early, at the age of thirty-seven, his beloved mistress supervised the collection of his letters and sermons, exercising what Beardsley describes as a powerful intellect that made part of her charm for Robertson whose death followed shortly after he decided to leave his wife.

In *Daniel Deronda,* George Eliot scrambles details of the Castletown family. Like Gwendolen and Grandcourt, the couple participated together on the hunting field. Like the Irish husband Mrs. Glasher leaves for Grandcourt, Lord Castletown served as an army officer. Like Lady Mallinger, Lady Castletown produced one daughter after another, but persevered through six (rather than three) births until the seventh produced a male. Like Gwendolen, Augusta conducted a relationship with a man in a role that included (in their case among other things) serious discussions and advice on finding meaning in the sort of ghastly, motiveless life described in their compact and assigned to Gwendolen by the *Deronda* narrator. Like Grandcourt, Wilson tolerated a relationship between his wife and a good-looking young man.

After the Castletown/Wingfield party departed as planned for Baden Baden, not to return until 5 October, the Leweses' social center of gravity dropped as they began a quieter week punctuated by headaches and the company of the "less grand." This group included S. D. Williams, Jr., a friend from long ago, whom they had encountered in Weimar on their honeymoon and mentioned as a welcome guest throughout their lives. It also included the Alfred Wigans and their son.

Actor, theater manager, playwright, Wigan had often performed on the London stage alongside his wife, especially during the 1860s. Victorians regarded him as a gentleman/actor. Montagu Williams, who sometimes shared the stage with him, quotes actress Mary Ann Keeley: "One of the pieces which I consider the most famous for individual acting was *Martin Chuzzlewit.* Mr. and Mrs. Wigan, Miss Fortescue (Lady Gardner), Miss Woogar, and Mr. Emery took parts. What a marvellous piece of acting was Wigan's Montague Tigg!" (136). In *Tracks of a Rolling Stone,* Henry Coke reports similar opinions about Wigan whom a friend believed "the best 'gentleman' he had ever seen on the stage. I think this impression was due in a great measure to Wigan's entire absence of affectation, and to his persistent appeal to the 'judicious' but never to the 'groundlings'" (299). Having retired from the theatrical life, Wigan and family came to Bad Homburg.

Wigan and Lewes spent much time in Homburg exchanging anecdotes during all-male interludes of lounging about the rooms and arcades and smoking, especially after dinner and on rainy days. Lewes, in the offhand tone he often adopts when emphasizing his indifference to the fashionable world to Charles Lewes, writes of employing the "strategy of a Von Moltke" (*GEL* 5:316) to elude the Wigans. But Lewes's strategies could not have matched the success of Helmuth Von Moltke's victory at Metz as one or the other or both of the Leweses spent time with one or more of the Wigans five out of the seven days the Castletowns and Mrs. Wingfield were gone.[5]

In Bad Homburg went forth all the rituals of the ultimate spa, including both therapy and recreation. Leubronn in *Daniel Deronda* offers the same rituals and similar scenes of all-male exchange, which in the novel take place between an insouciant aristocrat, Sir Hugo Mallinger, and an anecdotalist, Mr. Vandernoodt. In Homburg, Lewes and George Eliot spent the majority of their time with the mother–daughter pair, but Lord Castletown occasionally joined them for dinner or a drive. On several occasions, the single activity that Lewes consistently pursued away from George Eliot, his cigar smoking, he shared with Lord Castletown in the most characteristically male spaces. On 7, 8, and 10 October Lewes smoked his cigar with Lord Castletown in the billiard room.

After a few days indulging these pastimes, Lewes's journals begin to swell with anecdotes: about an American tourist, a German doctor, Mazzini's opinion of English food, the latter attributed to Wigan specifically.[6] Though he certainly had his own reputation for anecdotes, in his Bad Homburg journals Lewes becomes more anecdotal than ever in conversations among the male members of the party who smoked cigars, generally on the arcade in front of the Kurhaus. This repeated story telling suggests Wigan as partly a model for Mr. Vandernoodt who complains to Daniel that Grandcourt shows no respect for his anecdotes, abruptly turning his back and walking away during one which Vandernoodt considers among his best.

The group spent its remaining time drinking the waters, foregathering in the arcade or the Kursaal, hearing music, walking, and going out

---

[5] Lewes's antipathy could have proceeded from an incident in 1864 (*GEL* 2:222) when he wrote a play especially for Wigan to perform. The project did not come off, and Lewes's play did not debut until it opened in New York in 1864. The *New York Times,* in its "Amusements" column for 30 May 1864 anticipates the opening by calling it "a play of unusual promise" by "an English writer, of universal culture, whose labors have graced almost every branch of letters" (n.p.).

[6] Late in his life, Lewes packed his letters to Robert Lytton (*GHLL* 3) with anecdotes, always finishing them up with five or six examples of his best to cheer the burdened diplomat awash in his public duties and grieving the loss of two baby sons.

to dinner at the Hessicher Hof. George Eliot complained that the concerts occurred only in the afternoons, leaving the evenings unoccupied other than by gambling. But, for all her horror of greed and compulsion, it was also the atmosphere of the Kursaal that perturbed her: the hazy air produced and compressed in the gas-lit chambers. She mentions such details four times in chapter 1 of *Daniel Deronda*. The room is a "suitable condenser for human breath," containing a "visible haze" and people playing with "dull, gas-poisoned absorption." Later, in the evening the room is "stiflingly heated" and "brilliant with gas" (ch. 1).

George Eliot and her party went to see the gambling at least five times during their stay, a repetition that raises the question of why the abstainers so often drifted into the casino to observe the activity for which they had no taste. In Bad Homburg, geography helped make watching the gambling a usual occupation even for the non-gambling guests. The Kursaal devoted only one portion of its space to gambling and accommodated many rooms with other purposes, often serving as the site of the concerts as well. The building sat on the edge of the stately and attractive Kurpark, with its paths and springs, and made a logical stop for refreshment after a stroll or when driven inside by a sudden rain shower. Hence the guests might make a quick pass through the casino on their way elsewhere. In any event the crowds divided into the gamblers and the lookers on, the actors and the audience, all of which reinforces the theatricalization of the spa casino setting in which Gwendolen appears at the opening of the novel.

The gambling scene that opens *Deronda* includes many of the components that make up the descriptive portions of the nineteenth-century guides to German spas. Many authors, physician/authors as well as the writers for the standard guides, repeatedly mention two aspects of spa life. They nearly all describe the diversity of the groups that gather at the roulette table or the rouge et noir and accompany this observation with expressions of horror at the hazards of gambling. In the "Preface" to *The Spas and Their Uses,* Madden calls the "pilgrims to Hygeia" a mixed group socially (iii): "This cursaal always seemed to me by far the worst of the German gambling houses; there is no pretext of any other object" (26). He continues by observing that "struggling for places round the gaming tables of Baden may be seen noblemen and their grooms, ladies of high rank and spotless reputation and ladies of the 'demi-monde,' clergymen and blacklegs, all elbowing and pushing aside each other on terms of perfect equality" (261). George Eliot echoes this observation in *Deronda* as she concentrates in chapter 1 on the ethnic variety and social contrasts visible at the gaming tables in Leubronn.

The specific gamblers described by guide book authors are not always reckless young Gwendolens. Although the spa guides unanimously offer glimpses of young gamblers that convey strong disapproval, they differ in the kinds of young people they report having seen. Madden calls gambling "the black spot of German life" (62), observing its prevalence at spas where most guests participate out of feebleness, desperation, or compulsion. He illustrates his point with references to a young man he has watched lose all his stake, and concludes that gambling, because so exhausting, is especially bad for invalids. The young gambler need not be losing at the tables to convey the moral indignation of the guide authors. In *A Three Weeks' Scamper through the Spas of Germany and Belgium* (1858), Erasmus Wilson observes a "young girl" who "had a pile of silver coin before her; she had earned her week's lodging, and more . . . Alas! The destruction that that one night of gain might bring" (300). John Aldridge in *A First Trip to the German Spas and to Vichy* (1856) creates a more elaborate scene at Ems:

> I observed one young lady, of about three or four and twenty, handsome, but with a certain hardness and shrewish expression in her countenance, who seemed to be a gambling heroine in the estimation of her acquaintances. She always played gold herself, but would oblige a friend by staking a thaler or two for him. There she sat, amid a bevy of cavaliers, with some young girls, almost children, near her; and she laughed and talked with an air the most nonchalant, until suddenly an inspiration seemed to come on her; she would take a cue, push over her stake with determination to a selected part of the table; and then, relapsing into her former manner, appear heedless of the event. I watched her making several bets and she invariably won. But although the observation of this seeming good fortune for a certain number of events, I calculated the surprise that young lady's term of ill luck, if she continues to gamble, will most surely come. (47)

The opening scene to *Daniel Deronda* offers a similar view of a gambling young person, in that case both winning and losing. In her letters to Cross and Blackwood about the reckless gambler, as well as in her novel, George Eliot was working within an established guide book set piece.

The Castletown/Wingfield party, having returned from Baden Baden (and having anticipated Grandcourt's detour there in *Daniel Deronda*), dramatically increased their intimacy with the Leweses. On 6 October, during an evening together, "Lady C. gave curious sketch of her early life" (GHLJ). The following day Lewes read one of the sermons of Robertson of Brighton. On 9 October, after two visits to the springs in the park, a long walk, and a substantial recital and discussion featuring Lady Hildegard,

George Eliot listened with absorption to the confidences of Cecilia Wingfield, the wife who lived at spas apart from her husband. Later on that same day Lewes and Lady Castletown had their "deeply interesting talk" as they "promenaded in the corridor" (GHLJ 9 October 1872) after dinner. Their talk could not fail to touch on the subject of Robertson, whose sermon Lewes had just read, undoubtedly at the instigation of their de facto editor, his companion, Lady Castletown.

The mother–daughter intimacy, together with the problematic marriages of the pair, and even more the sequence of continental watering places they visited, brings Cecilia into the scramble of similarities between the Castletown family and events in Leubronn. In addition, the countess Hildegard makes a reasonable prototype for Catherine Arrowpoint, who, though far from beautiful as Hildegard, is a "thorough musician" who "made a softening screen for the oddities of her mother" (ch. 5). Describing Hildegard, Lewes calls the mother "a rattling, noisy, energetic, woman only tolerable on account of her lovely daughter" (*GEL* 5:317). Hildegard has "an exquisite face, the temperament of an artist, a large nature" (5:317). The important day together ended as the Leweses returned in a downpour of rain to their spacious rooms in the Obere Promenade for tea.

Such temporary and intensely intimate relationships with the fellow spa visitors help indicate how, in addition to forming the setting for three important chapters, the Black Forest spas contribute to the *Deronda* narrative in yet other, more pervasive and subversive ways. Gwendolen's time in Leubronn, when she pawns her necklace, is far from her first visit to such a place. The *Deronda* narrator remains vague on the circumstances of Gwendolen's childhood, mentioning only her mother's marriages and her family's "roving from one foreign watering place, or Parisian apartment, to another, always feeling new antipathies to new suites of hired furniture, and meeting new people under conditions which made her appear of little importance" (ch. 3). From girlhood, the spa has been one of Gwendolen's milieux where she has developed the sense of unimportance in others' eyes that she is planning to overcome as the novel opens.

Several circumstances of a young girl's residence at a sequence of nineteenth-century spas might convince her of her lack of consequence. As both Lewes and George Eliot mention, watering places frequently lack men. At Bad Peterstal in 1868, she comments, "The ladies are in the majority" (*GEL* 4:454). At Schwalbach, she observes the heavily female company: "There is a deficiency of men, children, and dogs" (*GEL* 5:278). In addition to women seeking therapy, wives who needed an excuse to live apart from unpleasant husbands swelled the female populations. Gwendolen, at a spa, could easily develop the "sense of empty benches" (ch. 11) she finds uninteresting among all-female companies, even though she has little respect for or interest in most of the men she captivates. When a schoolgirl at a spa, Gwendolen could hardly attract the attention she gains when she can enter the spielbank as an adult and theatrically place her bets. Moreover, a child-Gwendolen would have nourished her antipathy toward physical weakness among the genuinely sick people whose wheelchairs and nurses crowded the watering-place promenades and encumbered the paths of the Kurparks.

Possibly more importantly, Gwendolen knows well the components of the spas: the springs, the promenades, the conversation rooms, the gambling, the hotels, the pawn shops. She follows her preordained plot with fidelity in Leubronn, the plot of gambling loss, financial desperation, and furtive patronage of the pawnbroker.

Her knowledge of the spas also heightens Gwendolen's sense of herself as a star. Gwendolen gathers an audience, a huge audience as a matter of fact, for George Eliot places "fifty or sixty" people around Gwendolen who stands in the first rank behind the chairs, a large crowd for a gaming table only about eight or ten feet in length. If Gwendolen theatricalizes everything, she has been preparing her debut with a thorough knowledge of the stage she will occupy when she runs away from involvement with Grandcourt and toward the viewing and being viewed along the promenades, in the rooms, visiting the casinos, and, finally, patronizing the Leubronn pawn shop.

The following year, the Leweses and the Castletowns again returned to Bad Homburg for a substantial period of nearly two weeks. With the gambling temporarily in abeyance, and in quieter (and more expensive) lodgings, they experienced a less exciting and less social time. Nevertheless, the confidences of the previous year still occupied George Eliot's thoughts, as, according to Lewes, they discussed "The Wingfield story" (GHLJ 3 August 1873). But this time the company included only Lord and Lady Castletown, and, without the liveliness of the daughters' presence and the recitals by Lady Hildegard, the days also passed uncomfortably because of continuing illnesses and miserable weather. Whether Lord Castletown had a dampening effect on the smaller party or whether illness and the chilly rain were to blame, Lewes ended the 1873 stay with the exclamation that forms the motto for this chapter: "Last day and glad to leave!" (15 August). The Leweses had worn out Bad Homburg.

After the publication of *Deronda,* the Castletowns never returned to Sundays at the Priory. Although Lady Sebright, one of the daughters present at Bad Homburg in 1872, made an overture in 1875, her mother and her sister stayed away, having made their last visit the previous spring, on

7 March 1875. Lady Sebright invited the Leweses to her home in Hertfordshire near the end of that year, but George Eliot replied on New Year's Day 1876, tempering her refusal with a renewed invitation to Sundays at the Priory: "We are hermits, and rarely know anything of the world except through the stragglers from the crowd who visit our cell" (*GEL* 6:207). This wildly inaccurate metaphorical description of her salons, both the guests as "stragglers" and the Priory as a "cell," precedes her invitation, which she couples with an inquiry after Lady Castletown's health, apparently unimproved by the spa therapies she was still pursuing at Fontainebleau. Lady Sebright made one final appearance at the Priory the following September 1876, but her mother, father, and sisters stayed away.

Ironically, Lady Castletown, in whose presence Lewes had delighted in 1869, was far from the virtuous noblewoman he imagined her to be. In attending the salon of an illicit couple she was not raising the level of its respectability. Whether or not the Leweses, or their guests, knew of the gossip about the preacher of Brighton, she herself knew that she was only adding one more adulterer (for example, technically, Lewes himself, and, incorrigibly, Edward Burne-Jones) to the group.

1876:
Summer in Switzerland

In the summer of 1876, with *Daniel Deronda* finished, the Leweses followed their habit of initiating a long journey to celebrate the completion of a new George Eliot novel. Appropriately, given the novel's settings, their reward journey took them to one watering place after another. They stopped at Aix-les-Bain for five days and then paused at Chambéry, Lausanne, and Vevey. But they took for their main destination the mountains of eastern Switzerland where they spent most of July and August. By way of Berne and Zurich, they traveled to Bad Ragatz where they remained for more than two weeks. In August they moved on to Stachelberg for eleven days and then blundered on to Klönthal where the beauty of the landscape could not compensate for inadequate rooms, "noisy children who made the corridor their playground" (*GHLL* 2:225), and masses of annoying flies hovering around their frequently aching heads.

Although they longed for the well-remembered pleasures of Bad Peterstal, they despaired of finding rooms there. Nevertheless they proceeded back to the Schwarzwald northward by way of Zurich and Schaffhausen, both broiling in the summer sun, until they arrived at St. Blasien to remain for a week. But the long summer of strenuous travel brought only uneven improvements to their health, and the following year the purchase of their country home at Witley obviated the need for them to undertake the rigors of constant railway travel in the European mountains. And, although their health fluctuated, as with *The Spanish Gypsy,* their travels abroad had allowed them to keep themselves at a distance while the first reviews of *Daniel Deronda* were appearing in London.

Late Arrivals

During the final years of Sundays at the Priory, the guests included old friends, socialites, and some of the most important psychologists of that early, pre-Freudian age. Indeed the cutting edge psychological periodical, *Mind,* debuted in January 1876 as the project of a number of Priory guests. Alexander Bain, who financed it, visited the Priory occasionally between 1868 and the mid-seventies, one of the male guests who often came to St John's Wood along with his wife, Frances, who, like some of the other women guests, had helped encourage women's education, in her case through her involvement in the founding of Bedford College. George Croom Robertson, the first editor of *Mind,* also dated his attendance from an early age. Indeed, Robertson, a prodigy, began his work at University College London in his mid-twenties, the same age at which he became a conspicuously youthful Priory visitor as early as 1869. He, too, showed no reluctance to introduce his wife to the occasions. When queried, the Leweses replied with a warm invitation for the young couple, and Robertson often arrived with his wife, Caroline.

Unlike Bain and Robertson, their longtime colleague, James Sully, did not arrive at the Priory for his first Sunday until later in the decade. On 28 March 1875 he initiated a relationship that made him one of the most important of the psychologists growing increasingly thick on the Priory carpet during the mid-seventies. His training in Berlin and his 1874 publication of *Sensation and Intuition* gave him much in common with other guests and, especially, with his host, ever busy with such topics as "Laws of Sensibility" and "Organization of Impressions" for *Problems.* Having read *Sensation and Intuition* in February 1875, Lewes invited the young psychologist for a private visit, which occurred on a Monday, 22 February. He retained his importance after Lewes's death by supplying advice and proofreading skills while George Eliot was completing, as far as she could, the posthumous edition of Lewes's *Problems of Life and Mind.*

In 1877 Sully published *Pessimism: A History and a Criticism,* which George Eliot read right away (Fleischmann, "George Eliot's Reading" 66) and which devotes an Appendix to "Mr Lewes's View of Consciousness" that politely takes its stand in opposition to Lewes's theories. On the other hand, Sully placed a quotation from Lewes concerning the relationship between philosophy and personality as the motto to his first chapter. His welcome at the Priory after the appearance of *Pessimism* and its unflattering Appendix suggests Lewes's seriousness about reaching valid conclusions, his generosity of spirit, and his respect for his younger colleague, Sully.

Meanwhile, in another demonstration of journalistic incestuousness common at the Priory, Bain reviewed Sully's *Pessimism* in an October 1877 issue of *Mind* in a seven-page essay. Bain writes enthusiastically of one section: "This chapter is full of delicate psychological discriminations on the subjects of pleasure and pain, and the influences of temperament upon our judgment of the great matter at issue. The conclusion is a very graphic portraiture of the individualities of Schopenhauer and Harmann, and also of the circumstances in the European situation that favour the reception of their creed" (565). He adds that "Departing alike from optimism and from pessimism, the author rests finally in the watchword suggested to him by George Eliot—Meliorism" (565). Thus do the Priory hosts and guests come together in the pages of the new periodical.

In his mid-thirties at the time of his initiation, Sully continued visiting through 1878, with no variation as to pace, regularly once a month throughout subsequent Priory seasons. He had some luck in chancing upon celebrity guests. On 30 April 1876, he encountered Charles Darwin and wife, a most unusual visit, and also a late visit from Anthony Trollope who came more rarely now. Sully also visited on 28 May 1876 in a group of nearly thirty people, all or some of whom may have heard George Eliot read "two chapters of Daniel Deronda" (GHLJ 28 May 1876). On 25 March 1877, he found himself in the company of Tennyson and two of his sons.

Even after Lewes's death, Sully sustained his rigid objectivity in evaluating his Priory host's work. As Martha Vogeler has pointed out, George Eliot did not spend the first year of her bereavement in idleness but instead hard at work completing *Problems of Life and Mind*. Sully and Michael Foster reviewed the proofs for her (Vogeler 83). She tried to keep Lewes's reputation strong during the inevitable period of evaluation provided by the obituaries. According to Alexander Bain, "James Sully had been entrusted by her with the drawing up of a sketch of Lewes for publication in Magazine form" (343). Sully brought the proofs of his article along with him on a walking trip to Scotland he and Bain pursued that August, and Bain asserts that Sully showed him the proofs and asked advice of him.

The psychologists who made the Priory one of their important gathering places provided a ready-made set of likely reviewers for the posthumous publication of Lewes's last work. Henry Maine published a review whose moderate estimate of Lewes's philosophical powers disappointed George Eliot (Vogeler 83). Joseph Delboeuf's obituary appeared in *La Revue Scientifique* (1 February 1879, 730–33), and his review of the completed *Problem* in *La Nature* on 5 December 1879. Other obituaries followed the psychologists' pattern of placing him within their own groups. Frederic Harrison describes him in *The Academy* as an out-and-out Positivist. More literary authors singled out the *Biographical History of Philosophy* and his life of Goethe as his most significant contributions.

As for Sully, he also shared the proofs of his Lewes article with George Eliot. Vogeler summarizes George Eliot's exchanges with Sully about his article in the *New Quarterly Magazine* for October 1879. George Eliot thought Sully might delete some of the material about Lewes's acting, as well as the plot summary of the novel *Rose Blanche and Violet*. But she becomes serious about Sully's reports of Lewes's early critical responses to the work of poets who later became Priory visitors, notably Browning and Tennyson: "I beg you in his name and my own to omit the paragraph.... I know that he would have objected to have attention called to his early observations on two living poets—observations which his later mind would have considerably modified" (*GEL* 9:272–73). Her final two comments in this important letter concern Lewes's later work and the triumphant reception of the *Life of Goethe* in Germany. Throughout, she expresses her gratitude both for the content of the piece and for Sully's thoughtfulness in consulting her before publication.

But Vogeler concludes that Sully's essay did not "satisfy her" despite the author's more positive responses to Lewes's last two volumes of *Problems* (83). Simcox describes the situation more bluntly: George Eliot was "vexed" (103) at "the well-meant blundering way" of Sully's article "which she said was written by a clever man and a friend'" (103). Only once did George Eliot voice approval of Sully's work. To Cross, by this time her "best loved and loving one" (*GEL* 7:210), she mentions in passing that Sully's essay was "v well done" (164). During the year of her intense bereavement and hard work, Priory regulars, including Sully, Sidgwick, Foster, and Cross, continued to figure in her life despite the abolition of the Sunday afternoons.

While the psychologists at the Priory established the venue as an important site in the early and ever-less-shadowy history of psychology, the social side of Sunday at the Priory also gained cachet during the later seventies. Between 1875 and 1878, the Grosvenor cousins added a socially elite pair. Norman Grosvenor fit in well at the Priory. A fan of William Morris, he counted Leslie Stephen and Edward Burne-Jones among his friends. Described by his grandson as kindly and gentle with a streak of romantic melancholy, he reveled in several occupations that competed for his time. In addition to enjoying grouse hunting, "he was happiest dressed in his oldest clothes, going fishing or studying harmony and counterpoint" (quoted in Lownie 94). During the same period he was participating in Sundays at the Priory, he launched his successful project of bringing classical music to London's poorer neighborhoods. According to J. A. Fuller-Maitland, " In 1878 the Honourable Norman Grosvenor, with a handful of amateurs like-minded with himself tried the experiment of giving classical music concerts in the East End of London . . . nothing but the best music was good enough for their purpose" (317). Their organization, the People's Concert Society, charged a penny per concert and survived until 1936. He began visiting the Priory regularly in 1876 at the age of thirty-one and continued through 1878.

After a few Sundays, Norman Grosvenor began to arrive with his cousin Richard. Although both at different times MPs (Norman, member for Chester, 1869–74; Richard, for Flintshire, 1861–86), during their period as Priory guests they shared the more emotional bond of being unhappily single. Richard was mourning his first wife, Beatrice Vesey, who died in 1876 shortly after giving birth to their daughter Elizabeth. He remarried in 1879, and his second wife, Eleanor Hamilton-Stubber, bore five more children. Norman Grosvenor was waiting with as much patience as possible to marry Caroline Stuart Wortley, whom he first met in 1875. But Norman's father survived into 1893, postponing or eliminating whatever chance a younger son might have at an inheritance, and the couple waited until 1882 to marry. Meanwhile, both temporarily single cousins spent many afternoons at the Priory.

In 1876 another philosopher/scientist (and, eventually, archaeologist), Charles Waldstein, began joining the company. Lewis S. Feuer assigns an important role to Waldstein's presence at the Priory for he believes that Waldstein encountered there ideas responsible for a major shift in the thinking of Karl Marx. Feuer describes how the meeting between Priory visitor Edwin Ray Lankester and Marx resulted in a friendship that demonstrates how "in his last years, Marx appears to have been longing to evolve from ideology to science" (646). The short biography that Feuer includes in his essay narrates Waldstein's rather wandering vocational path from studying philosophy at Heidelberg, moving to London to write his dissertation on Kant and Hume, and somehow ending up delivering a series of art lectures at the British Museum during the winter of 1876–77.

He first turned up at the Priory on 29 October 1876, the same day as a visit by Maxim Kovalevsky who, according to Waldstein, introduced him to Marx, making possible in turn the pivotal Lankester introduction (Feuer 645).[7]

Waldstein went on to become known as an archaeologist and eventually Slade Professor of Art at Cambridge, but when he remembers his years at the Priory he emphasizes his youth.[8] Two of his publications reflect his experiences as a young visitor to George Eliot's salon. The more direct appeared in Charles Dudley Warner's 1896 *Library of the World's Best Literature Ancient and Modern* for which Waldstein wrote the section on George Eliot. Warner's format called for a critical biography followed by excerpts from George Eliot's novels.

Probably because of his reading of Cross's *Life in Letters,* Waldstein narrates the youth of his subject with far less inaccuracy than so many of the Priory guests produced in their 1881 obituaries. When he comes to George Eliot's later life, he describes how the Sunday afternoons reassured him: "The present writer remembers with grateful piety how, when he was a very young man struggling to put a crude thought into presentable form before these giants of thought and letters, she would divine his meaning even in its embryonic uncouthness of expression, and would give it back to him and to them in a perfect and faultless garb; so that in admiring and worshipping the woman, he would be pleased with his own thoughts and think well of himself" (5364). He places his analysis of her work in an Arnoldian Hebraic/Hellenic frame, putting her on the Hebraic side of the binary and praising her as a novelist and poet but "above all a social philosopher" (5364). When he writes on *Daniel Deronda,* he confines his interest largely to Gwendolen, identifying the subject of the novel "the development of her soul" (5374). Lewes himself, he concludes, ratified his interpretation: "When she comes out of the final soul's tragedy we feel that the woman has stood the test of fire, and has realized the greatness and overwhelming vastness of the spiritual world. G. H. Lewes, to whom

---

[7] Feuer suggests that either Darwin or Huxley might have introduced him at the Priory, but Lewes's notes fail to support this. Darwin attended the Priory only twice, once in 1873 and once in 1876; Huxley does not appear on Lewes's list at all. Waldstein himself suggests the Darwin/Huxley possibility in his essay on George Eliot for the *Library of the World's Best Literature Ancient and Modern* in which he describes Sundays at the Priory: "I might meet in one and the same afternoon Charles Darwin, Robert Browning, Tennyson, Robert Wagner, Joachim the violinist, Huxley, Clifford, Du Maurier and Turgénieff" (5363). Waldstein uses his "might" judiciously, since that particular group never assembled all at once on any given Sunday.

[8] See Collins's excerpt from Waldstein's *Truth: An Essay in Moral Reconstruction* (1919), which also dwells on his gratitude to George Eliot for her helpfulness as he attempted to express himself effectively at the Priory (*George Eliot* 90).

the writer communicated this conception of 'Daniel Deronda,' assured him that he had grasped the central idea which George Eliot had in her mind, and the actual history of the story's construction" (5374). His segment on George Eliot concludes with excerpts from *The Mill on the Floss, Silas Marner,* and *Romola.*

In 1894, Waldstein, born in New York to Jewish parents, published anonymously *The Jewish Question and the Mission of the Jews.* His analysis vastly underestimates the force of European anti-Semitic movements of which he concludes, "they are artificial and false in their origin and ephemeral in their vitality, and they are doomed to die soon" (4), but he also engages the possibility of a homeland in Palestine, a matter he leaves untouched in his analysis of *Daniel Deronda* for the *World's Best Literature* volume. He distances himself from the matters he discusses through consistent third-person references, including his chapter titles: "The Mission of the Jews," "Money and the Jews." The future "Sir Charles Walston," whose path took him from New York through Heidelberg and London and on to Cambridge, learned and benefitted from his attendance at the Priory, but he did not share George Eliot's more accurate (in the light of history) ideas about the future of European Jewry.

The women regulars during the Priory's last two years drew from the usual groups: Pre-Raphaelites, singers, and Bodichon's protégées. Henrietta Rintoul's 1905 obituary in *The Mercury,* published in Hobart, Tasmania, devotes most of its space to her father, Robert Stephen Rintoul, longtime editor of *The Spectator.* Once courted by William Michael Rossetti, she corresponded with Christina Rossetti, who never came near the Priory. Within the musical contingent, another woman guest, Augusta Redeker, sang with Liebreich to a large group of twenty-seven on 14 April 1878. The following year she married one of the guests in the audience that afternoon, Sir Felix Semon. The new Lady Semon won fervent praise from P. McBride, her husband's biographer, who eulogized Sir Felix in 1913. He describes her as "charming," talented, and, what's more, devoted to her domestic duties. Artist Emily Greatorex, friend to both Bodichon and Marks, later committed herself to assuring that Girton College accepted and exhibited Bodichon's portrait (Hirsch 307–8).

Lord Acton began turning up at the Priory only during its last days as a Sunday salon in the spring of 1878, but his effects on the legacy of George Eliot persist out of all proportion with the length and depth of their social relationship. A highly active, almost a professional Catholic, Acton spent much of his intellectual life embroiled in the controversies facing Victorian Catholicism, in particular the Vatican decree of papal infallibility. He survived with the possibility of excommunication ever hovering about his publications and lectures.

During the early 1880s, Lord Acton immersed himself in George Eliot's life and works, assembling a mass of note cards now in the Cambridge University Library. They suggest that Acton may have projected a biography of his own. Indeed he participated actively in the writing of John Cross's *Life in Letters,* which Cross worked on partly while wintering on the French Riviera. In 1892 Queen Victoria selected Acton as her Lord-in-Waiting. His performance in this undemanding role, which consisted largely of sharing the Queen's evening meals, enabled him to reverse financial woes and retain his home in Shropshire, as well as his chalet in Germany and La Madeleine, his villa in Cannes (Hill 343). He delighted in the crowning joy of his life when he became Cambridge University Regius Professor of Modern History in 1895, despite his Catholicism, supported by old Priory friend Henry Sidgwick (367) and in competition with Oscar Browning, by this point generally regarded as a figure of fun (368).

Selected Futures

Sundays at the Priory, in the form Lewes and George Eliot conducted them for nearly ten years, ended abruptly in November 1878. Lewes's death occurred on a Saturday night. Several friends—Browning, Tennyson, Spencer, Maine—anticipating the devastation George Eliot would suffer, hesitated to forward their sympathy notes right away. Du Maurier, too, feared "to intrude on her grief" (*GEL* 7:84). He wrote instead to Charles Lee Lewes, his friend and neighbor, telling about how he actually set out from his home in Hampstead Heath for Sunday at the Priory on 1 December, rehearsing along the way a song adapted from Lewes's *Life of Goethe* with which he hoped to please his host. Charles Kegan Paul's letter of condolence mentions that, like Du Maurier, he had "intended calling at the Priory yesterday afternoon" (ms. letter, Beinecke, 2 December 1878). Indeed the condolence letters that piled up awaiting George Eliot's ability to read them, as well as the list of mourners who attended the services at Highgate Cemetery, read like one of Lewes's diary lists of frequent visitors to Sundays at the Priory.

After Lewes's death, the Sundays ceased, although George Eliot remained in isolation for many months. But by March 1879 the old standbys were beginning to call on random days of the week, first the men involved in the George Henry Lewes Studentship, then a few women: her daughter-in-law Gertrude Lewes, Maria Congreve, and Georgiana Burne-Jones. From 22 May until 1 November, she stayed at Witley where callers were frequently local, including Tennyson and other neighbors.[9]

Among the people who mourned the death of Lewes and remained on social terms with George Eliot afterwards, some did not outlive their Priory hosts for long, while others went on to change their lives and find pursuits that took them in surprising directions, sometimes directions that showed the influence of their participation at the Priory and their acquaintance with the people that gathered there. Among their contemporaries, Trollope (1882), Browning (1889), Bodichon (1891), and Tennyson (1892) did not make it into the twentieth century while Burton (1900) and Spencer (1903) died in their mid-eighties. Bice Trollope married in 1880, but died young, the year following her wedding.

Of the Leweses' other juniors, the most long-lasting popular fame of all came to the modest cartoonist songbird with the weak eyes. Taken together, Du Maurier's three 1890s novels have yielded a variety of twentieth-century dramas, movies, operas, and television productions, but among the three, *Trilby* takes the lead in indelible popularity. The style of hat to which it gave its name has still not gone completely out of style in the twenty-first century.

Artist Felix Moscheles describes the youthful hijinks he shared with Du Maurier in his reminiscences of "Bohemia with Du Maurier," as experiences that he believes provided the material for *Trilby*'s Parisian setting and plot events. He concludes that his own ability to mesmerize in those distant days impressed Du Maurier. Of his mesmeric abilities, he expresses his confidence "that du Maurier was inoculated with the germs that were eventually to develop into Trilbyism and Svengalism" (59). But during the years between the 1850s in Paris and the writing of *Peter Ibbetson, Trilby,* and *The Martian* in the 1890s, Du Maurier had multiple opportunities to observe, discuss, question, and become inspired to plot spiritualism, hypnotism, and reincarnation into his fiction by the company he shared at the Priory, especially Myers, Sidgwick, and Gurney,

---

[9] *Impressions of Theophrastus Such,* crowded with authors of varying degrees of reliability and success, set in many a drawing room, and written during the last days of Sundays at the Priory, offers a tempting array of possibilities for characters drawn from George Eliot's own salon. But they provide at once too much and too little information to establish similarities between, say, "The Too-Ready Writer" and Leslie Stephen who, in writing for the *Cornhill Magazine* tackled topics ranging from touring in the Alps to Shakespeare or "Too Young" to Croom Robertson, who stuck with coming to the Priory long enough to have outgrown his singularizing precocity. While George Eliot's coded communications may have offered telling details for her in-crowd of guests, the identifying significance of the fall of a lock of hair here or a broken bootstrap there lies beyond the twenty-first-century investigator.

who embraced the various processes represented in Du Maurier's novels. The Priory days did not remove thoughts of such things from Du Maurier's memories of an artistic youth, but rather intensified them during the decades between youthful experimentation and the creation of the relationship between Svengali and Trilby that has delighted and terrified audiences throughout the years since its publication by the late-blooming novelist.

Not only his plot but Du Maurier's plentiful allusions in *Trilby* also show signs of his regular Priory attendance. While Du Maurier's mentions of names such as Burne-Jones and Rossetti make likely references in a novel about artists irrespective of their mutual socializing with its author, Priory-related literary references turn up in *Trilby* as well. On Little Billee's train journey to Devonshire to visit his mother and sister, he provides himself with reading matter that includes the work of three participants in Priory society: *Silas Marner, Origin of Species,* and *Punch,* although the character gives most of his attention to the first. Meanwhile, Du Maurier's anti-Semitic construction of Svengali himself reveals that the cartoonist-become-novelist did not completely accept the message of respect George Eliot delivers in *Daniel Deronda*.

Edmund Gurney's death in the Brighton hotel did not paralyze the psychical group. F. W. H. Myers and his friends pursued spiritualism, and they became increasingly known for his psychical research. Myers died 1901 in Rome and is memorialized with a plaque in the A-Catolico Cemetery near the Porta Paolo. His wife, Eveleen, born in 1856, became a photographer, often including wistful portraits of her children among her subjects.

In addition to Du Maurier, other ex-Priory guests wrote novel after novel. Betham-Edwards continued writing novels and travels. Lucy Clifford wrote children's stories, while Lewis Strange Wingfield and Charles Hamilton Aidé also continued to turn out fiction. William Allingham's poetry received a high compliment when W. B. Yeats edited his volume of "Sixteen Poems" in 1905. Kate Field continued her journalism and between 1890 and 1895 edited her own newspaper, *Kate Field's Washington,* which appeared weekly (Scharnhorst 25).

After a lifetime suggesting domestic submission, continued self-sacrifice, and patience with her erring husband, Georgiana Burne-Jones became what she had little reason to believe part of her future: a politician and an author. She won election to the parish council in Rottingdean Surrey where the Burne-Joneses had made their refuge from London and the Grange at Fulham. Then, at the age of 65, after her husband's death, she wrote his *Memorials,* still consulted today for its biography of one of the most famous and productive of the Pre-Raphaelites who was also a constant visitor at the Priory.

James Sully concentrated his later efforts on child psychology and the publication of text books in 1884, '85, '95, and '97, before returning to a subject more typical of his Priory days: *An Essay on Laughter* (1902). As late as 1923 Sully demonstrated evidence of his easy relationship with the Leweses. In a departure from his usual topics, a set of *Italian Sketches,* he refers offhandedly to the Leweses' travels. He mentions in particular their 1860 journey as part of a decade that drew many important *Inglesi* to Italy and that marked "the triumph of the long struggle of the Italians for freedom and national unity" (61). In his arrangement of important visitors to Italy during that time, the Leweses come after Henry Taine and before J. A. Symonds and Herbert Spencer.[10] He mentions how the Leweses had to plan their movements to avoid the campaigns of Garibaldi, and he praises George Eliot's eye for the colors of the ruins of Paestum, its three ancient temples rising out of meadows of wildflowers she also admired. His casual references this late in the game suggest he has no need to boast of the friendship; it was a matter of course to link the Leweses and 1860s Italy.

Phoebe Sarah (Hertha) Marks became the second wife of her professor, W. E. Ayrton, and stepmother to Edith Ayrton who married author Israel Zangwill. She enthusiastically joined a family circle active in the late nineteenth-century women's suffrage effort (Rochelson 15). Described as a "scientist, writer, and lecturer in London" (15), she later successfully invented and sold a fan that she designed to disperse poisonous gases from World War I trenches. She named her daughter after Barbara Bodichon.

Charles Waldstein continued his distinguished work as an archaeologist. Knighted in 1913, he took the honor under the name Sir Charles Walston (Feuer 644). But his most unusual achievement for a Priory visitor occurred in 1896 when he participated in the Summer Olympics. A member of the committee formed to revive the games in 1894, he was everywhere when they actually took place in Athens two years later. He participated in shooting events and, though he won no medals, organized athletic and gymnastic competitions, and served as referee for bicycling and tennis.

Edith Simcox, despite a huge pile of achievements, never found happiness. During the first seven years after George Eliot's death, she

---

[10] Like Waldstein's contributions to the *Library of the World's Great Literature,* Sully here contributes to one of the many Victorian collective biographies Alison Booth calls prosopographies and which often include George Eliot. While most authors who attended the Priory Sundays include her among sketches of famous people the authors have known, Sully narrows his process of selection to famous people he can also present as Italophiles.

remained preoccupied with her love, going over memories of this day or that, pondering the beliefs expressed in the novels, and making pilgrimages to places associated with George Eliot. She met with George Eliot's old friends, including Barbara Bodichon, Cara Bray, Sara Hennell, and, during a lasting friendship, Maria Congreve. She traveled to Warwickshire where she failed to persuade Isaac Evans that she, not Johnny Cross, should write the biography of his sister. Although she eventually gave up both supervising Hamilton and Company and also her membership on the School Board, she remained active in workers' groups, meeting with miners, visiting sweatshops, and traveling to conventions. She continued writing, including the *Vignettes,* her allegories of love for George Eliot.[11]

For four years Simcox waited anxiously for the appearance of Cross's book. When it finally came, she first reacted with relief: "the blasphemers I think will be at a loss for anything to take hold of and the invention of the arrangement is good," although "I could have spared all the references to myself especially the last, which seems to me in questionable taste" (211). Afterward, she kept the volumes by her, rereading George Eliot's letters as a source of comfort.

Then, in 1888, references to George Eliot cease: her last reference, in March 1887, identifies herself and Lewes as "worshippers at one dear shrine" (241). This reference in the *Autobiography* follows up a long reflection about growing up without romantic interest in boys and precedes a detailed report concerning the International Workman's Congress in London and Paris. It then yields to a long narrative of her mother's decline and death. Even when referring to Maria Congreve in 1891, when George Eliot's old friend taught Simcox to ride horseback (and again later in 1894), she does not mention her lost love. Notes concerning former Priory guest George Romanes in 1895 do not prompt reflections concerning the beloved hosts of the Sunday salons. In the end, the *Autobiography* concentrates almost exclusively on her mother's slow death, after which she concludes that "I rank her above my other love in perfection for all human relations" (280). The diary ends ominously with the statement that "[t]he few pages that remain will serve to report if any work gets done in the few years that remain" (280). The disturbing absence of further entries suggests that her last year and a half of life yielded little satisfaction. She died 15 September 1901.

The later experiences of the Priory visitors confirm that at the same time George Eliot was drawing on her acquaintances and experiences

---

[11] Rosemarie Bodenheimer's "Autobiography in Fragments: The Elusive Life of Edith Simcox" describes the *Autobiography* as "a struggle with George Eliot" (2) and a search for an "acceptable life plot" (3) for herself.

there to create her composite characters, those acquaintances were participating in a literary atmosphere that kept many of them writing in various genres and for various audiences, often even more intensely than when they were actually in attendance. Into the eighties and nineties, many of them continued to move in the same circles that visited in St John's Wood on Sundays, circles likely to take an interest in their specialized activities, such as Cobden Sanderson's Doves Press or Sully's child psychology. In addition to Cross's biography, extensive sets of their notes suggest unachieved biographical ambitions on the parts of Acton and Simcox, while dozens of the guests produced their versions of Sundays at the Priory, sometimes as a minor detail in a memoir and sometimes as a chapter in a propsopography devoted to famous people the author has known. If George Eliot turned to her guests for creative inspiration, it worked both ways when, after the salons ceased, Priory guests inserted long or short descriptions of Sundays at the Priory to add the sparkle of celebrity name-dropping to their letters, memoirs, and autobiographies.

CHAPTER 6

John Cross and the Last Spa

> As thus I spoke,
> Servants announced the gondola, and we
> Through the fast-falling rain and high-wrought sea
> Sailed to the island where the madhouse stands.
> We disembarked.
>
> —Percy Bysshe Shelley, *Julian and Maddalo*

George Eliot demonstrated her confidence in Continental spas most convincingly on her disastrous honeymoon with John W. Cross in 1880. After Cross had his breakdown in Venice, which supposedly included a desperate, perhaps suicidal, jump into the Grand Canal, she moved him as quickly as possible to the Schwarzwald, ending up at the spa at Bad Wildbad. George Eliot's decision to marry John Walter Cross has invited various interpretations, most of them based on its inexplicability. They range from Haight's belief that "she was not fitted to stand alone" (530) to Phyllis Rose's belief in an act of bravery that asserted her independence as a woman (211).

George Eliot's own accounting for her marriage coincides with advice she also delivered to Edith Simcox (and others), when she chided that unlikely marriage candidate for resisting her own belief that only marriage between man and woman can engender the best kind of love, tender, sympathetic, dutiful. Of her engagement, she confided to Maria Congreve that as a widow, "instead of any former affection being displaced in my mind, I seem to have recovered the loving sympathy that I was in danger of losing. I mean that I had been conscious of a certain drying up of tenderness in me, and that now the spring seems to have risen again" (*GEL* 7:296). At that point and to that degree, she could present the marriage and the subsequent honeymoon positively.[1]

---

[1] Bodenheimer interprets the rhetoric of the letters George Eliot wrote about her engagement and concludes that Cross's attractions included his abilities as a business manager.

For Cross's part, he, too, at the outset of the honeymoon, expressed nothing but satisfaction, at least at the journey's launch: "I don't know what people generally complain so much of in their wedding journeys—ours has certainly been very full of delight and it goes on increasing and I hope will go on jusqu'à la fin—she is a very inexhaustible storehouse" (*GEL* 9:312). His wife, too, created a positive picture. Writing to Cross's brother in the United States, she creates a charming epistolary scene: "I wish you could see Venice this morning; or any other morning like it, in the clear calm light of half past nine o'clock, and have a gondola waiting below to take you wherever you liked to be guided by a picturesque gondolier in blue and white. This is our luxurious lot, and Johnnie seems as happy and well as possible under this regime" (*GEL* 7:292). At the same time, Hughes and Bodenheimer accurately point out that Cross lost a considerable amount of weight as the wedding approached (341;xxx). Indeed George Eliot mentions this twice, first to her stepson Charles Lewes, then to the distant brother. And, in the end, the only people who mention any physical contact, actual or potential, between the newlyweds are two of the Cross sisters, Emily and Florence. Emily writes to her brother, "kiss her well for me," while Florence, the youngest Cross, writes to them: "Please give each other all the kisses and love that we send you each" (ms. letter, Beinecke 7 May 1880). In doing so, Florence and Emily depart from the pattern of joyous references to the sights of the honeymoon itinerary into the realm of actual physical contact, though physical contact among the family members, rather than just the couple themselves.

At any rate, the entire tendency of George Eliot's life at the time was a family affair with the Crosses. They had been intimate friends for more than a decade. Financially and emotionally, they already considered themselves "family." Two of the sisters and a cousin named their children for George Eliot and for characters she created. Emily Cross Otter called her daughter Gwendolen Otter, and Anna Cross Druce named her little boy Eliot. Elinor Sellar, related to the Crosses through the Denistouns, named her daughter Eppie.

The eldest Cross sister, Elizabeth, nicknamed Zibbie, was, according to her cousin Eleanor Sellar, the star of the family and the sister whose loss George Eliot's marriage to Johnny helped make up for. Sellar describes them all in superlatives: a wise father and "handsome, lively, humorous mother" (74), but the oldest girl is "the peerless Zibbie" (74) and "one of the most charming and brilliant women I have ever known" (52). Cross reports that Zibbie Cross Bullock sang one of George Eliot's *Spanish Gypsy* songs on the important day in August of 1869 on which the lifelong intimacy between the Crosses and Leweses sprang up full blown.

Simcox suggests that Zibbie Cross never felt comfortable in the company of the family idol, although the Cross brothers and sisters detected many strange and portentous resemblances between their eldest sister and George Eliot (70). Eleanor Cross informed Simcox that when Elizabeth Bullock died, both her bereaved husband, William Henry Bullock, and her brother, Johnnie, were "drawn" to George Eliot because of a "strange likeness" (70) between the two women, one just turning fifty the other dead in her thirties. When the family showed George Eliot Elizabeth's book of extracted passages from literature, it turned out that both had copied many of the same ones. Bereavement brought the two families together again in 1878 when Anna Cross and Lewes died within days of each other.

Consequently, the marriage between George Eliot and Cross did not just add one more sister to the family-like group. Instead, the Crosses regarded it as the replacement of a specific sister, their departed Zibbie. When George Eliot became Mary Ann Cross, Eleanor Cross wrote in terms that show she was still connecting her late sister and her new relative: "it is most delicious to have an *oldest sister* again!" (ms. letter, Beinecke, 6 May 1880; my italics). Rather than participating in a general restoration of the condition of sister, George Eliot was expected to take the place of the particular sister they had connected with her since the afternoon Zibbie sang the song from *The Spanish Gypsy* in the house at the foot of St George's Hill on Weybridge Heath, henceforth a second home for the Leweses.

The wedding of George Eliot and Johnnie Cross was a family affair. On 6 May 1880, a group of eight people gathered in the late-morning light at St George's. Popular for society weddings, it had an east Mayfair location convenient to some of the best neighborhoods in London. Although the porch atop the series of Corinthian columns offered shelter out front in the event of a rainy day, the bright weather meant that this party had no serious need of it. Coming together in the church's wide aisle, dwarfed by the towering pulpit, they encircled the bride and groom, making but a small party in the broad aisle. The setting for a wedding that was already puzzling literary and social London earned George Eliot additional negative comment for her choice of an Anglican church despite her famous agnosticism (Haight 543).

A last-minute change introduced a single Lewes into the Cross-dominated occasion. Before the wedding, George Eliot had asked Alfred Druce, Anna Cross's husband, to give her away. Then she had a last-minute talk with Charles Lee Lewes. Consequently the role he assumed implies approval of and respect for his stepmother's plans. Druce attended the wedding, but Charles gave her away. The couple departed under clear skies toward Dover. They spent their wedding night at the King's Head, eschewing the Lord Warden, so often the first or last stop on journeys to or from the Continent. As the day ended, they walked along the beach below the white cliffs agreeing on the blessedness of their wedding (*GEL* 7:272).

To a certain degree, the honeymoon was a family affair as well. Letters from bride and groom crisscrossed with return letters from Weybridge. Writing directly after the wedding, the sisters' letters to George Eliot contain a strain of relief, and a suggestion that their brother needed caring for, side by side with references to the combination of sorrow and joy the event was prompting. Eleanor writes: "We bless you with our whole hearts for all you are giving to our best beloved. You must not think that we cannot understand the sorrow as well as the joy. We do indeed and we love you the more if that were possible for all you have suffered for him" (ms. letter, Beinecke). On 6 May, after the wedding, Eleanor returned home to Weybridge and immediately sent off a letter to the bride, a letter that acknowledges the Cross servants' concerns about the bridegroom: "Amelia and Delia were so sympathetic when I got home and I had to tell them every detail I could think of. The former was much relieved to hear that the bridegroom's brother had packed his things for him. She evidently has misgivings as to their future fate." On 10 May, the youngest sister Florence sounds the same note: "You can't think what a weight it is off our minds getting rid of our mauvais sujet of a brother and how good of you to tell us how the three days passed . . . as to the keys I hope you will not trust them to Johnnie." For all his efficient handling of finances and real estate, his sisters hardly trusted him to pack his trunk.

Did Johnny Jump?

As for the central event of the honeymoon, Cross's mental breakdown in Venice and accompanying jump into the Grand Canal, most of George Eliot's early biographers, including Mathilde Blind (1883), Oscar Browning (1890), Leslie Stephen (1902), and Charles Olcott (1911), do not mention the Grand Canal incident in any way. By mid-century, several authors (Ramieu in 1932, the Hansons in 1952, and Crompton in 1960) do mention Cross's sickness in Venice but leave out the jump. By the 1990s, all biographers felt the need to confront the question of whether fear of sex with George Eliot prompted Cross to take this supposed plunge. Taylor, Karl, Ashton, and Hughes all consider the possibility.[2] Brenda Maddox, draw-

---

[2] Aside from being the result of twentieth-century preoccupations with sex, the prurient version owes much to Terence de Vere White's fictionalized account of the honeymoon in which he creates Cross as a tormented creature, retreating into madness when faced by his

ing an intense if not fanciful version of the event, follows the pattern of the more popular, least scholarly biographies that embrace the progress from illness to leap, from leap to suicide, from suicide to sexual terror.[3]

Barbara Hardy, among others, has raised questions about whether the jump occurred at all (104). Contemporary versions, on which Haight relies with undue confidence, come from people, most of them in England at the time of the event, who heard about it by rumor or report. These include Lord Acton and Walter Sichel who agree that Cross had shown signs of mental illness previous to the incident. Acton and Sichel, however, also include demonstrably false details in their versions that conflict with the illness, jump, suicide attempt, and sexual repulsion that has become irretrievably part of the story. Lord Acton concludes, "At Venice she thought him mad," and mentions that she reported to Dr. Richetti, the hotel doctor, that Cross had a mad brother. Acton goes on to assert that during the doctor's presence in their hotel rooms, she "just then heard that he had jumped into the canal" (quoted in Haight 544). No other version supports Acton's conclusion about the doctor's presence at the time of the jump.

Sichel (who also believed that Agnes Jervis Lewes was shut up in "a lunatic asylum" [186]) in later years played bridge with Cross at the Sheridans' Club. He found him unforthcoming, either about his excellent handling of the cards or about his honeymoon with George Eliot, and in any event he introduces his version with a disclaimer: "The silliest gossip was bruited about their honeymoon. It was rumoured that after a prolonged course of Dante at Venice he had cast himself into the Grand Canal and begged the gondoliers not to rescue him. But such inventions were probably due to the ignorance of thickheads who could not understand how a literary man of business became united to a genius through a worship of

---

wife's sexual expectations. George Griffith (email to author) locates versions of the story in the American periodical *Literary World,* while K. K. Collins mentions its publication in the *Examiner* shortly after George Eliot's death and adds George Howard, Caroline Jebb, Hallam Tennyson, and Bertrand Russell as sources for sometimes conflicting accounts. Despite the prurient cruelty with which White treats George Eliot, he accurately emphasizes the almost daily intimacy the Crosses shared with William Bunney, Ruskin's protégé in Venice, creating a possible Ruskinian link to the honeymoon events. The timing of the Crosses' visit suggests that, along with purchasing one of Bunney's paintings for the Heights, his connection with them may have provided the occasion for them to read *Fiction Fair and Foul,* with its harshness regarding *The Mill on the Floss,* available in Venice, at this crucial point in the honeymoon.

[3] Collins accepts the story of the jump because of Maddox's research coup: her discovery of stories concerning the incident in Italian newspapers and a police report that appear to corroborate Cross's jump and his refusal of help from the gondoliers (218). Nevertheless, the inflamed style of Italian journalism, together with the possibility that Cross did not need help because he could swim perfectly well, qualify this evidence as the final word.

mind and character" (186).[4] Simcox secured her version of Venice from the Cross sisters at Weybridge but does not mention any Grand Canal jump, only an attack of mental illness. On hearing a report of Cross's crisis, she hastened out to the house on the Heath where she learned that the brother had a history of mental illness. She and Eleanor Cross "spoke a little about the marriage," and Eleanor reported "that they had been very anxious before their marriage, he was so worn and ill" (128). Simcox regarded this as the explanation for George Eliot's decision because it identified a plausible reason for admiring her plucky young husband handling a mental illness with fortitude. Also, with Cross losing weight and looking ill, a journey abroad, more conveniently undertaken by a married couple, might have the objective of helping to restore his health.

John Dalberg-Acton shared no close friendship with either George Eliot or Lewes. After a brief meeting in 1872, he did not turn up at Sunday at the Priory until late spring1878, and then for but two visits, neither of which coincided with Johnny Cross's. Nevertheless, Acton formed a relationship with Cross himself during the writing of his late wife's biography. He also took a rarely noticed active part in its composition. When George Eliot's widower settled down to doing the *Life in Letters,* he composed a good deal of it while wintering on the Riviera where Acton kept a villa in Cannes. Turning to the Catholic historian/moralist, Cross accepted Acton's active interest and considerable anxieties about his project. According to Acton, in his letters to Mary Gladstone, "They tell me that Mr. Cross is here. If so, I hope to have a talk with him about the difficult life he is writing." On 7 March 1883, Acton writes from his home in Cannes, that "Cross is in great force, writing the biography and wanting me to read the papers" (*Letters* 117). Two weeks later, Acton ventures his opinion of Cross's now-famous collage of excerpts from letters occasionally interrupted by his own narrative passages, describing the method on 31 March 1883 as a "v. interesting stringing together" (166).

As his project advanced, Cross continued to consult Acton. On 9 December 1884, Acton was reviewing Cross's draft when he spoke to "a young Englishman [who] described the Grasse Hotel to me, where he had lived with Cross who was writing a book" (*Letters* 198). Acton was amused that the young man "did not discover that it was the book in my hand" (198). He entered into his work on Cross's draft with thoroughness: "I have sent it back with some considerable suggestions" (198). Finally, on 22 January 1885, Acton was looking forward to seeing the publication to which he had contributed first hand. At his home in Cannes, La Made-

---

[4] Most versions of this passage truncate the disclaimers.

leine, he writes in anticipation, "Cross is coming with his book next week" (205).

Acton's worries about the biography probably helped result in its turning out, as famously described by William Gladstone, a disappointing "reticence in three volumes." Uneasy about her union with Lewes and with her agnosticism, yet devoted to her novels, he fretted over counsel that could not fail to concern containing potential scandal.

On the other hand, the winters on the Riviera and the intimacy between Cross and Acton provide just a little room for remaining doubt. Who knows but that some afternoon or evening among the palm trees Cross did not confide in Acton about a jump into the Grand Canal?

Henry Sidgwick also suggested revisions to the project to which Cross responded positively. Cross forwarded volume 3 to Sidgwick on 11 December 1884 urging him to review it quickly as the printer's deadline was approaching. Cross points out that "no one outside his own family, aside from Lord Acton, has yet seen it" and claims that he shall feel it "greatly strengthened by [HS's] revision" because he does not know anyone "whose judgment [his] wife would have trusted more" (Cambridge Trinity Add. Ms. c/93/102). Cross ended up accepting Sidgwick's revision to one of the most important narrative passages that link the excerpts from the letters, the passage that pinpoints the beginning of his romantic relationship with George Eliot. On 12 December, having read the forwarded material, Sidgwick suggests, "The 1st sentence of what you have written might perhaps suggest to stupid or careless readers ideas which you did not intend, and would not desire, to suggest" (ms. letter, Beinecke). He offers as a revision the statement: "From this time forward I saw her 'constantly' or some such phrase" (ms. letter, Beinecke). Although neither piece of correspondence reveals the phrasing of Cross's original passage, he accepted Sidgwick's revision word for word. Following a quotation from a letter from George Eliot, he inserts: "From this time forward I saw George Eliot constantly" (JWC 3:292). Like Acton, Sidgwick was making an effort to protect George Eliot's moral reputation.

Meanwhile Acton's letters to Mary Gladstone contain the interesting detail that Cross did some of his writing in Grasse while living with the "young Englishman." While this could mean only that they stayed at the same hotel, it could also mean what it says: that the widower-biographer and the young man lived together. While providing no more than a thread of possible support for Haight's story about a jump into the Grand Canal, Acton's letter may supply the key to the marriage itself. If Cross sought love in the arms of a young man at the Grasse Hotel, he perhaps did enter the marriage to George Eliot in the spirit of an alliance between two close friends, the younger one without interest in the opposite sex, who joined together for the sake of health, convenience, and platonic affection.

Simcox, though apprehensive about Cross's version of her beloved's life, upon its publication expressed relief. Not until the second edition did she mention a serious objection, an objection directly concerning Acton. In both editions Cross acknowledges the service of Acton whom he calls "a friend always most kindly ready to assist me with valuable counsel and with cordial generous sympathy" ("Preface"). On 17 January 1886, Simcox notes bitterly, "I don't forgive Mr. Cross for leaving the reference to Lord Acton in the preface to the new edition" (228). Simcox does not account for her irritation with Cross's acknowledgment of Acton, but it did not improve her touchy relationship with him despite her affection for his sisters Mary and Eleanor. No reference to the supposed jump appears in Cross, Blind, Simcox's journal, or the article-length intellectual biography of George Eliot which Acton published in *The Nineteenth Century* in March 1885, where he reviewed the very book to whose composition he claims to have contributed substantially.

Meanwhile, Kathleen Adams departs from the happy-extended-family version of the marriage. In *Those of Us Who Loved Her,* she reports a family tradition contrary to the one suggested by the letters of Mary, Eleanor, and Florence Cross. According to this interpretation, gained from John Cross's great-niece Joan O'Conner, "who knew him well during his latter years" (v), the Cross sisters regarded George Eliot as "a very autocratic old lady" (175). Adams goes on: "If they were right in thinking that George Eliot had, even subtly, persuaded him into the marriage, then their subsequent view that Johnnie had, on his honeymoon, suddenly realised that he was saddled with an old lady of powerful intellect and a will of her own, and deeply regretted the trip in which he found himself, would seem amply justified" (175). Hughes also suspects a hint of danger in George Eliot's report of Cross's severe weight loss in the year leading up to the event (341).

Two incidents on the honeymoon support Adams's suggestion of a connection between a panicking groom and an "autocratic old lady" (175). One of George Eliot's letters home, from Milan, mentions a concession she made to follow her new husband's inclinations rather than her own: "Last evening, to satisfy J's curiosity, we went to see Rossi in Hamlet" (*GEL* 7:288). She had already seen the performance in London, and in Milan she reported, "Anything so unintelligent, so—*drunken* [her emphasis] as the performance last night I never saw on any stage English or foreign. In the scene with his mother he roared (hoarsely) and stamped, and pulled the poor women's arms as if he meant to put them out of joint" (*GEL* 7:289).

The intemperance of the language in the evaluation of Rossi makes a departure from the generally contented tone of the honeymoon letters and suggests George Eliot may have blamed Cross for the unpleasant evening undertaken solely to humor him.

The second suggestion of autocracy concerns swimming. Three days before the plunge into the Grand Canal, the couple crossed the lagoon in their gondola to visit the Lido where they sat on the sands and watched the waves. At the Lido, as George Eliot wrote to the Cross sisters, her bridegroom expressed a desire for some sea bathing: "J rather longs to have a swim there" (7:298).[5] She remains vague about the reasons for his not gratifying this desire, speaking of it as having to do with insufficient temperatures of the air: "But though the temperature is agreeable it has not the sort of heat that makes a plunge in cold water as good as a drink to the thirsty" (7:298). According to her letter, only excessive heat might justify swimming, not the need for exercise.

If John Cross did make the jump so long associated with the honeymoon, his motivations, though connected with a mental illness, need not have included suicide. Supposing, for example, Cross, known for his athleticism, was a swimmer.[6] Prevented from doing so at the Lido for whatever reason, a plunge could have been a defiant gesture rather than a suicide attempt. His own version blames heat, filth, and lack of exercise, and when the couple departed from Venice, they sought to reverse these conditions. Indeed their longest stop on their return journey remedied the specific lack Cross identifies, for Bad Wildbad, among all the spas, was renowned for its piscine swimming baths.

Bad Wildbad

As the couple fled homeward, they paused for more than a day or two at a time in only two locations: Innsbruck, Austria, and Wildbad, Germany. After stopping for one night each in Verona, Trent, and Bolzano, they arrived in Innsbruck on Saturday, 26 June 1880. They were seeking

[5] Note that George Eliot mentions a *swim*, rather than a *bath* or a *bathe*.

[6] Cross's obituary emphasizes his athleticism, but does not mention swimming: "Cross was accustomed to outdoor exercise; he played tennis for some years at Prince's, though he took up 'the game of kings' too late in life to attain proficiency. Later he took to golf, at which he was a respectable performer; and for a season or two he tried mountaineering, but found that this was too strenuous a pursuit for a man well over 59 to take up for the first time" (*Times* 4 November 1924). Nevertheless novelist Weisgall, whatever her sources (and otherwise she uses Harris & Johnston scrupulously) makes his ability to swim a pivotal part of the plot of her novel, *The World Before Her*.

therapies that would address the causes Cross assigns to his illness: lack of exercise and bad air (JWC 3:331). In Innsbruck and Bad Wildbad, they could reverse both of these conditions.

Indeed Innsbruck offered surroundings exactly the opposite to those of Venice. Instead of air the English regarded as tinged with malaria, they had mountain freshness. Instead of water famous for its impurity, they had mountain streams. The Crosses waited a few days for the rain to cease, then they started making drives in several directions to take the air: toward the Mariabrunn forest monastery, along Engadine Road, southward toward Italy (H&J 207). To the end, George Eliot (and George Henry Lewes before his death) sustained a belief in the therapeutic benefits of the right air, and Innsbruck's mountain location offered the clarity and briskness the Crosses sought.

After six days in Innsbruck, the couple began the journey to a second mountain destination where they remained longer. George Eliot left no account of why she chose Bad Wildbad, and she had no firsthand knowledge of the spot, not having visited there with Lewes.[7] But the guide books to German spas, at least two of them written by acquaintances of George Eliot, chorus their approval of Bad Wildbad for its popular English physician, its romantic situation, and its swimming baths.

On the journey toward Bad Wildbad, the honeymooners moved a bit more slowly than they did on the leg to Innsbruck. The Leweses had usually interrupted their stays at the spas to visit places such as Stuttgart and Karlsruhe where they could supplement the spa concerts with some full-scale opera, and now the Crosses traveled by train to stops in Munich, Augsburg, and Stuttgart. In 1868, the railway from Pforzheim had reached the formerly remote spa town of Bad Wildbad, tucked away in a deeply carved river valley. Now many more guests could enjoy its views and surrender themselves to the waters of its thermal springs. Its popularity with English patients led to the establishment of an English Church in 1865 (Bechtle 44), whose vicar, Burckhart, became one focal point for the physically feeble members of the expatriate community. When the train carried George Eliot and John Cross through the valley into the station near the Kurplatz, she took satisfaction that Bad Wildbad supplied all the "commodities" (*GEL* 7:303) she felt they needed.

Bad Wildbad addressed its patients' health problems more seriously than many of the other nineteenth-century Black Forest watering places George Eliot had visited. Even its myth of origin differs from those of

---

[7] On the other hand, the unnamed book of poems by Ludvig Uhland she received as a good-bye present from Gustav Schöll in Weimar in 1854 might have been the volume that contains "Der Uberfall im Wildbad," set in the remote Schwarzwald town.

Figure 14. Bad Wildbad, the Bad Hotel on the Kurplatz

the more frivolous spas. Baden Baden, for example, emphasizes its Roman origins, a bathing culture with as many social dimensions as therapeutic. Bad Wildbad's legend, on the other hand, features a wounded boar that heals himself in the waters of the thermal spring. One patient, Egyptologist Georg Ebers, in describing his convalescence in Bad Wildbad, provides a reminder that many patrons of the spas had more wrong with them than gout. He reminisces about a young woman he met there with whom he shared a poignant evening as they both looked on from their wheelchairs at a dance in the Kursaal. A year later, Ebers's lovely young companion had died.

Among the various therapies offered—exercise, drinking waters, and the care of respected physicians—the pride of Bad Wildbad was the swimming baths, the feature that singularized this serious spa among Schwarzwald watering places. The baths occupy a large building on the Kurplatz kitty-corner from Klumpp's Hotel. Madden approves of these baths as "the most perfect bath establishment in Europe for its size" (256). The building stands out conspicuously from the staid hotels with which it shares the Kurplatz because of its size, architecture, and color. A deep dusky red, the stone contrasts with the green hills that provide its backdrop and with the more neutrally colored hotels all around the perimeter of the square. Tall arched windows admit the light on all sides, and its porch repeats the arches to the front. Within, Moorish decoration provides color and exoticism. Wilson finds the Bad Wildbad baths "patterns of their kind" (289). Madden estimates at least 80,000 baths taken there in a single season.

It was the construction of the baths that distinguished this Bad Hotel from Bad Homburg or Baden Baden (although Schlangenbad, too, had swimming baths). Julius Althaus describes them as "large reservoirs the soil of which is covered with fine sand, through which the water rises from the depth at a temperature just suitable for bathing." According to Madden, the water "percolates" through solid granite rock of building (251). Wilson notes that because the Bad Wildbad waters are "chiefly taken in so-called piscines, or swimming-baths . . . It is therefore not necessary to heat or cool the water, and a constant renewal of it is also rendered easy" (40). Wilson regards swimming as a major contribution to good health. He laments the lack of swimming baths in Britain and calls for swimming schools as well (40). He describes the pleasantness of a bathe in the Wildbad water where "[b]ubbles of nitrogen in which the Bad Wildbad water is very rich, continually glide along the surface of the body, and produce a sort of titillation which is by no means unpleasant. If the stay in the bath is too prolonged, weariness, fatigue, vertigo, headache, and febrile symptoms are apt to follow" (253). He also prefers swimming baths to bathrooms: "Baths are either taken in single rooms or in common reservoirs, the so-called 'piscines' or swimming-baths, in which exercise is possible." Unable, for whatever reason, to bathe at Venice, John Cross had ample opportunity to do so at the beautiful facility in Bad Wildbad.

In keeping with their reputation for seriousness, Bad Wildbad waters had a reputation for addressing a great variety of disorders. Madden's list begins with "old gunshot wounds, and contractions resulting from this cause; some forms of paralysis, especially of the lower extremities" (256). After mentioning "neuralgia, sciatica, and some other nervous affections," Madden comes to the only one relevant to Cross's difficulties, but associated exclusively with women: "hysteria and other diseases peculiar to females, when dependent upon the obstruction of certain functions." He mentions effectiveness for skin diseases and "above all, in chronic gout and rheumatism" (256). But because Madden's taxonomy depends on therapies no longer recognized by physicians or psychologists, Bad Wildbad might have had some efficacy for male nervous disorders and offer Cross the exercise he sought as well.

George Eliot found Bad Wildbad completely satisfactory. The party of three checked into the foremost hotel, Klumpp's "the chief hotel in Wildbad . . . one of the most comfortable and cleanest hotels in Germany" (Madden 250). Many of Bad Wildbad's inns face the river or the Kurplatz; Klumpp's faced both. Ebers admired the Kurplatz and its smooth-faced hotels where "one stately building of lighted sandstone adjoins another" (ch. 25). The Crosses' rooms overlooked the platz and its hotels and, to the right, the baths. Directly across the square stood what George Eliot called the ugliest church in town. Nevertheless, the views of pine-covered mountains stretched outward and upward in all directions, while the kurpark paths began nearby before extending out of the town along the rocky river. A path suitable for wheelchairs formed the river's immediate border, with a steep rise on the other side of the path for more challenging climbing.

In the location she hoped would "put the finishing touch to Johnny's recovery" (*GEL* 7:303), George Eliot's new husband improved steadily. After four days, he had gained enough health so that Willie Cross left them and returned to England. The Cross household, reduced by the death of the mother and the recent marriages of Emily, Anna, and John, was moving from Weybridge Heath, their beloved location at the foot of breezy St George's Hill, to London. Having inspected a property in Kent Terrace Regent's Park, not far from the Priory, they decided instead on one in Redcliffe Gardens, considerably closer to the house the newlywed

Crosses had bought at 4 Cheyne Walk overlooking the Thames. These considerations of proximity would keep George Eliot even closer to the Crosses now that they had formalized the family relationship through the marriage.

The couple themselves remained in Bad Wildbad nine days, walking extensively every day. They sometimes drove out of town and over the mountains for dinner. After a few days, George Eliot wrote to Elma Stuart, who often traveled on the Continent, to recommend Bad Wildbad for Stuart's chronic ailments. On the thirteenth, a thunderstorm cut short their planned excursion into the hills for lunch: "I never saw so incalculable a state of weather as we have in this valley. One quarter of an hour the blue sky is only flecked by lightest cirrhus [*sic*] clouds, the next it is almost hidden by dark rain clouds" (*GEL* 7:305). Nevertheless, "Johnnie is quite well again but is inclined to linger a little in the sweet air of the Schwarzwald which comes to one on gently stirred wings laden with the scent of the pine forests" (7:304). On hearsay, she then recommends Bad Weiler to Lewes's son Charles in preference to Wildbad as "much more lovely than this place" (7:305).

After more than a week at Bad Wildbad, the couple resumed the journey home and crossed the hills on the day-long drive to Baden Baden. George Eliot, having boarded trains more days than not since leaving Venice, had grown weary of traveling by railways and anticipated the slower, quieter pace of the carriage along its scenic route. Halfway there, another spa town, Bad Herrenalb, offered the opportunity for a *mittenessen*. After a journey of seven hours, the honeymooners' vehicle came within sight of Baden Baden.

Back in Baden Baden again after many years, George Eliot discovered that elaborate new baths, the Friederichsbad, more than a decade in the building, had opened three years previously. If the couple followed her previous practices, they drank the waters and took their baths. But the Kursaal and trinkhalle still drew guests to the other side of the little river, familiar to the new Mrs. Cross from her time there in 1868. When the Crosses walked along the colonnade fronting the trinkhalle and especially from the steep gardens behind it, they could view the town and the hills opposite, one of them crowned with the medieval Schloss towards which George Eliot and Lewes had climbed on their healthiest day at Baden Baden twelve years previously.

During the Middle Ages, the Altes Schloss had sheltered the margraves who held Baden Baden through force and authority from the eleventh century on. A few centuries later, the family had mellowed and moved away to the town in the valley into an elaborate establishment called the

Neues Schloss. High on the mountain, the old Schloss remained to remind Bad Wildbad of the Middle Ages. Half cliff, half castle, the unusual structure commands the kind of view necessary for observing enemy armies as they advance through the valley below. It stands among its sister cliffs of pinkish irregular stones in mellow contrast with the pines surrounding it.

Seen from below, the Schloss rises like a pueblo, presenting a formidable outline against the sky. Close up, it loses little of its ferocity. Its empty rocky window frames, filled with nothing but views of more rocks, made it a somewhat gloomy destination for a man recovering from a psychological jolt. Nevertheless, the Schloss added to the opportunities Cross craved for exercise, even though the couple, unlike the Leweses, drove to its base rather than climbing up through the woods. Once entered, however, Baden's Schloss, built in three separate stages over many years, required an ascent up hundreds of steps to reach the top. Again, the journey home was providing exercise for Cross.

Refreshed by Bad Wildbad, exercised at Baden Baden, the couple departed for England the next day, Monday 19 July. A week later they were back home at Witley.

Soon after their return to England, George Eliot wrote letters complaining about travels abroad, about European noise, and, to a certain extent, about foreignness in general. On 28 July, to the Hollands, their neighbors at Witley, she praises "the delicious stillness here, which seems to us to make life a new thing after the noise of continental towns" (*GEL* 7:307). To Barbara Bodichon on the first of August she again expresses her contentment at Witley as "a delight to be at home, and enjoy perfect stillness after the noisiness of foreign bells and foreign voices indoors and out" (7:308). Her choices here, the solemn or joyous chime from the churches of Catholic countries and the multilingual human talk around her, hardly intrinsically annoying sounds, have become so for her.

After his honeymoon, Johnny Cross never omitted his exercise again. His description of his illness in Venice names "riding or rowing" as his usual methods of exercise. But at Witley, he had less opportunity for rowing than he did at Weybridge, and he makes no mention of horse riding anywhere. Instead, the final letters of George Eliot bulge with references to Johnny's tennis. At Witley, at Weybridge, in Brighton, he played with the Crosses, including his sister Florence (7:325); again with family members at Sevenoaks; and, as had Lewes, at Six Mile Bottom when visiting the Halls. He booked into the public courts at Brighton, and the couple made plans for their own tennis at Witley (7:337). At home in Surrey, they laid out a new private court, and Cross chopped down trees in preparation for its installation, sustaining vigorous activity even before the court could be built. George Eliot remained vigilant about his exercise and fitness. Neither wanted a recurrence of whatever happened in Venice.

Although George Eliot never again traveled abroad, her last months took her away from home for days at a time as the couple duly made their wedding visits to family: the Cross sisters who lived at Sevenoaks, Ranby, and Newmarket, followed by another journey to Brighton. The new house in Chelsea stood waiting for them on the banks of the Thames to offer a welcome back to town for the winter-to-spring season. If life in a London townhouse prevented Johnny from exercising with his tennis, the river could not have been more convenient for rowing. But the healthful life on the river bank never materialized. George Eliot lived only nineteen days in the house overlooking the Thames, the same river that, farther upstream, had inspired Maggie Tulliver's rowing scenes and, from Kew Bridge to Blackfriars, supplied settings for *Daniel Deronda*. Most importantly, the river overlooked by the house in which she died had carried Marian Evans off to Belgium in 1854 to begin her joined life with George Henry Lewes, traveling abroad. The travels begun then, together with their Sunday salons, placed the Leweses within a group of people who not only constituted the Society of their era, but also contributed to some of the most important scientific, philosophical, social, artistic, and literary expressions of late Victorian culture.

Conclusion

Collins concedes of his additions to the forty most often-gleaned biographical sources that "[i]t would be an exaggeration to say that these unfamiliar sources demand a radical revision of the George Eliot, complex and contradictory, who emerges from the familiar ones. But they do complicate her character and circumstances even further, often in richly modulated ways" (xviii). He specifies her more detailed childhood, her earlier novelistic ambitions, and how in Weimar and Berlin, "she comes into her own conversationally and socially, almost as if she is rehearsing in a foreign tongue for her impending role as one of the most private of public figures back home" (xviii). Similarly, the version of George Eliot created through additional information about the Priory and the travels abroad creates a more socially active person who surrounded herself with men and women who both contributed to her creative imagination, especially as she (and her characters) moved upward in social status, and engaged her interest, affection, and sympathy. They also help humanize her by revealing the impatience she sometimes felt toward her less charming guests and the measures she took to smooth hurt feelings after a Sunday salon at which disappointments, frictions, or mild or serious confrontations occurred. The guests themselves also made use of the Priory to gain material for their writing, to gather audiences for their projects, to engage in fruitful intellectual exchange, to enjoy musical performances, and, possibly, to fall in love. The "unfamiliar sources" confirm that the mature George Eliot of the 1870s ill deserves a reputation as reclusive. Rather, during the winter social season, she and Lewes together indefatigably conducted one of the most visited, vital, and influential London salons of the decade.

APPENDIX

The Leweses' Travels Abroad
A Chronology

Note: Because George Eliot sometimes stopped at a watering place for as little as a few hours or a single day, the list below includes in brackets only her slightly longer periods at the European spas. In addition, because most Britons traveling in Europe passed through either France or Belgium, unless the couple spent an unusually long time in stops along the way, the list omits these necessary, transient locations.

The Leweses

1854–55 July–March	Germany: Weimar and Berlin [Ilmenau, 5 days]
1857–58 April–September	Germany
1860 March–June	Italy
1861 April–June	France, Italy, Switzerland
1864 May–June	Italy
1865 August–September	France: Normandy and Brittany
1866 June–July	Belgium, Netherlands, Germany [Schwalbach and Schlangenbad, 4 weeks]
1866–67 December–January	France [Biarritz, 3 weeks]
1867 January–March	Spain
1867 August–September	Germany [Cologne and Ilmenau, 2 weeks]
1868 May–July	Germany and Switzerland [Baden Baden, 9 days; Bad Peterstal, 3 weeks; Sankt Märgen, 4 days]

1869 March–April	France and Italy
1870 March–April	Germany and Austria
1872 September–October	Belgium, Germany [Bad Homburg, 23 days], France
1873 June–August	Belgium, Germany [Bad Homburg, 13 days], France
1876 June–September	France [Aix, 8 days], Switzerland [Bad Ragatz, 2½ weeks; Stachelberg 11 days; Klönthal, 8 days; St. Blasien, 1 week], Germany

The Crosses

1880 May–July	France, Italy, Austria [Innsbruck, 6 days], Germany [Bad Wildbad, 9 days; Baden Baden, 2 days]

BIBLIOGRAPHY

Acton, John Dalberg. Add. Mss. 4607. Cambridge University Library.

———. "George Eliot's Life," *19th Century* (March 1885).

———. Letters to and About George Eliot. Ms. Vault Collection. Beinecke Rare Book and Manuscript Library, Yale University.

———. *Letters of Lord Acton to Mary Gladstone.* Edited by Paul Herbert. London: George Ellen 1904.

Adam, Ian, ed. *This Particular Web.* Toronto: Toronto University Press, 1975.

Adams, Harriet. "George Eliot's Deed: Reconciling an Outlaw Marriage." *Yale University Library Gazette* 75 (2000): 1–2, 52–63.

———. "Prelude and Finale to *Middlemarch.*" *Victorian Newsletter* 68 (1985): 9–11.

Adams, Kathleen. *Those of Us Who Loved Her: The Men in George Eliot's Life.* Coventry: George Eliot Fellowship, 1980.

Aidé, Charles Hamilton. *A Nine Days' Wonder.* Boston: James R. Osgood, 1875.

Aldrige. John. *A First Trip to the German Spas and to Vichy.* Dublin: McGlasken and Gill, 1856.

Allingham, William. *Sixteen Poems.* Edited by W. B. Yeats. Dundrum: The Dun Emer Press, 1905.

———. *Songs Ballads and Stories.* London: 1877.

———. *William Allingham: A Diary.* Edited by Helen Allingham and D. Radford. Intro. by John Norwich. London: Macmillan, 1907.

Althaus, Julius. *The Spas of Europe.* London: Trubner and Son, 1862.

Amberley, John Russell, Patricia Helen (Spence) Russell Russell, and Katharine Louisa Stanley Russell. *The Amberley Papers.* Richmond: Hogarth Press, 1937.

Anderson, Nancy Fix. *Women against Women in Victorian England: A Life of Eliza Lynn Linton.* Bloomington: Indiana University Press, 1987.

Andres. Sophia. "Gendered Incongruities in George Eliot's Pre-Raphaelite Paintings." *The Journal of Pre-Raphaelite Studies* 5 (Fall 1996): 46–55.

———. "The Turn of Fortune's Wheel in *Daniel Deronda:* Sociopolitical Turns of the British Empire." *Victorians Institute Journal* 24 (1996): 87–111.

Ashton, Rosemary. *142 Strand: A Radical Address in Victorian London.* London: Chatto and Windus, 2006.
———. *George Eliot: A Life.* London: Hamish Hamilton, 1996.
———. *George Henry Lewes: A Life.* Oxford: Clarendon University Press, 1991.
Bain, Alexander. *Autobiography.* London: Longmans, Green, 1904.
Baker, William, and John C. Ross. *George Eliot: A Bibliographical History.* Newcastle, Delaware: Oak Knoll Press and London: The British Library, 2002.
———. *The George Eliot–George Henry Lewes Library: An Annotated Catalogue of Their Books at Dr Williams's Library.* New York: Garland Publishing, 1977.
———. *George Eliot and Judaism.* Salzburg: Universität Salzburg, 1975.
———. *The Libraries of George Eliot and George Henry Lewes.* Victoria: University of Victoria Press, 1981.
Beardsley, Christine. *Unutterable Love: The Passionate Life and Preaching of FW Robertson.* Cambridge: Lutterworth, 2009.
Beaty, Jerome. "*Middlemarch* from Notebook to Novel: A Study of George Eliot's Creative Method." Urbana: University of Illinois Press, 1960.
Bechtle, Götz. *Wildbad von A bis Z.* Bad Wildbad: Univeräbderter Nachdruck, 2001.
Beer, Gillian. *Darwin's Plots: Evolutionary Narrative in Darwin, George Eliot and Nineteenth-Century Fiction.* London: Ark Paperbacks, 1983.
———. *George Eliot: Key Women Writers.* Edited by Sue Roe. Bloomington: Indiana University Press, 1986.
Beer, John. *Providence and Love: Studies in Wordsworth, Channing, Myers, George Eliot, and Ruskin.* Oxford: Clarendon Press, 1998. Web 2 June 2010, p. 232.
Betham-Edwards, Matilda. *Mid-Victorian Memories.* Intro. and personal sketch by Sarah Grand. London: John Murray, 1919.
Bilski, Emily D., and Emily Braun. *Jewish Women and Their Salons: The Power of Conversation.* New York: The Jewish Museum; New Haven, CT: Yale University Press, 2005.
Birch, Dinah. "The Scholar's Husband." *Essays in Criticism* 54 (2004): 205–15.
Blair, Kirstie. "Priest and Nun?: George Eliot, *Daniel Deronda,* and Popular Anti-Catholicism," *The George Eliot Review* 32 (2001): 45–50.
Blake, Kathleen, ed. *Approaches to Teaching* Middlemarch. New York: MLA, 1990.
Blind, Mathilde. *George Eliot.* Boston, 1883.
Bodenheimer, Rosemarie. "Autobiography in Fragments: The Elusive Life of Edith Simcox." *Victorian Studies* 44, no. 3 (2002): 399–422.
———. *The Real Life of Mary Ann Evans: George Eliot, Her Letters and Fiction.* Ithaca, NY: Cornell University Press, 1994.
Bodichon, Barbara. "An Easy Railway Journey in Spain." *Temple Bar* (January 1869): 240–49.
Booth, Alison. *How to Make It as a Woman: Collective Biographical History from Victoria to the Present.* Chicago: University of Chicago Press, 2004.
Brewer, William Dean, and Jay Fosey, eds. *Mapping Male Sexuality: Nineteenth-Century England.* Cranbury, NJ: Associated University Presses, 2000.
Brooks, Shirley. Diary for 1872. Transcribed by Patrick Leary. London, British Library.
Broomfield, Andrea, and Sally Mitchell. *Prose by Victorian Women: An Anthology.* New York: Garland Publishing, 1996.
Brown, Catherine. "Why Does Daniel Deronda's Mother Live in Russia?" *George Eliot—George Henry Lewes Studies* 58–59 (2012): 26–42.

Browning, Oscar. *Life of George Eliot.* London: Walter Scott, 1890.

———. *Memoirs of Sixty Years at Eton Cambridge and Elsewhere.* London: John Lane, 1910.

Buchanan, Robert. Review of *George Eliot's Life as Related in Her Letters and Journals* by John Cross. In *A Look Round Literature.* London: Ward and Downey, 1887.

Burne-Jones, Georgiana. *Memorials of Edward Burne-Jones.* 2 vols. London: Lund Humphries, 1893.

Buzard, James. *The Beaten Track: European Tourism, Literature, and the Ways to Culture, 1800–1918.* Oxford: Oxford University Press, 1993.

Carroll, Alicia. *Dark Smiles: Race and Desire in George Eliot.* Athens: Ohio University Press, 2003.

Carroll, David. *George Eliot and the Conflict of Interpretations: A Reading of the Novels.* Cambridge: Cambridge University Press, 1992.

Chard, Chloe. *Pleasure and Guilt on the Grand Tour: Travel Writing and Imaginative Geography 1600–1830.* Manchester: Manchester University Press, 1999.

Chisolm, Monty. *Such Silver Currents: The Story of William and Lucy Clifford, 1845–1929.* Cambridge: Lutterworth, 2002.

Clifford, Lucy. "A Remembrance of George Eliot." *The Nineteenth Century and After: A Monthly Review* 74 (June 1913): 109–18.

Clough, Blanche Athena. *A Memoir of Anne Jemima Clough.* London: Edward Arnold, 1897.

Cobden-Sanderson, T. J. *Credo.* London: Doves Press, 1909.

Coke, Henry. *Tracks of a Rolling Stone.* London: Smith Elder, 1905.

Collins, K. K., ed. *George Eliot: Interviews and Recollections.* Basingstoke: Palgrave Macmillan, 2010.

———. "Reading George Eliot Reading Lewes's Obituaries." *Modern Philology* 85, no. 2 (November 1987): 153–69.

Colvin, Sidney. *Memories & Notes of Persons & Places 1852–1912.* London: Edward Arnold and Company, 1921.

Cracroft's Peerage: The Complete Guide to the British Peerage and Baronetage. 20 August 2012. www.cracroftspeerage.co.uk/online/content/Castletown1869.htm.

Crompton, Henry. *The Festival of Holy Women. A Sermon Preached by Henry Crompton at the Church of Humanity.* London: A Bonner, 1893.

"Henry Crompton 1836–1904." 22 August 2010. www.jihc.info/cromptonhenry1904.htm.

Crompton, Margaret. *George Eliot: The Woman.* London: Cassell, 1960.

Cross, Elizabeth D. *An Old Story and Other Poems.* London: Longmans, 1868.

Cross, John Walter. *George Eliot's Life as Related in Her Letters and Journals.* Edinburgh: William Blackwood and Sons, 1885.

———. *Impressions of Dante and of the New World.* Edinburgh: Blackwood, 1893.

———. *The Rake's Progress in Finance.* Edinburgh: Blackwood, 1905.

Cross, Mary. "Marie of Villefranche." *Macmillan's* (August 1871).

Dakers, Caroline. *Business, Art and the Morrisons.* New Haven: Yale University Press, 2011.

Cunningham, Sir Henry Stewart. *Lord Bowen: A Biographical Sketch.* Private Circulation, 1896.

David, Deirdre. "Getting Out of the Eel Jar: George Eliot's Literary Approximation of Abroad," in *Creditable Warriors: 1830–1876,* edited by Michael Cotsell. London: Ashfield, 1990.

De Gaury, Gerald. *Travelling Gent: The Life of Alexander Kinglake (1809–1891)*. London: Routledge and Kegan Paul, 1972.
Deacon, Richard. *The Cambridge Apostles*. London: Farrar, Strauss and Giroux, 1986.
Deakin, Mary. *The Early Life of George Eliot*. Manchester: Manchester University Press, 1913.
De Coverly, E. L. *Cobden-Sanderson Bookbinder*. A paper read by Mr. E. L. de Coverly to the Master Binders' Association about the year 1912. Leicester College of Art School of Printing, 1951.
Dell, Elizabeth, and Jay Fosey. "Introduction." In Brewer and Fosey.
Dellamora, Richard. *Masculine Desire: The Sexual Politics of Victorian Aestheticism*. Chapel Hill: University of North Carolina Press, 1990.
Dewes, Simon. *Marian: The Life of George Eliot*. London: Rich & Cowan, 1939.
Dickens, Charles. *The Letters of Charles Dickens*. Edited by Graham Story, Margaret Brown, and Kathleen Tillotson. Oxford: Oxford University Press, 2002.
Dolin, Tim. *George Eliot (Authors in Context)*. Oxford: Oxford University Press, 2005.
Du Maurier, Daphne. "Introduction." *The Young George Du Maurier: A Selection of His Letters*. Garden City, NY: Doubleday and Company, 1952.
Du Maurier, George. *Trilby*. Oxford: Oxford University Press, 2009.
Easley, Alexis. "Poet as Headliner: George Eliot and *Macmillan's Magazine*." In Hadjiafxendi, 107–25.
Ebers, Georg. *The Story of My Life: From Childhood to Manhood*. New York: Appleton and Company, 1893.
Ellman, Richard. *Golden Codgers: Some Biographical Speculations*. Oxford: Oxford University, 1973.
Epperson, Gordon. *The Mind of Edmund Gurney*. London: Associated University Presses, 1997.
Evans, Marian (George Eliot). *Adam Bede*. New York: Riverside, 1980.
———. Autograph Ms. Diary. June 1861–December 1879. New York Public Library.
———. *Brother Jacob*. London: Virago Classics, 1989.
———. *Daniel Deronda*. New York: Penguin Books, 1967.
———. *The Essays of George Eliot*. Edited by Thomas Pinney. New York: Columbia University Press, 1963.
———. *Felix Holt*. New York: Penguin Books, 1968.
———. *The George Eliot Letters*. 9 vols. Edited by Gordon S. Haight. New Haven, CT: Yale University Press, vols. 1–7, 1954; 8–9, 1979.
———. *George Eliot: Selected Essays, Poems and Other Writings*. Edited by A. S. Byatt and Nicholas Warren. London: Penguin Books, 1990.
———. *George Eliot's Blotter: A Commonplace-Book*. Edited by Daniel Philip Waley. London: The British Library 1980.
———. *George Eliot's* Middlemarch *Notebooks: A Transcription*. Edited by John Clark Pratt and Victor A. Neufeldt. Berkeley: University of California Press, 1979.
———. *Impressions of Theophrastus Such*. Edited by Nancy Henry. Iowa City: University of Iowa Press, 1994.
———. *The Journals of George Eliot*. Edited by Margaret Harris and Judith Johnston. Cambridge: Cambridge University Press, 1998.
———. *The Lifted Veil*. London: Virago Classics, 1985.
———. *Middlemarch*. Boston: Houghton Mifflin Company, 1956.
———. *The Mill on the Floss*. Boston: Houghton Mifflin Company, 1961.

———. *Quarry for* Middlemarch. Edited by Anna Kitchel. Berkeley: University of California Press, 1950.

———. *Romola*. New York: Penguin Books, 1980.

———. *Scenes of Clerical Life*. New York: Penguin, 1972.

———. Some George Eliot Notebooks: An Edition of the Carl H. Pforzheimer Library's George Eliot Holograph Notebooks. Mss 707, 708, 709, 710, 711. Ed. William Baker. Salzburg: Institut für Engklische Sprache und Literatur, 1976–85.

———. *The Spanish Gypsy by George Eliot*. Edited by Antonie Gerard van den Broek and William Baker. London: Pickering & Chatto, 2008.

———. *Silas Marner*. New York: Penguin Books, 1968.

———. *A Writer's Notebook, 1853–1879 and Uncollected Writings*. Edited by Joseph Wiesenfarth. Charlottesville: University of Virginia Press, 1981.

Evans, Robert. Unpublished diaries. The Nuneaton Public Library and Robin Evans, Tiverton.

Fawcett, Millicent Garrett. *Fitzjames Stephen on the Position of Women*. London: Macmillan, 1873.

Feuer, Lewis S. "The Friendship of Edwin Ray Lankester and Karl Marx: The Last Episode in Marx's Intellectual Evolutions." *Journal of the History of Ideas* 40, no. 1 (1979): 633–48.

Field, Kate. *Selected Letters*. Edited by Carolyn J. Moss. Carbondale: Southern Illinois University Press, 1996.

Fitzgerald, Penelope. *Edward Burne-Jones*. London: Hamish Hamilton, 1989.

Fleischman, Avrom. *George Eliot's Intellectual Life*. Cambridge: Cambridge University Press, 2010.

———. "George Eliot's Reading: A Chronological List." *George Eliot–George Henry Lewes Studies*, 54–55 (September 2008): 1–106.

Fremantle, Anne. *George Eliot*. London: Duckworth, 1933.

Fuller-Maitland, J. A. "People's Concert Society." *The Musical Times* 77 (April 1936): 317–18.

Garratt, Peter. *Victorian Empiricism: Self, Knowledge, and Reality in Ruskin, Bain, Lewes, Spencer, and George Eliot*. Madison, NJ: Fairleigh Dickinson University Press, 2010.

Gilbert, Sandra. "From Patria to Matria: Elizabeth Barrett Browning's *Risorgimento*." *PMLA* 99 (1984): 194–211.

Gilbert, Sandra M., and Susan Gubar. *The Madwoman in the Attic: The Woman Writer and the Nineteenth-Century Literary Imagination*. London: Oxford University Press, 1979.

Gouws, Dennis S. "George Eliot's enthusiastic bachelors: topical fictional accounts of nineteenth-century homoerotic Christian masculinities and the manhood question." *Forum on Public Policy: A Journal of the Oxford Round Table* 4, no. 2 (2008): 1–16.

Grant Duff, Montstuart Elphinstone. *Notes from a Diary 1892–1895*. London: John Murray, 1904.

Green, Vivian. *Love in a Cool Climate: The Letters of Mark Pattison and Meta Bradly, 1879–1884* Oxford: Oxford University Press, 1985.

Gwenllian, F. Palgrave. *Francis Turner Palgrave: His Journals and Memories of His Life*. London: Longmans, Green,1899.

Hadjiafxendi, Kyriaki, ed. "Introduction: George Eliot and the Poetics of Disbelief." *George Eliot–George Henry Lewes Studies: The Cultural Place of George Eliot's Poetry* 60–61 (September 2011): 7–16.

Haight, Gordon S. *George Eliot: A Biography*. New York: Oxford University Press, 1968.
———. *George Eliot and John Chapman, with Chapman's Diaries*. New Haven, CT: Yale University Press, 1940.
———. "George Eliot's 'eminent failure,' Will Ladislaw." *This Particular Web: Essays on* Middlemarch. Edited by Ian Adam. Toronto: University of Toronto Press, 1975.
———. *George Eliot's Originals and Contemporaries*. Ann Arbor: University of Michigan Press, 1992.
Hall, Trevor H. *The Strange Case of Edward Gurney*. London: Duckworth, 1964.
Hamerton, Philip Gilbert, and Eugénie Gindriez Hamerton. *Philip Gilbert Hamerton, an Autobiography, 1834–1858, and a Memoir by His Wife, 1858–1894*. Cambridge, MA: Harvard University Press.
A Handbook for Travellers on the Continent. London: John Murray, 1854.
A Handbook for Travellers on the Continent. London: John Murray, 1873.
A Handbook for Travellers in Switzerland and Alps of Savoy and Piedmont. 8th ed. London: John Murray, 1858.
Handley, Graham. *George Eliot: State of the Art: A Guide through the Critical Maze*. Bristol: The Bristol Press, 1990.
Hanson, Lawrence, and Elisabeth Hanson. *Marian Evans and George Eliot*. London: Oxford University Press, 1952.
Hardy, Barbara. *George Eliot: A Critic's Biography*. London: Continuum, 2006.
Harris, Margaret. "What George Eliot Saw in Europe: The Evidence of her Journals." In Rignall, *George Eliot and Europe*.
Harrison, Frederic. "Mr Lewes's *Problems of Life and Mind*." *Fortnightly Review* (July 1874): 89–101.
———. Obituary of George Henry Lewes. *Academy*. 7 December 1878. George Henry Lewes Special Files. Ms. Vault Collection. Beinecke Rare Book and Manuscript Library. Yale University.
———. "Reminiscences of George Eliot." In *Memories and Thoughts: Men, Books, Cities, Art*. New York: Macmillan, 1906, 134–49.
Hartley, Eeyan. "A Country House Connection: George Eliot and the Howards of Castle Howard."*George Eliot–George Henry Lewes Studies* 22–23 (September 1993): 17–21.
Hazlitt, William Carew. *Four Generations of a Literary Family*. London: G. Redway, 1897.
Henley, Dorothy. *Rosalind Howard Countess of Carlisle*. London: Hogarth, 1958.
Henry, Nancy. *The Cambridge Introduction to George Eliot*. Cambridge: Cambridge University Press, 2009.
———. *George Eliot and the British Empire*. Cambridge: Cambridge University Press, 2002.
———. "George Eliot, George Henry Lewes, and Comparative Anatomy." In Rignall, *George Eliot and Europe*.
———. *The Life of George Eliot*. Oxford: Wiley Blackwell, 2012.
———. "The *Romola* Code: 'Men of Appetites' in George Eliot's Historical Novel." *Victorian Literature and Culture* 39, no. 2 (2011): 327–48.
Hertz, Neil. *George Eliot's Pulse*. Stanford: Stanford University Press, 2003.
———. "Recognizing Casaubon." In *The End of the Line*. New York: Columbia University Press, 1985.
Hill, Roland. *Lord Acton*. New Haven, CT: Yale University Press, 2000.

Hirsch, Pam. *Barbara Leigh Smith Bodichon: Feminist, Artist and Rebel.* London: Pimlico: 1999.
Hodgson, William Ballantyne. *Life and Letters of William Ballantyne Hodgson.* Edited by J. M. D. Meiklejohn. Edinburgh: David Douglas, 1883.
Hughes, Kathryn. *George Eliot: The Last Victorian.* London: Fourth Estate, 1999.
Hughes, William, and Andrew Smith. *Empire and the Gothic: The Politics of Genre.* Basingstoke: Palgrave Macmillan, 2003.
Jebb, Caroline Reynolds. *With Dearest Love to All: The Life and Letters of Lady Jebb.* Edited by Mary Reed. London: Faber and Faber, 1960.
Johnston, Judith. "*Middlemarch*'s Dorothea Brooke and Medieval Hagiography." *The George Eliot Review* 23 (1992): 405.
Jones, Alan W. *Lyulph Stanley: A Study in Educational Politics.* Waterloo, Ontario: Wilfrid Laurier University Press, 1979.
Karl, Frederick. *George Eliot: Voice of a Century.* New York: W. W. Norton, 1995.
Kehler, Grace. "Armgart's Voice Problems." *Victorian Literature and Culture* 34 (2006): 147–66.
Kenyon, Frank William. *The Consuming Flame: The Story of George Eliot.* London: Hutchinson, 1970.
Knoepflmacher, U. C. "Fusing Fact and Myth: The New Reality of *Middlemarch*." *Essays on* Middlemarch: *This Particular Web.* Edited by Ian Adam. Toronto: Toronto University Press, 1975.
Knoepflmacher, U. C. "*Middlemarch:* An Avuncular View." *Nineteenth Century Fiction* 30 (1975): 43–72.
———. "Mr. Haight's George Eliot: '*Wahreit und Dichtung.*'" *Victorian Studies* 12 (1969): 422–30.
———. "On Exile and Fiction: The Leweses and the Shelleys." In *Mothering the Mind: Twelve Studies of Writers and Their Silent Partners,* edited by Ruth Perry and Martine Watson Brownley. New York: Holmes and Meier, 1984.
Kovalevskaia, Soph'ia V. "A Memoir of George Eliot." *Yale Review* 73 (Summer 1984): 533–50.
Kuhn, William M. *Henry and Mary Ponsonby: Life at the Court of Queen Victoria.* London: Duckworth, 2002.
La Porte, Charles. "George Eliot, the Poetess as Prophet." *Victorian Literature and Culture* 31 (2003): 159–79.
Lehmann, John. *Ancestors and Friends.* London: Eyre and Spottiswood, 1962.
Lehmann, Rudolph. *An Artist's Reminiscences.* London: Smith Elder, 1894.
Levine, George, ed. *The Cambridge Companion to George Eliot.* Cambridge: Cambridge University Press, 2001.
Lewes, George Henry. Journals X, XI, XII and Diaries 1–8. Ms. Vault Collection, Beinecke Rare Book and Manuscript Library, Yale University.
———. *The Letters of George Henry Lewes.* 3 vols. Edited by William Baker. Victoria: University of Victoria Press, 1995, 1999.
———. *The Life and Works of Goethe: With Sketches of His Age and Contemporaries.* Boston: Ticknor and Fields, 1856.
Linton, Eliza Lynn. "George Eliot." *Temple Bar* (April 1885).
Litzinfer, Boyd, ed. *The Letters of Robert Browning to Frederick and Nina Lehmann, 1863–1889.* Baynore Browning Interests, Armstrong Browning Library Baylor University, 1975.

Locker-Lampson, Frederick. *My Confidences: An Autobiographical Sketch Addressed to My Descendants.* 2nd ed. London Smith Elder, 1896.

———. *London Lyrics.* London: C. Kegan Paul, 1878.

Lownie, Andrew. *John Buchan: The Presbyterian Cavalier.* Jaffrey, NH: David R. Godine, 2003.

Madden, Thomas. *The Spas of Belgium, Germany, Switzerland, France, and Italy; a Handbook of the principle Watering Places on the Continent, descriptive of Their Nature and Uses in the Treatment of Chronic Diseases, With Notices of Spa Life, and Incidents of Travel.* London, 1867.

Maddox, Brenda. *George Eliot: Novelist, Lover, Wife.* London: Harper, 2009.

Martin, Carol. *George Eliot's Serial Fiction.* Columbus: Ohio State University Press 1995.

Martin, Theodore. *Helen Faucit Lady Martin.* Edinburgh & London: Blackwood, 1890.

Masson, Flora. *Victorians All.* London and Edinburgh: W. & R. Chambers,1931.

McCobb, E. A. "*Daniel Deronda* as Will and Representation: George Eliot and Schopenahauer." *Modern Language Review* 80 (1985): 533–49.

———. *George Eliot's Knowledge of German Life and Letters.* Salzburg: Universität Salzburg, 1982.

McCormack, Kathleen. *George Eliot and Intoxication: Dangerous Drugs for the Condition of England.* Basingstoke: Macmillan, 2000.

———. *George Eliot's English Travels: Composite Characters and Coded Communications.* New York: Taylor & Francis; London: Routledge, 2005.

———. "George Eliot's Wollstonecraftian Feminism." *Dalhousie Review* 63 (Winter 1983–84): 602–15.

———. "*Middlemarch:* George Eliot's Husbands in the Vatican Museums." *Victorians Institute Journal* 20 (1992): 79–91.

———. "Wollstonecraft: George Eliot's 'Judicious Person with Some Turn for Humour.'" *English Language Notes* 9 (September 1981): 44–46.

McKay, Brenda. *George Eliot and Victorian Attitudes to Racial Diversity, Colonialism, Darwinism, Class, Gender, and Jewish Culture and Prophecy.* Lewiston, Queenston, Lampeter: The Edwin Mellen Press, 2003.

Meikle, Susan. "Fruit and Seed: The Finale to *Middlemarch.*" In Smith, xxx.

Michael, Virginia Surtess. *The Artist and the Autocrat: George and Rosalind Howard.* Wilby Norwich: Michael Russell, 1988.

Nadel, Ira Bruce. "George Eliot and Her Biographers." In *George Eliot: A Centenary Tribute,* edited by Gordon S. Haight and Rosemary T. VanArsdel, 107–21. Totowa, NJ: Barnes & Noble, 1982.

Nestor, Pauline. *Female Friendships and Communities: Charlotte Brontë, George Eliot, Elizabeth Gaskell.* Oxford: Clarendon Press, 1985.

Newton, K. M. "Historical Prototypes in *Middlemarch.*" *English Studies* 56 (1975): 403–8.

Nicholes, Joseph. "Dorothea in the Moated Grange." *Victorians Institute Journal* 20 (1992): 93–124.

———. "Vertical Context in *Middlemarch.*" *Nineteenth -Century Literature* (1990): 144–75.

Novick, Sheldon. *Henry James: The Mature Master.* New York: Random House, 2007.

Novikoff, Olga. *Is Russia Wrong? A Series of Letters by a Russian Lady.* London: Hodder & Stoughton, 1878.

O'Gorman, Francis. "George Eliot's *Middlemarch.*" *The Explicator* 60, no. 3 (2002): 137–38.

Olcott, Charles S. *George Eliot: Scenes and People in Her Novels.* London: Cassell, 1911.
Oldfield, Sybil. *Jeanie, an "Army of One": Mrs Nassau Senior, 1828–1877, The First Woman in Whitehall.* Brighton: Sussex University Press, 2008.
Parkes, Bessie Rayner. "Dorothea Casaubon and George Eliot." *The Contemporary Review* (February 1894): 207–16.
Paterson, Arthur. *George Eliot's Family Life and Letters.* London: Selwyn, 1928.
Paxton, Nancy.*George Eliot and Herbert Spencer: Feminism, Evolutionism, and the Reconstruction of Gender.* Princeton, NJ: Princeton University Press, 1991.
Pemble, John. *The Mediterranean Passion: Victorians and Edwardians in the South.* Oxford: Oxford University Press, 1987.
Perry, Ruth, and Martine Watson Brownley, eds. *Mothering the Mind: Studies of Writers and Their Silent Partners.* New York: Holmes and Meier,1984.
Peterson, Linda H. "*The Spanish Gypsy* as George Eliot's Poetic Debut." In Hadjiafxendi, 31–46.
Pratt-Smith, Stella. "Inside-Out: Texture and Belief in George Eliot's 'Bubble-World.'" In Hadjiafxendi, 62–76.
Putzell-Korab, Sara M., and Martine Watson Brownley. "Dorothea and Her Husbands: Some Autobiographical Sources for Speculation." *Victorian Newsletter* 68 (Fall 1985): 15–19.
Qualls, Barry. "George Eliot and Religion." In Levine, xxx.
Ramieu, Emile and Georges. *The Life of George Eliot.* London: Cape, 1932.
Reade, Brian. *Sexual Heretics: Male Homosexuality in English Literature from 1850 to 1900: An Anthology.* London: Routledge & Kegan Paul, 1970.
Redinger, Ruby. *George Eliot: The Emergent Self.* New York: Knopf, 1975.
Reed, John, and Jerry Herron. "George Eliot's Illegitimate Children." *Nineteenth Century Fiction* 40 (1985): 175–86.
Reed, Joseph W., Jr. *Barbara Leigh Smith Bodichon: An American Diary 1857–8.* London: Routledge & Kegan Paul, 1972.
Rendall, Jane. "Friendship and Politics: Barbara Leigh Smith Bodichon (1827–91) and Bessie Rayner Parkes (1829–1925)." In *Sexuality and Subordination: Interdisciplinary Studies of Gender in the Nineteenth Century,* edited by Susan Mendus and Jane Rendall, 136–70. London: Routledge 1989.
Richards, Jeffrey. *Sir Henry Irving.* New York: St. Martin's Press, 2005.
Rignall, John. *George Eliot, European Novelist.* Farnham Surrey: Ashgate, 2011.
———. "George Eliot and the Idea of Travel." *Yearbook of English Studies* 36, no. 2 (2006): 139–152.
———. "George Eliot and Weimar." *George Eliot Review* 37 (2006): 7–16.
———, ed. *George Eliot and Europe.* Aldershot: Scolar Press, 1997.
———, ed. *Oxford Reader's Companion to George Eliot.* Oxford: Oxford University Press, 2000.
Roberts, Charles. *The Radical Countess: The History of the Life of Rosalind Countess of Carlisle.* Carlisle: Steel Brothers, 1962.
Rochelson, Meri-Jane. *A Jew in the Public Arena: The Career of Israel Zangwill.* Detroit: Wayne State University Press 2009.
———. "The Weaver of Raveloe: Metaphor as Narrative Persuasion in *Silas Marner.*" *Studies in the Novel* 15 (1983): 35–43.
Röder-Bolton, Gerlinde. *George Eliot in Germany 1854–55: "Cherished Memories."* Aldershot: Ashgate, 2006.

Romano, Terrie M. *Making Medicine Scientific: John Burdon Sanderson and the Culture of Victorian Science*. Baltimore: Johns Hopkins University Press, 2002.

Rose, Phyllis. *Parallel Lives: Five Victorian Marriages*. New York: Knopf, 1983.

Roundell, Charles. *England and Her Subject Races, with Special Reference to Jamaica*. London: Macmillan, 1866.

Sacks, Glenda. "George Eliot's Boudoir Experiment: Dorothea as Embodied Learner." *George Eliot–George Henry Lewes Studies* 56–57 (September 2007): 19–27.

Scharnhorst, Gary. "Kate Field on George Eliot and George Henry Lewes." *George Eliot–George Henry Lewes Studies,* 52–53 (September 2007): 19–27.

Schultz, Bart. *Henry Sidgwick, Eye of the Universe: An Intellectual Biography*. Cambridge: Cambridge University Press, 2004.

Sedgwick, Eve. *The Epistemology of the Closet*. Berkeley: University of California Press, 1991, 2008.

Seifert, Siegfried. *Weimar: A Guide to European City of Culture*. Berlin: Edition Leipzig, 1999.

Sellar, E. M. *Recollections and Impressions*. Edinburgh: Blackwood, 1907.

Shaffer, Elinor. *"Kubla Khan" and* The Fall of Jerusalem*: The Mythological School in Biblical Criticism and Secular Literature 1770–1880*. Cambridge: Cambridge University Press, 1975.

Sichel, Walter. *The Sands of Time: Recollections and Reflections*. London: Hutchinsons and Company, 1923.

S[idgwick, A[rthur] and E[leanor].M[ildred]. *Henry Sidgwick: A Memoir* by A.S. and E.M.S. London: Macmillan, 1906.

Simcox, Edith. *A Monument to the Memory of George Eliot: Edith Simcox's Autobiography of a Shirtmaker*. Edited by Constance Fulmer and Margaret Barfield. New York: Garland, 1998.

Smith, Anne, ed. *George Eliot: Centenary Essays and an Unpublished Fragment*. London: Vision Press, 1980.

Spencer, Herbert. *An Autobiography*. 2 vols. London: Williams and Norgate, 1901.

Stange, G. Robert. "The Voices of the Essayist." *Nineteenth-Century Fiction* 35 (1980): 312–20.

Steen, Michael. *Enchantress of Nations: Pauline Viardot—Soprano Muse and Lover*. Cambridge: Icon Books, 2007.

Stephen, Leslie. *English Men of Letters: George Eliot*. London: Macmillan, 1902.

Stern, Kimberly J. "The Poetics of Criticism: Dialogue and Discourse in George Eliot's Poetry." In Hadjiafxendi, 91–106.

Stockton, Kathryn Bond. *God between Their Lips: Desire between Women in Irigaray, Brontë, and Eliot*. Stanford: Stanford University Press, 1994.

Suhn-Binder, Andrea. 2009. "Great Teachers." 28 August 2012. www.cantabile.de/teachers/teachers.html.

Sully, James. *My Life and Friends: A Psychologist's Memories*. London: T. Fisher Unwin, 1918.

Szirotny, June Skye. "Edward Casaubon and Herbert Spencer." *George Eliot Review* 32 (2001): 29–43.

Taylor, Ina. *A Woman of Contradictions: The Life of George Eliot*. New York: Morrow, 1990.

Thomas, Henry, and Dana Lee. *Living Biographies of Famous Women*. Garden City, NY: Doubleday, 1942.

Thompson, Andrew. *George Eliot and Italy*. Basingstoke: Macmillan, 1998.

Tromp, Marlene. "Gwendolen's Madness." *Victorian Literature and Culture* 28 (2000): 45167.
Trollope, Thomas A. *What I Remember.* 3 vols. London, 1887–89.
Tucker, Herbert F. "Quantity and Quality: The Strange Case of George Eliot, Minor Poet." In Hadjiafxendi, 17–30.
Turner, Frank. *The Greek Heritage in Victorian Britain.* New Haven, CT: Yale University Press, 1981.
Uglow, Jennifer. *George Eliot.* New York: Pantheon, 1987.
Vipont, Elfrida. *Towards a High Attic: The Early Life of George Eliot.* London: Hamilton, 1970.
Vogeler, Martha. "George Eliot as Literary Widow." *Huntingdon Library Quarterly* 51 (1988): 72–87.
Waddington, Patrick. "Mary Elizabeth Mohl." *Oxford Dictionary of National Biography.* Oxford: Oxford University Press.
Waldstein, Charles. "George Eliot." *Library of the World's Best Literature Ancient and Modern.* Vol. 13. Edited by Charles Dudley Warner. New York: The International Society, 1896.
———. *The Jewish Question and the Mission of the Jews.* New York: Harper & Brothers, 1894.
Ward, Wilfrid. *Ten Personal Studies.* London: Green, 1908.
Weisgall, Deborah. *The World Before Her.* Orlando, FL: Houghton Mifflin, 2008.
West, Rebecca. "George Eliot: A New Reading: The Domestic Urge." Reviews of Arthur Henry Paterson's *George Eliot's Family Life and Letters.* George Eliot. Writings About. Ms. Vault Collection. Beinecke Rare Book and Manuscript Library. Yale University.
White, Terence de Vere. *Johnnie Cross: A Novel.* New York: St. Martin's Press, 1983.
Whiting, Lilian. *Kate Field: A Record.* London: Sampson Low, Marston,1899.
Williams, Blanche Colton. *George Eliot.* New York: Macmillan, 1936.
Williams, David. *Mr. George Eliot: A Biography of George Henry Lewes.* London: Hodder & Stoughton, 1983.
Williams, Montagu. *Later Leaves: Being the Further Reminiscences of Montagu Williams, Q. C.* London: Macmillan, 1891.
Wilson, Erasmus. *A Three Weeks' Scamper through the Spas of Germany and Belgium.* London: John Churchill,1858.
Witemeyer, Hugh. *George Eliot and the Visual Arts.* New Haven, CT: Yale University Press, 1979.
———. "The Province of Scandal: Gordon S. Haight's Conception of the Biographer's Task." *George Eliot–George Henry Lewes Studies* 24–25 (September 1993): 76–90.
Wood, T. Martin. *George Du Maurier: The Satirist of the Victorians. A Review of His Art and Personality.* London: Chatto and Windus, 1913.
Woolf, Virginia. *A Room of One's Own.* New York: Harcourt Brace Jovanovich, 1929.
Wortham, Hugh Evelyn. *Oscar Browning.* London: Constable and Company, 1927.
Wright, T. R. *George Eliot's* Middlemarch. Hemel Hempstead: Harvester Wheatsheaf, 1991.
———. "The Woman at the Window" *George Eliot Review* 31 (2000): 79.
Wrigley, Richard, and George Revill. *Pathologies of Travel.* Amsterdam: Rodopi, 2000.
Young, Kay. *Imagining Minds: The Neuro-Aesthetics of Austen, Eliot, and Hardy.* Columbus: The Ohio State University Press, 2010.

INDEX

The Academy, 75n19, 76, 107–8, 127
Acton, John Dalberg, 130–31, 136, 141, 142–44, 157, 162
Adam, Ian, 60, 157, 162, 163
Adams, Harriet, 157
Adams, Kathleen, 144, 157
Aidé, Charles Hamilton, 87–88, 89, 94, 99, 133, 157
Aldridge, John, 121, 157
Alighieri, Dante, 60n3, 141
Algiers, 93
Allbutt, Clifford, 59, 67
Allingham, Helen, 7n7, 67n10, 70–72, 157
Allingham, William, 65, 67n10, 70–72, 74n18, 110, 133, 157
Althaus, Julius, 148, 157
Amberley, John Russell, 157
Amberley, Kate, 7n7, 65
Anderson, Nancy Fix, 93, 157
Andres, Sophia, 157
Annan, Noel, 100
Appleton, Charles, 74–75n19, 76
Arnold, Matthew, 20
Arnott, Neil, 20
Ashton, Rosemary, 3, 3n2, 19–20, 40n1, 66n8, 140, 158
Athens, 134
Athenaeum, 16

Austria, 145, 156; Innsbruck, 145–56, 156; Vienna, 69, 106, 107
Ayrton, Edith, 134
Ayrton, W. E., 134

Bagehot, Walter, 23
Bain, Alexander, 7n7, 20, 23, 58, 125, 126, 158, 161
Bain, Frances, 7n7, 58, 125
Baker, William, 2n1, 34, 71n15, 158, 161, 163
Baudissin, Agnes, 49
Baudissin, Gräfin Ida, 8, 38, 49
Beardsley, Christina, 117–18, 158
Beaty, Jerome, 158
Bechtle, Götz, 158
Bedford College, 125
Beer, Gillian, 158
Beer, John, 158
Beesly, Edward Spencer, 7n7, 67, 77
Beesly, Emily, 7n7, 67, 77
Beethoven, Ludwig von, 37
Belgium, 15, 33n23, 45, 121, 152, 155, 156; Aix, 45; Bruges, 45; Chaudfontaine, 43n5, 45; Ghent, 45; Liège, 45; Louvain, 45; Ostend, 45
Belloc, Bessie Raynor Parkes, 7n7, 59, 67, 165

Benzon, Elizabeth, 7n7, 10, 59, 82, 87, 115
Benzon, Ernst, 7n7, 10, 59, 82, 87, 115
Berlin, Miriam Haskell, 68, 69n11, 70n13
Betham-Edwards, Matilda, 4n4, 7n7, 31–33, 67n20, 90–91nn10–11, 133, 158
Bilski, Emily D., 21, 158
Birch, Dinah, 158
Blackwood, John, 48, 55, 74, 76, 76n20, 107, 112, 113, 121
Blagden, Isa, 15, 88
Blair, Kristie, 158
Blind, Mathilde, 8, 12, 140, 144, 158
Blythe, Isabella, 66, 67, 93
Bodenheimer, Rosemarie, 3, 4n2, 45n7, 135n11, 137n1, 138, 158
Bodichon, Barbara Leigh Smith, 7n7, 22, 23, 28, 30–32, 58, 62, 66–68, 80, 89, 90n10, 93, 102, 130, 132, 134, 135, 151, 158, 163, 165
Bodichon, Eugène, 58, 89, 93
Booth, Alison, 17–18n12, 134n10, 158
Bowen, C. S. C., Baron, 159
Bowen, Lady Emily Frances, 159
Bradly, Meta, 161
Brandt, Marianne, 91
Braun, Emily, 21, 158
Bray, Cara, 51, 135
Bray, Charles, 51
Bremer, Frederika, 19
Brewer, William Dean, 158, 160
Brooke, Stopford, 117, 118
Brooks, Shirley, 158
Broomfield, Angela, 32, 158
Brown, Catherine, 82n3, 158
Brown, Margaret, 160
Browning, Elizabeth Barrett, 161
Browning, Oscar, 8, 32, 33, 68, 94, 99, 101–2, 100n19, 105, 106, 131, 140, 159, 167
Browning, Robert, 8, 12, 20, 23, 35, 38, 57–58, 61–62, 73, 77, 82, 88, 100n19, 127, 129n7, 131–32, 163
Brownley, Martine Watson, 163, 165
Bruyère, Jean de la, 17
Buchanan, Robert, 9–10, 12, 31, 159

Buchanan, Sir Andrew, 107
Bullock-Hall family, 83, 151
Bullock, William Henry, 82, 139
Bulwer-Lytton, Edward, 107
Bunney, William, 141n2
Burckhart, Karl, 146
Burne-Jones, Edward, 9, 10, 65, 71, 82, 85n6, 124, 128, 133, 159, 161
Burne-Jones, Georgiana, 7n7, 12, 32, 60n1, 65, 71, 79, 82nn5–6, 132, 133–34, 159
Burton, Frederic, 6, 12, 15, 23, 30, 37, 58, 62, 77, 132
Bury, John, 52
Buzard, James, 159
Byatt, A. S., 160
Byron, Lady, 117
Byron, Lord, 45, 53, 60n3, 113

Call, Rufa Brabant, 7n7, 20
Cambridge University, 66, 94, 95, 97, 99, 105, 130, 131, 143
Carlyle, Thomas, 41–42, 71
Carroll, Alicia, 159
Carroll, David, 159
Casaubon, Isaac, 60n3
Casaubon, Meric, 60n3
Castletown, Bernard, 115
Castletown family, 110, 113n2, 118
Castletown, John Wilson Fitzpatrick, Baron, 73, 90n9, 115, 116–18
Castletown, Lady Augusta, 7n7, 30, 73, 82, 88n7, 90, 90n9, 111–13, 115, 117–18, 122–23
Chambers, Robert, 87
Champneys, Basil, 33
Chapman, Frederick, 59
Chapman, John, 16, 19, 20, 162
Chard, Chloe, 159
China, 116
Chisolm, Monty, 159
Clifford, Lucy Lane, 4n4, 8n7, 12, 31, 33, 60n1, 133, 159
Clifford, W. K., 12, 68, 129n7, 159
Clough, Anne Jemima, 7n7, 67–68
Clough, Arthur Hugh, 67–68, 97
Clough, Blanche, 68, 159

Collins, K. K., 3, 4, 9, 23n17, 31, 32, 69n12, 87, 113n2, 129n8, 141nn2–3, 152, 159
Colvile, Lady Frances, 7n7, 73
Colvile, Sir James, 73
Colvin, Sidney, 8, 9, 12, 28, 66, 77, 159
Congreve, Maria, 52–58, 67, 93, 110, 132, 135, 137
Congreve, Richard, 52, 58, 110
Cornhill Magazine, 71n4, 132n9
Cortes, G. W., 6
Cotsell, Michael, 159
Cracroft's Peerage, 115, 115n3, 159
Craig, Isa, 7n7, 59
Craik, George, 20
Crompton, Henry, 7n7, 12, 28, 30, 58, 110, 159
Crompton, Lucy, 7n7
Crompton, Margaret, 110, 159
Croom Robertson, Caroline, 125
Croom Robertson, George, 9, 77, 125, 132n9
Cross, Anna, 112, 121, 139
Cross, Eleanor, 7n7, 72, 74, 75, 77, 94, 139, 140, 142, 144
Cross family, 15, 70, 75, 138–40
Cross, Florence, 72, 138, 140, 144, 151
Cross, John Walter, 1, 9, 14, 15, 23, 28, 31, 35, 44, 52, 62, 66, 66n9, 71, 72, 75, 80, 94, 97, 98, 127, 129, 131, 135, 136–52, 142, 144, 159
Cross, Mary, 7n7, 28, 72, 74n18, 77, 79, 89, 94, 144, 159
Cross, William, 72, 149
Cunningham, Sir Henry Stewart, 159

Dakers, Caroline, 73n16, 159
D'Albert-Durade, François, 51–52
Daniels, Samuel, 60n3
Darwin, Charles, 70n13, 126, 129n7, 133, 158
Darwin, Emma, 126
Daubigny, Charles François, 80–81
David, Deirdre, 159
Davies, Emily, 67
Dawson, Vesey, 115
Deacon, Richard, 98n17, 160

Deakin, Mary, 3n2, 160
De Coverley, E. L., 72, 160
De Gaury, Gerald, 160
De Lieven, Princess Dorothea, 109
Delboeuf, Joseph, 127
Dell, Elizabeth, 92n12, 160
Della Robbia, Giovanni, 37
Della Robbia, Luca, 37
Dellamora, Richard, 105–6n21, 160
Derrida, Jacques, 44n6
Deutsch, Emmanuel, 30, 31n19, 66
Dewes, Simon, 160
Dickens, Charles, 20, 23, 70, 76, 87–88, 160
Dolin, Tim, 160
Douglas, Archibald, 115
Druce, Alfred, 139
Druce, Anna Cross, 7n7, 72, 138, 149, 151
Druce, Eliot, 138
Du Maurier, Daphne, 83, 160
Du Maurier, Emma Wightwick, 7n7, 83
Du Maurier, George, 7nn7, 83–87, 89, 90, 91, 103, 129n7, 131, 132–33, 160

Easley, Alexis, 61n5, 63n7, 160
Ebers, Georg, 148, 149, 160
Edinburgh, 76, 87
Edinburgh Review, 28, 87
Ellman, Richard, 79, 160
Emerson, Ralph Waldo, 20
England, 17, 41, 42, 71, 73, 88, 141, 148, 149, 150; Brighton, 88, 98, 115, 117, 121, 124, 151, 152; Channel Islands, 42; Chislehurst, 89; Coventry, 44, 51, 64; Devonshire, 133; Dover, 139; Flintshire, 128; Freshwater, 71; Fulham, 133; Godalming, 96; Greenwich, 58, 116; Hampshire, 41; Hampstead Heath, 131; Harrogate, 45, 59; Hertfordshire, 107, 124; Ilfracombe, 42; Leamington, 44; Leeds, 67, 68; Liverpool, 68; London, 2, 6, 15, 16, 19, 20, 21n15, 22, 30, 31n20, 36, 38, 43, 54, 57, 59, 59n1, 62, 64, 68, 70n13, 74n18, 75, 80, 81, 82, 83, 85, 99, 100, 101, 102, 106, 109, 113,

115, 118, 125, 128, 130, 134, 135, 144, 149, 152, 153; Lymington, 70; Malvern 20, 38, 44, 59; Manchester, 68; Marylebone, 52; Mayfair, 139; Newmarket, 152; Oxford, 59; Ranby, 152; Red Hill, 89, 111; Richmond, 41; Rottingdean, 133; Ryde, 107; Scilly Isles, 42; Sevenoaks, 152; Shropshire, 131; St John's Wood, 4, 20, 22, 23, 31, 52, 57, 58, 67, 75, 77, 83, 125, 136; St. Leonards, 38; Surrey, 1, 2, 68, 89, 111, 115, 133, 151; Sydenham, 85; Torquay, 59; Tunbridge Wells, 38; Wandsworth, 52, 58; Warwickshire, 44, 52, 135; Watford, 89; Weybridge, 72, 75, 76, 76n20, 80, 94, 139, 140, 142, 149; Witley, 23, 71, 125, 132, 151

English Woman's Journal, 93

Epperson, Gordon, 98, 160

Eton College, 100, 101

Eugénie, Empress, 45

Europe, 15, 16, 21, 37, 38, 43, 80, 148, 155

European salons, 17–19, 21–22

Evans, Isaac, 135

Evans, Marian (George Eliot), biographies and early life, 3–4, 3n2; composite characters, 3–4, 6, 34n24, 50–51, 79–80, 82n3, 88–89, 90, 98, 112, 117–22, 132n9; Cross biography, 9, 14, 31, 62, 66n9, 71, 72, 129, 131, 136, 137–45; early social life, 19–20; marriage to Cross, 16, 137–52; "marriage solution," 99–106; ostracism, 1, 4, 7, 40–41, 40n4

—Sundays at the Priory: antagonisms and conflicts, 23, 28–30, 152–53; and character creation, 35, 36, 78, 79–80, 89, 91, 95–96, 98, 105–6; conversation, 19, 22–23, 28, 36, 59, 68; dullness, 2, 8–10, 35–56; and previous entertaining, 58–59; European guests, 4n4, 7n7, 8, 12, 69–71, 69nn11–12, 74n18, 81–83, 82nn3–5, 91, 106–10, 128–31, 130n8; gay and lesbian guests, 3, 35, 80, 92–106; and guests' writing material, 63, 85–92, 106–8, 132–34, 154; and influences on guests' later lives, 35, 72, 73, 98, 131–36; launch of, 34–35, 37–38, 59; liveliness, 8–12; later guests, 125–31; location, 30–33, music, 3, 14, 15, 80–92; new faces, 66–70, 70–73, 76, 78; poetry, 14, 35, 57, 60–64, 73–74; positivism and psychology, 66, 125–30, 134; reading aloud, 14, 64, 74n17, 74–75, 77; refreshments, 14, 21n15, 33, 90; regulars, 15, 23, 30, 58, 62, 67, 70–74, 75n19, 76; romantic encounters, 12–14, 67, 153; and Thornton's illness, 66–68; and promotion of George Eliot's writing, 3, 28, 61, 63, 64–66, 75–77; publishing business and journalism, 3, 23–24, 36, 58, 74, 76, 125–27; titled/society guests, 2, 30, 35, 64–66, 110, 128; scandal, 3, 7–8, 35, 65; sources regarding, 2–3, 4–6, 8–12, 14, 34, 130–31; spiritualism, 94–98; stiffness, 2–3, 9, 12, 14, 22–23, 36; women guests, 2–3, 4, 7n7, 12, 67–70, 130–31

—travels, 14–16; as celebrations, 42, 111, 124; and character creation, 4, 15, 34, 36, 47–50, 53–54, 112, 24; European (*see* Austria, Belgium, Germany, Italy, Netherlands, Switzerland); guide books, 34, 44, 47, 53, 121; *Murray's,* 34, 55; Galignani, 55; and social life, 37–38, 40, 113–24; and scandal, 41–42; to spas, 15–16, 37–48, 53–56, 111–24, 145–51. *See also* Aix, Aix les Bains, Bad Bercka, Bad Herrenalb, Bad Homburg, Bad Peterstal, Bad Ragatz, Bad Weiler, Bad Wildbad, Baden Baden, Biarritz, Bonn, Chambéry, Chaudfontaine, Ems, Fontainebleau, Ilmenau, Interlaken, Klönthal, Lausanne, Sankt Märgen, Schlangenbad, Schwalbach, St. Blaisin, Strachelberg, Vevey, Vichy

—works: *Adam Bede,* 2, 42; "Agatha," 44, 48–63, 74n17, "Armgart," 44, 45, 61nn5–6, 64; "Brother and Sister Sonnets," 74; "A College Breakfast

Party," 61n5; *Daniel Deronda,* 2, 4n2, 14, 15, 30, 34, 34n24, 35, 38, 44, 45, 47, 53–55, 66, 77–80, 82n3, 85, 87–92, 90n9, 95–96, 98, 105, 105n21, 108–13, 111n1, 116–26, 129–30, 133, 152; *Felix Holt,* 43, 60, 74n18; "How Lisa Loved the King," 62, 64–66, 74n17; *Impressions of Theophrastus Such,* 2, 18, 36, 132n9; "In a London Drawing Room," 31n20; "The Legend of Jubal," 61n5, 74; *The Legend of Jubal and Other Poems,* 61; *Middlemarch,* 2, 3n2, 4n2, 8, 14, 18–19, 28, 34n24, 35, 44, 45, 54, 55, 60, 60n3, 73–80, 74n17, 89, 92, 101, 105, 106, 111, 111n1, 115; *The Mill on the Floss,* 34n24, 42, 52, 106, 130, 141n2, 152; "Modern Housekeeping," 33, 58; "Notes on Form in Art," 60; "O May I Join the Choir Invisible," 95; "Recollections of Berlin 1854–1855," 21; "Recollections of Weimar," 42; *Romola,* 35n25, 42, 61n5, 71, 99n18, 105n21, 130; *Silas Marner,* 35, 105, 130, 133; "Silly Novels by Lady Novelists," 18; *The Spanish Gypsy,* 28, 54–56, 59, 61, 61n4, 62, 65, 72, 125, 138, 139; "On Versification," 60; "William Lecky: *The Influence of Rationalism,* 58; "Worldliness and Otherworldliness: The Poet Young," 95; "Woman in France: Madame de Sablé," 16–19
Evans, Robert, 52, 79, 161
The Examiner, 141

Faithfull, Emily, 93n14
Faucitt, Helen, 10, 58, 62, 77, 164
Fawcett, Millicent Garrett, 23, 161
Ferrière le Vayer, Marquis, 41
Feuer, Lewis S., 128–29, 129n7, 161
Field, Kate, 7n7, 12, 65, 92, 133, 161, 166, 167
Fiske, John, 6–8
Fitzgerald, Penelope, 161
Fleischman, Avrom, 74, 74n18, 75n19, 82, 125, 161

Forman, Henry Buxton, 61, 61n6
Fortnightly Review, 28, 58, 107
Fosey, Jay, 92n12, 158, 160
Foster, Michael, 97, 126, 127
Foucault, Michel, 92
France, 15, 17, 33n23, 48, 80, 85, 109, 155, 156; Aix les Bains, 124, 156; Biarritz, 38, 155; Brittany, 155; Cannes, 131, 142; Chambéry, 124; Fontainebleau, 124; Grasse, 142–43; Normandie, 155; Paris, 21, 22, 82, 83, 99; Pau, 38, 87; Riviera, 131, 142; Vichy, 121
Franklin, Mary, 63
Franklin, Rebecca, 63
Fraser's, 71
Fremantle, Anne, 161
Froude, J. A., 20, 108
Fuller-Maitland, J. A., 128, 161

Garibaldi, Giuseppe, 134
Garratt, Peter, 9, 161
Gaskell, Elizabeth, 164
Gentpath, Doctor, 45
The Germ, 63
Germany, 15, 16, 17, 33n23, 39, 40, 42, 43, 59, 80, 81, 109, 121, 127, 131, 146, 155, 156; Appenweier, 55; Arnstadt, 39; Augsburg, 146; Bad Bercka, 39, 42, 43; Bad Wildbad, 44, 137, 145–51, 156; Bad Weiler, 150; Bad Herrenalb, 150, Bad Homburg, 15, 45, 47, 53–54, 90, 90n9, 111–13, 115, 117–20, 123, 156; Bad Peterstal, 48, 54–56, 122, 124, 148, 155; Baden Baden, 15, 38, 44, 45, 47, 48, 53–55, 81, 83, 108, 111, 118, 120, 121, 150–51, 155, 1565; Berlin, 20, 21, 22, 40, 41 42, 43n5, 44, 45, 46, 81, 91, 105n21, 125, 152, 155; Black Forest (Schwarzwald), 34, 35, 44, 45, 58, 113, 122, 124, 137, 146, 150; Bonn, 43, 45, 47, 55, 115; Coblenz, 45; Cologne, 45, 155; Dresden, 42; Ems, 121; Freiburg, 8, 48, 50, 53; Heidelburg, 69, 128, 130; Ilmenau, 39–40, 41, 155; Karlsruhe, 146; Munich, 42,

146; Pforzheim, 146; Sankt Märgen, 38, 48–51, 53, 56, 155; Schlangenbad, 43–48, 148, 155; Schwalbach, 43, 45–48, 113, 122, 155; Stuttgart, 146; Weimar, 16, 39, 40, 41, 42, 118, 152, 155
Gilbert, Sandra, 161
Gimson, Sidney A., 28
Girton College, 67, 68, 89, 130
Gladstone, Mary, 142–43, 157
Gladstone, William, 109, 143
Goethe, Wolfgang Johann, 39, 40, 42, 53, 63, 90, 127, 163
Gortchakov, Prince Aleksander, 107
Gouws, Dennis, 35n25, 92–93n13, 105n21, 161
Grant Duff, Elphinstone Montstuart, 20, 74, 75, 161
Grant, Frances Elinor (Lady Colvile), 73
Gray, Beryl, 32n22
Greatorex, Emily, 67n10, 130
Greeley, Horace, 19
Green Vivian, 161
Griffith, George, 141n2
Grosskuth, Phyllis, 98–99
Grosslob, Emil, 38
Grosvenor, Beatrice Vesey, 128
Grosvenor, Eleanor Hamilton-Stubber, 128
Grosvenor, Elizabeth, 128
Grosvenor, Norman, 91, 127–28
Grosvenor, Richard, 91, 127–28
Gruppe, Otto, 41
Gubar, Susan, 161
Guest, Edwin, 60
Gully, James, 44
Gurney, Edmund, 65, 94, 98, 102–3, 105, 110, 133, 160, 162
Gurney, Kate Sibley, 8n7, 105
Gwenllian, F. Palgrave, 161

Hadjiafxendi, Kyriaki, 161, 165, 166
Haight, Gordon S., 3, 3n2, 6, 6n1, 7, 8, 10, 14n10, 20, 21, 31, 31n19, 32, 32n22, 34, 34n24, 40, 53, 58, 60, 61n5, 62, 66, 69n11, 73, 74, 79, 92– 93, 94, 98, 101n20, 106, 108, 109, 137, 139, 141, 143, 160, 162, 164, 167
Hall, Trevor, 97–98, 162
Hamerton, Eugénie, 162
Hamerton, Philip Gilbert, 20, 162
Handley, Graham, 162
Hanson, Elisabeth, 140, 162
Hanson, Lawrence, 140, 162
Hardy, Barbara, 4n2, 79, 141, 162
Hardy, Thomas, 167
Harris, Margaret, 34, 38, 40, 42, 52, 58, 62, 145n6, 146, 160, 162
Harrison, Ethel, 7n7
Harrison, Frederic, 7n7, 67, 74n18, 110, 127, 162
Harrison, Mary, 104
Hartley, Eeyan, 162
Haydn, Joseph, 37
Hazlett, W. C., 109, 162
Helps, Alice, 8n7, 42, 110
Helps, Arthur, 41
Henley, Dorothy, 162
Hennell, Charles Christian, 20
Hennell, Sara, 63–64, 135
Henry VIII, 115
Henry, Nancy, 3n2, 34n24, 35n25, 38n1, 73n16, 79n1, 99n18, 105n21, 160
Herbert, Paul, 157
Herron, Jerry, 165
Hertz, Neil, 162
Higginson, Florence, 115
Higginson, Sir George Wentworth
Hill, Roland, 162
Hirsch, Pam, 67, 71, 89, 163
Hodder and Stoughton, 108
Hodgson, William Ballantyne, 20, 163
Holland, Lady Margaret, 151
Holland, Sir Henry, 151
Hornby, J. J., 100–101
Houghton, Lady Annabel, 21
Howard, George, 9, 65, 141n2, 162, 164
Howard, Rosalind, 7n7, 32, 65, 162, 164, 165
Hughes, Kathryn, 3, 3n3, 6n6, 34n24, 138, 140, 144, 162
Hughes, William, 4, 163
Hume, David, 128
Hunt, Thornton, 20

Huth, Augusta, 7n7, 60n1, 109
Huth, Henry, 7n7, 60n1, 109
Huxley, Thomas Henry, 20, 128n7

India, 73, 74; Bengal, 73, Calcutta, 73
Ireland, 71, 73, 115; Donegal, 70; Kildare, 116; Limerick, 116; Lisduff, 117–18; Queen's County, 116, 118; Upper Ossory, 115
Italy, 15, 17, 33n23, 34, 42, 134, 146, 155, 156; Bellosguardo, 15; Bolzano, 145; Camaldoli, 37; Florence, 33n23, 37, 67, 88; La Verna, 37; Lakes, 15; Milan, 15, 144; Padua, 15; Paestum, 42, 134; Rome, 15, 43n5, 133; Trent, 145; Turin, 15; Venice, 15, 16, 37, 44, 94, 137–38, 140–45, 149, 151, 152; Verona, 15, 145
Irigaray, Luce, 166

James, Henry, 66, 99, 164
Jebb, Caroline Reynolds, 141n2, 163
Jeffreys, John Gwyn, 58
Jerrold, Douglas, 20
Joachim, Joseph, 129n7
Joan of Arc, 18n12
Johnston, Judith, 34, 38, 40, 42, 52, 53, 58, 62, 96, 145n6, 146, 160, 163
Jones, Alan W., 64, 163
Jones, Owen, 31
Jowett, Benjamin, 97n15, 110

Kant, Immanuel, 128
Karl, Frederick, 3, 3n2, 140, 163
Kate Field's Washington, 133
Keeley, Mary Ann, 118
Kehler, Grace, 163
Kenyon, Frank William, 163
Kinglake, Alexander, 94, 105, 108–9, 160
Kitchel, Anna, 161
Knoepflmacher, U. C., 60, 60n2, 163
Kovalevsky, Maxim, 129
Kovalevsky (Kovalevskaia), Soph'ia, 4n4, 12, 31, 68–70, 70n13, 163

Kovalevsky, Vladimir, 68–69, 70n13
Kuhn, William, 93, 163

Lankester, Edwin Ray, 128–29, 161
La Porte, Charles, 61n5, 163
Leary, Patrick, 158
Lecky, William, 58
Le Brun, Louise, 109
Lee, Dana, 166
Lehmann, Amelia Chambers, 10, 10n9, 87, 89, 91, 103
Lehmann, Frederic, 38, 87, 163
Lehmann, John, 87, 163
Lehmann, Nina Chambers, 38, 87, 163
Lehmann, Rudolph, 10, 10n9, 12, 87, 163
Leigh, Geraldine, 45, 53, 113, 133n2
Leigh Smith, Nannie, 7n7, 66, 67, 93
Leighton, Frederic, 7n7, 71n14, 90, 115
Levin, Rahel, 21–22
Levine, George, 163, 165
Lewes, Agnes Jervis, 20, 141
Lewes, Bertie, 73n16
Lewes, Blanche, 32
Lewes, Charles Lee, 12, 23, 30, 32, 46, 52, 61, 61n4, 64, 73, 85, 97, 119, 131, 138, 139, 150
Lewes, George Henry: anecdotes, 12, 199; death, 1, 35, 131; early social life, 20–21, 81; liveliness, 6, 10–12, 14, 23, 25; material for Du Maurier, 85; promotion of George Eliot; promotion of Lytton, 107–8; and physiological psychology, 3, 9, 9nn8–9, 27–28, 125–27; publishing business and journalism. *See also* Sundays at the Priory.
—works: *Biographical History of Philosophy,* 127; *Life of Goethe,* 127, 131; *Rose, Blanche and Violet,* 127; *Problems of Life and Mind,* 9, 28, 35, 125, 126–27; *Sea-side Studies,* 42
Lewes, Gertrude, 64, 132
Lewes, Thornton, 35, 66, 66n8, 73n16
Lewes, Vivian Byam, 74
Liebreich, Richard, 7n7, 85–87, 89, 90, 90n10, 91, 130
Lincoln, Abraham, 70

Linton, Eliza Lynn, 7n7, 20 66, 66n8, 80, 93, 163
Liszt, Franz, 41, 91
Literary World, 141
Litzinfer, Boyd, 87, 163
Locker-Lampson, Eleanor, 10, 103
Locker-Lampson, Frederick, 10, 20n16, 74n18, 83, 103, 164
Lowell, James Russell, 61
Lownie, Andrew, 128, 164
Lushington, Godfrey, 7n7, 20
Lushington, Vernon, 7n7, 20
Lytton, Edith, 107
Lytton, Robert, 20, 34n24, 81, 82, 106–8, 119n6

Macmillan's Magazine, 61n5, 63
Madden, Thomas, 43, 44, 45, 46, 120, 121, 148–49, 164
Maddox, Brenda, 140–41, 141n3, 164
Magniac, Augusta, 115
Magniac, Charles, 115–16
Magnus, Edward, 40
Magnus, Heinrich, 40
Main, Alexander, 76
Maine, Sir Henry, 74, 127, 131
Maitland, F. W., 97
Marks, Phoebe (Hyrtha Ayrton), 8n7, 67n10, 89, 130, 134
Marshall, Annie, 103
Marshall, James, 41
Martin, Carol, 75–76, 164
Martin, Theodore, 58, 62, 164
Marx, Karl, 128–29, 161
Masson, Flora, 164
Mazzini, Giuseppe, 119
McBride, Peter, 130
McCobb, E. A., 15, 164
McCormack, Kathleen, 33n23, 38n2, 44n6, 79, 79n1, 164
McKay, Brenda, 164
Meikle, Susan, 164
Mendus, Susan, 165
The Mercury, 130
Meres, Frances, 60n3
Metternich, Princess, 106
Michael, Virginia Surtees, 65, 164

Mill, John Stuart, 97
Millais, John Edward, 9, 71
Milnes, Richard Monckton (Lord Houghton), 20–21, 66, 77
Milton, John, 61
Mind, 125, 126
Mitchell, Sally, 23, 158
Mohl, Mary Clarke, 22
Morris, William, 31, 54, 128
Morrison, Alfred, 7n7, 73, 159
Morrison, Mabel, 7n7, 73, 159
Moscheles, Felix, 132
Moss, Carolyn J., 161
Murray, Edith, 115
Murray, Sir Charles Augustus, 115
Myers, Eveleen Tennant, 103, 105, 133
Myers, F. W. H., 67, 68, 94, 95, 98, 99, 101–4, 105, 133, 158

Nadel, Ira Bruce, 164
La Nature, 127
Nestor, Pauline, 164
Netherlands, 45, 155; Amsterdam, 45; The Hague, 45; Leyden, 45; Rotterdam, 45
Neuberg, Joseph, 58
Neufeldt, Victor A., 160
New Quarterly Magazine, 127
New York Times, 119
Newnham College, 66–68, 97
Newton, K. M., 164
Nicholes, Joseph, 164
Nineteenth Century, 144
Noel, Alice de Broe, 105
Noel, Roden, 79, 94, 98–99, 105
Norton, Charles Eliot, 6–8, 59, 60
Norton, Susan, 61
Norwich, John, 71, 157
Novick, Sheldon, 88, 99, 164
Novikoff, Olga, 7n7, 82n4, 106–9, 164

O'Conner, Joan, 144
O'Gorman, Francis, 164
Olcott, Charles S., 140, 165
Oldfield, Sybil, 79, 165
Olfers, Hedwig, 40–41

Olfers, Ignaz, 40–41
D'Orleans, Mlle, 17
Orr, Alexandra, 7n7, 62, 83
Otter, Emily Cross, 7n7, 14, 28, 72, 74, 75, 77, 82, 138, 149, 152
Otter, Francis, 14
Otter, Gwendolen, 138
Oxford University, 74, 75n19

Paget, Violet (Vernon Lee), 93
Palestine, 130
Palgrave, Francis Turner, 61, 161
Pall Mall Gazette, 54, 58, 63
Pascal, Blaise, 18
Paterson, Arthur, 32, 71, 72, 165, 167
Pattison, Emilia, 7n7, 34n24, 65, 79, 92, 96
Pattison, Mark, 34n24, 61, 62, 75n19, 77, 79, 161
Paul, C. Kegan, 74n18, 100, 131
Paxton, Nancy, 30n18, 69n12, 165
Payne, John Burnell, 62–63
Payne, Joseph Frank, 59, 62, 64, 77
Pelly, Lewis, 58
Pemble, John, 165
Perry, Ruth, 163, 165
Peterson, Linda, 61n5, 165
Pigott, Ned, 59
Pinney, Thomas, 16–17, 40, 160
De Pisan, Christine, 17n12
Podmore, Frank, 97–98
Ponsonby, Henry, 163
Ponsonby, Mary, 93, 163
Pratt, John Clark, 160
Pratt-Smith, Stella, 9n8, 165
Putzell-Korab, Stella, 165

Qualls, Barry, 165

Radford, D., 157
Ralston, William Sheddon, 68, 74n18, 82, 82n4
De Rambouillet, Marquise, 17
Ramieu, Emile, 140, 165
Ramieu, Georges, 140, 165

Rathbone, Richard, 20
Rauch, Christian, 41
Reade, Brian, 99, 165
Récamier, Juliette, 21–22, 32, 109
Redeker, Augusta (Lady Semon), 130
Redinger, Ruby, 3, 3n2, 165
Reed, John, 165
Reed, Joseph W. Jr., 165
Reed, Mary, 163
Rendell, Jane, 165
Revill, George, 167
La Revue Scientifique, 127
Ricchetti, Giacomo, 141n2
Richards, Jeffrey, 58, 99, 165
Rignall, John, 4n2, 162, 165
Rintoul, Robert Stephen, 130
Roberts, Charles, 165
Robertson, Frederick William, 117–18, 121–22, 158
Rochelson, Meri-Jane, 89n8, 134, 165
Röder-Bolton, Gerlinde, 21, 40, 165
Roe, Sue, 158
Rolleston, George, 59
Romanes, George, 9, 23, 94, 98, 135
Romano, Terry, 166
Rose, Phyllis, 137, 166
Ross, John C., 71n15, 158
Rossetti, Christina, 130
Rossetti, Dante Gabriel, 71, 85n6, 133
Rossetti, William Michael, 63, 130
Rossi, Ernesto, 144–45
Roundell, Charles, 7n7, 166
Roundell, Julia, 7n7
Rubenstein, Anton, 34n24, 91
Ruskin, John, 20, 23, 141n2, 158, 161
Russell, Bertrand, 141n2
Russell, Katharine Louisa Stanley, 157
Russell, Patricia Helen (Spence) Russell, 157
Russia, 106, 108, 109; St. Petersburg, 107

De Sablé, Madeleine, 22n16, 18
Sacks, Glenda, 9n8, 166
De Sade, Marquis, 21
Saturday Review, 58, 74
Sauppe, Emilie, 41
Sauppe, Hermann, 41

Scharnhorst, Gary, 133, 166
Schöll, Gustav Adolf, 41, 146n7
Schöll, Mathilde, 41
Schultz, Bart, 97–98, 98nn16–17, 99, 101, 103, 166
Sebright, Lady Olivia, 115, 123–24
Sebright, Sir John Gale Saunders, 115
Sedgwick, Eve, 92, 92n12, 166
Seifert, Siegfried, 166
Sellar, Eleanor, 7, 7n7, 138, 166
Sellar, Eppie, 138
Sellar, William, 7
Semon, Sir Felix, 130
Senior, Jane, 79, 165
Seymour, Danby, 58
Shaffer, Elinor, 166
Shakespeare, William, 60n3, 132n9, 144
Shelley, Percy Bysshe, 137
Sichel, Walter, 9, 80, 141, 166
Sidgwick, Arthur, 67, 94–95, 98, 166
Sidgwick, Eleanor Balfour, 105, 106
Sidgwick, Henry, 67, 94–97, 99, 101, 104, 105, 131, 143, 166
Sidney, Philip, 60n3
Simcox, Edith, 6n1, 7n7, 12, 23, 32, 33, 76, 93, 94, 99, 103, 104–5, 107, 127, 134–35, 136, 137, 142, 143, 144, 157, 166
Simcox, George Augustus, 107–8
Smith, Andrew, 4, 163
Smith, Anne, 164, 166
Smyth, Colonel Edward Skeffington, 90, 115
Smyth, Ethel, 93
Smyth, Gertrude, 7n7, 90, 91, 115
Solmar, Henriette, 20, 21, 22, 41
Solomon, Simeon, 100
Spain, 17, 21, 22, 33n23, 34, 38, 55, 58, 155
The Spectator, 130
Spencer, Herbert, 12, 20, 23, 30, 58, 63, 69–70, 69n12, 74n18, 110, 131, 132, 134, 161, 165, 166
Spinoza, Baruch, 41
Stahr, Adolf, 41, 91
Stahr, Fanny Lewald, 91
The Standard, 109
Stange, G. Robert, 18, 166

Stanley family, 64–66
Stanley, Henrietta, 66
Stanley, Lyulph, 64, 163
Stanley, Mary Bell, 65
Steen, Michael, 81, 166
Stephen, James Fitzjames, 23, 100, 161
Stephen, Leslie, 8, 10–11, 23, 74n18, 128, 132n9, 140
Stern, Kimberley J., 61n5, 166
Stockton, Kathryn Bond, 166
Stoddard, Charles Warren, 31n21
Story, Graham, 160
Strachey, General Richard, 73
Strachey, Jane, 7n7, 73
Stuart, Elman, 8n7, 23, 28, 110, 150
Stummer, Juda, 59
Suhn-Binder, Andrea, 166
Sully, James, 4n4, 9, 23, 28, 31n21, 125–27, 134, 134n10, 136, 166
Swinbrune, Charles Algernon, 20–21
Switzerland, 15, 48, 51, 53, 124–25; Bad Ragatz, 124, 156; Bauen, 52; Berne, 52, 124; Einsiedeln, 50–51, 53; Fluellen, 53; Geneva, 51; Hofwyl, 52; Interlaken, 53; Klönthal, 124, 156; Lausanne, 124; Lucerne, 52–53; Rütli, 52–53; Schaffhausen, 124; St. Blaisin, 124, 156; Stachelberg, 124, 156; Thun, 53; Treib, 53; Vevey, 124; Zollikoffen, 52; Zurich, 50, 124
Symonds, Catherine North, 105
Symonds, John Addington, 68, 94, 97, 98, 99, 103, 105, 134
Szirotny, June Skye, 166

Taine, Henry, 134
Taylor, Ina, 3, 3n2, 140, 166
Temple Bar, 22
Tennyson, Hallam, 141n2
Tennyson, Lionel, 10
Tennyson, Lord Alfred, 12, 23, 70, 71, 97, 126, 127, 129, 129n7, 131, 132
Thackeray, William Makepeace, 28
Thomas, Henry, 166
Thompson, Andrew, 166
Tillotson, Kathleen, 160
The Times, 16, 43, 116, 116n4, 145n6

Trollope, Anthony, 8, 12, 23, 59, 73n18, 80, 82, 126, 132
Trollope, Beatrice, 8n7, 15, 88–89, 132
Trollope, Frances Eleanor Ternan, 88
Trollope, Theodosia, 37, 44, 88
Trollope, Thomas A., 15, 37, 88, 167
Tromp, Marlene, 167
Trübner, Nikolaus, 66, 97
Tucker, Herbert, 61n5, 167
Turgenev, Ivan, 74n18, 81–83, 107, 108
Turkey, 108
Turner, Frank, 97n15, 167

Uglow, Jennifer, 167
Uhland, Ludwig, 146n7
United States, 6, 70, 109, 138; Massachusetts, 61; New York City, 119n5, 130
University College London, 125
University of Edinburgh, 7, 20
Usedom, Lady Hildegarde, 121–23

Van Den Broek, Antoine Gerard, 161
VanArsdel, Rosemary T., 164
Vanity Fair, 63
Varnhagen von Ense, Karl, 21, 41
Viardot, Louis, 81
Viardot, Pauline, 81–83, 91
Victoria, Queen, 116, 131, 158
Vipont, Elfrida, 3n2, 167
Voltaire, 18, 107
Von Moltke, Helmuth, 119

Waddington, Patrick, 167
Waldstein, Charles, 4n4, 128–30, 129nn7–8, 134, 134n10, 167
Wales, 34; Tenby, 20, 42
Ward, Wilfrid, 167
Ward, William, 64
Warner, Charles Dudley, 129, 129n7, 130
Warren, Nicholas, 160
Warton, Thomas, 60

Watts, G. F., 22, 59n1, 112
Weisgall, Deborah, 145n6, 167
West, Rebecca, 81–82, 167
Westminster Review, 16, 20, 61, 95
Westphal, Carl, 105n21
White, Terence de Vere, 140–41n2, 167
Whiting, Lilian, 12, 167
Whitman, Walt, 61, 97, 99
Wiesenfarth, Joseph, 161
Wigan Alfred, 118–19, 119n5
Wigan family, 118
Wiley, Daniel Philip, 160
Williams, Blanche Colton, 167
Williams, David, 167
Williams, Montagu, 118, 167
Williams, Samuel D., 41, 118
Willim, Elizabeth, 58
Wilson, Erasmus, 45, 121, 167
Wilson, Thomas, 41
Wingfield, Cecilia, 7n7, 30, 90–91, 110–11, 113, 115–16, 122
Wingfield, Lady Elizabeth Jocelyn, 115
Wingfield, Lewis Strange, 30, 110n16, 116n4, 133
Wingfield, Richard (Viscount Powerscourt), 115
Witemeyer, Hugh, 167
Wollstonecraft, Mary, 18, 18n13
Wood, T. Martin, 83, 167
Woolf, Virginia, 4, 167
Wordsworth, William, 60n3, 97, 157
Wortham, Hugh Evelyn, 167
Wortham, Thomas, 100
Wright, T. R., 167
Wrigley, Richard, 167

Yale Review, 69
Yeats, William Butler, 133, 157
Young, Kay, 9n8, 167

Zambaco, Maria, 82n5
Zangwill, Israel, 134, 165

www.ingramcontent.com/pod-product-compliance
Lightning Source LLC
Chambersburg PA
CBHW031628160426
43196CB00006B/332